Ross 78°10'
Erebus & Terror
82°17'
Shackleton 1909
88°23'
C T I C A
Pole
Amundsen Dec.
1911
Charcot Ld.
Alexander I Ld.

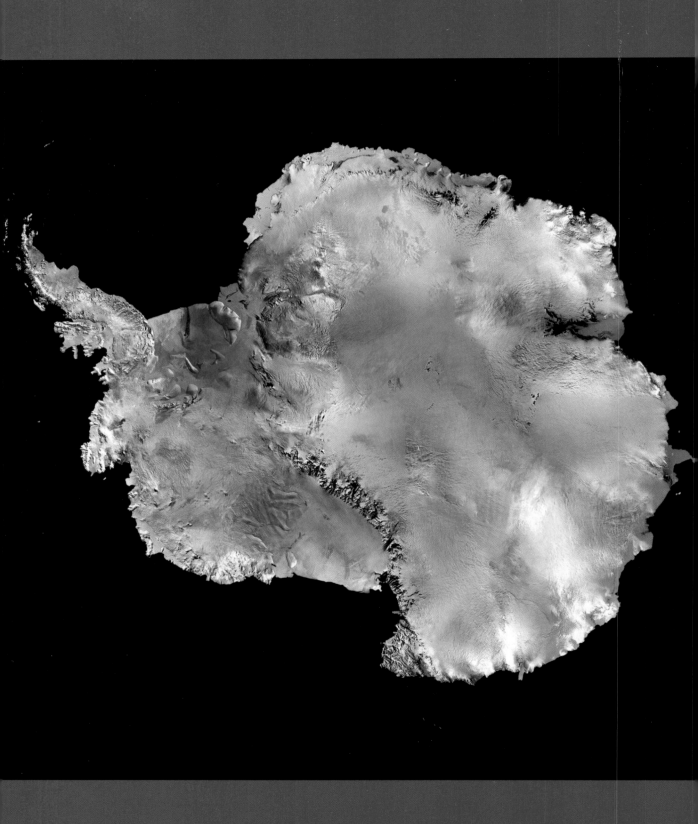

GREAT ENDEAVOUR
Ireland's Antarctic Explorers

To Ireland

Also by Michael Smith:

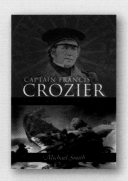

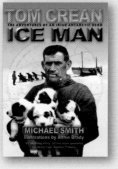

GREAT ENDEAVOUR

Ireland's Antarctic Explorers

MICHAEL SMITH

The Collins Press

FIRST PUBLISHED IN 2010 BY
The Collins Press
West Link Park
Doughcloyne
Wilton
Cork

British Library Cataloguing in Publication Data
Smith, Michael, 1946-
  Great endeavour : Ireland's Antarctic explorers.
  1. Antarctica–Discovery and exploration–Irish.
  2. Explorers–Ireland–Biography.
  I. Title
  919.8'9'04-dc22

ISBN-13: 9781848890237

Design and typesetting by Burns Design
Typeset in Bembo
Maps by Design Image
Printed in Malta by Gutenberg Press Limited

Jacket photographs
Front and spine: *Endurance* trapped in the ice off Antarctica, 1915
Back jacket: (top:) Shackleton's party at start of journey towards the South Pole, 1908;
(top row, l–r) Francis Crozier, Robert Forde, Ernest Shackleton, Mortimer McCarthy;
(bottom row, l–r): Tom Crean, Patrick Keohane, Beyond Endurance team; Mike Barry (Mike Barry);
(bottom) the first all-Irish party to trek to the South Pole (Pay Falvey).
Back flap: (clockwise from top): Patrick Keohane's sledging flag (Plymouth Museum); Tom Crean's Albert Medal
(Crean family); Mortimer McCarthy's navy ID card (McCarthy family).

Endpapers: map of Antarctica (iStockphoto.com); NASA satellite image of Antarctica.

Photograph on p. i: Pat Falvey sledge-hauling in the Antarctic (Pat Falvey).

CONTENTS

ACKNOWLEDGEMENTS

A considerable number of people from many corners of the world have contributed to this project and I am enormously grateful to everyone for the kind support and generous assistance. It is no exaggeration to say that this book would not have been possible without their help.

In many respects, this book is the result of a lifetime's interest in the history of Polar exploration and it would not be possible to list all those who have assisted me over the years, particularly those who helped with my earlier research into the lives of Thomas Crean, Francis Crozier and Ernest Shackleton. I am grateful to you all and any omissions are unintentional.

More specifically, I wish to extend my sincere thanks to Sheila Bransfield who generously shared her knowledge of Edward Bransfield and helped to sketch in many details about his life. I was also given much assistance and encouragement by Ursula O'Mahony and Marie Guillot of the Cloyne Literary & Historical Society. I am also pleased to pass on my thanks to Richard J. Campbell for permission to reproduce the painting of *Williams* by the late Commander G. W. G. Hunt, which was first published in his book, *The Discovery of the South Shetland Islands*.

I must extend my deep appreciation to the many people who assisted me in researching the life of Patrick Keohane. I was given valuable help by Patrick Madigan and Mary Underwood, two of Keohane's grandchildren, who generously shared their memories, family papers and personal photographs. Nora Hickey, a member of the extended Keohane clan, was enormously patient and generous with her knowledge of the family and local history. I am also very grateful to Michael O'Brien who kindly showed me around the Keohane family homeland and shared his knowledge of the area. My thanks are due to Michael O'Connell of the Clonakilty Museum and to Micheál Hurley for his enthusiastic support and for sharing his knowledge of the Courtmacsherry lifeboat. My thanks also to Mike O'Shea of the Irish Explorers Trust who kindly allowed me access to Keohane documents and material held in the Kerry County Museum, Tralee, where I was given courteous support by Helen O'Carroll and Griffin Murray. Cyril Hart and Peter Woods in Cornwall were valuable sources of information about the Coverack lifeboat. I am also indebted to Nigel Overton and Dawn Trewhella at Plymouth Museum and to Paul Davies for his helpful advice.

I am particularly grateful for the enthusiastic support and encouragement of the McCarthy family in New Zealand, notably Gerard McCarthy, son of Mortimer McCarthy, and Mortimer's grandsons, Peter and Andrew McCarthy. They were immensely patient with my enquiries and generously shared their recollections, private papers and photographs. Terry Connolly was an important source of information, for which I am very grateful. Others who helped were Kerry McCarthy, Joanna Condon and Jane Myhill at Canterbury Museum and Baden Norris, the museum's Emeritus Curator of Antarctic Collections, who very kindly shared his personal memories of Mortimer McCarthy. Thanks to you all.

ACKNOWLEDGEMENTS

I wish to extend particular gratitude to John Hennessy who was an important source of information regarding Robert Forde. He supported my research with great enthusiasm, willingly shared his own knowledge and personal recollections of Forde and generously took the time to show me the places in Cobh most associated with Forde. I am very grateful. I must also acknowledge the helpful assistance of Scott Porter.

Special mention should be made to the present generation of travellers and adventurers who have contributed by deeds and words to this book. I salute their courage and endurance in dealing with the Antarctic and I offer my sincere thanks for the generous assistance to my research.

In particular, I wish to thank Mike Barry who was obliging and helpful with my enquiries and allowed me access to personal photographs. Frank Nugent and Jarlath Cunnane generously shared their experiences of the South Arís expedition, for which I am grateful. Clare O'Leary was patient and considerate in response to my enquiries and I must also pass on my grateful thanks to Pat Falvey. A special note of thanks must go to Niall Foley for all his special help. Mark Pollock and Simon O'Donnell gave me wholehearted support and assistance, including access to photographs. I am grateful to you all and my apologies if I have forgotten to mention anyone.

It is not possible to measure fully Mary O'Connell's important contribution to this book. Her encouragement and advice was vital and I will always be enormously grateful.

My thanks are also due to Nan Keightley and I wish to acknowledge Shirley Sawtell and Naomi Boneham at the Scott Polar Research Institute who were courteous and very helpful with my enquiries. I was also given valuable advice and encouragement by Robert Burton, Robert Headland and Rob Stephenson. A special word of thanks is due to the estimable Joe O'Farrell who cast a knowing eye over the manuscript and offered his thoughtful and constructive advice.

Where possible, I have identified all known sources of the material used in this book and provided accreditation where it can be properly established. Any omissions are unintentional and I would be pleased to correct any errors or oversights.

I have never been able to produce a book without the invaluable support of my lads, Daniel and Nathan, whose patience and understanding of their father's technological limitations (a source of bewilderment to them) are a great comfort to me. Finally, I must say how much I value the continuing support and understanding of Barbara.

Michael Smith
June 2010

CHRONOLOGY OF EVENTS

1773   James Cook's ships, *Resolution* and *Adventure*, make first crossing of Antarctic Circle

1785   Edward Bransfield born, Ballinacurra, Cork

1796   Francis Crozier born, Banbridge, Down

1820   Bransfield in *Williams* and von Bellingshausen's ships, *Vostok* and *Mirnyi*, separately sight the Antarctic continent

1839–43   Crozier and Ross in *Erebus* and *Terror* penetrate Antarctic pack ice and discoveries include Ross Sea, Victoria Land, Cape Crozier, McMurdo Sound, Mount Erebus, Ross Island and the Ross Ice Shelf

1848   (*circa*) Crozier dies

1852   Bransfield dies

1874   Ernest Shackleton born, Kildare

1875   Robert Forde born, Cork

1877   Thomas Crean born, Anascaul, Kerry

1879   Patrick Keohane born, Barry's Point, Cork

1882   Mortimer McCarthy born, Kinsale, Cork

1888   Timothy McCarthy born, Kinsale, Cork

1895   Henryk Bull's *Antarctic* expedition makes first recorded landing on Antarctic continent outside the Peninsula

1898   Adrien de Gerlache's *Belgica* expedition, trapped in pack ice off Antarctic Peninsula, is the first party to overwinter in Antarctic seas

1899   Carsten Borchgrevink's *Southern Cross* expedition first to overwinter on mainland Antarctica

1901   Shackleton and Crean join *Discovery* expedition

1901-04   Scott, Shackleton and Wilson establish 'furthest south' of 82·17° S

1907   Shackleton launches *Nimrod* expedition

1908-09   Shackleton and three companions reach 88·23° S, only 97 nautical miles (111½ geographical miles or 179 km) from South Pole

1910   Crean, Forde and Keohane join Scott's *Terra Nova* expedition and Mortimer McCarthy joins ship's crew

1911   Amundsen and four companions reach South Pole on 14 December

1911   Keohane, a member of First Supporting Party, turns back from Polar march at 85° S, about 350 miles (560 km) from Pole

CHRONOLOGY OF EVENTS

1912   Crean, a member of Last Supporting Party, turns back 150 geographic miles (172 statute miles or 240 km) from the Pole

1912   Scott and four companions reach South Pole on January 17 and all five die on return journey

1912   Crean saves lives of Lt Evans and Lashly by walking 35 miles (56 km) to fetch help

1912   Forde invalided out of Antarctica after suffering severe frostbite

1912   Crean and Keohane in search party that finds Scott's body

1913   Mortimer McCarthy completes last of *Terra Nova*'s three voyages to Antarctic

1914   Shackleton launches Imperial Transantarctic Expedition

1914   Crean and Tim McCarthy join *Endurance*

1915   *Endurance* trapped in Weddell Sea and sinks

1916   Shackleton and McCarthy in *James Caird* and Crean in *Stancomb Wills* sail to Elephant Island

1916   Shackleton, Crean and Tim McCarthy sail *James Caird* to South Georgia

1916   Shackleton, Crean and Worsley cross interior of South Georgia

1916   Tim McCarthy returns to UK

1916   Shackleton and Crean rescue twenty-two companions from Elephant Island

1917   Tim McCarthy dies

1922   Shackleton dies

1938   Crean dies

1950   Keohane dies

1955–58   First coast-to-coast crossing of Antarctica by Commonwealth Trans-Antarctic Expedition under Vivian Fuchs

1959   Forde dies

1967   Mortimer McCarthy dies

2004   Mike Barry is first Irishman to walk overland to the South Pole

2008   First all-Irish expedition (Pat Falvey, Shaun Menzies, Jonathan Bradshaw and Clare O'Leary) reaches South Pole on foot. O'Leary is first Irishwoman to walk to the Pole

2009   Mark Pollock is first blind Irishman to reach South Pole on foot

AUTHOR'S NOTE

For much of the period covered in this book temperatures were measured in Fahrenheit and for guidance approximate conversions to the modern Celsius scale are generally shown. For the purposes of consistency, the same form — Fahrenheit first — is used throughout the book, even though the Celsius scale is now in wider use.

The same applies to the measure of distance and weight used for much of the period covered and conversion to modern measures is given where appropriate. Distances are generally shown in statute miles, with conversions to the metric scale. Weights are shown in the previously common avoirdupois scale with conversion to metric where appropriate.

Facing page: ice ridges in the Antarctic. PAT FALVEY

INTRODUCTION

IRELAND STANDS at the heart of Antarctic exploration, a dramatic and captivating episode in history, which surpasses all other tales of discovery to any place in the world. While every ocean, continent or mountain has its own special tale to tell, none can match exploration of the Antarctic for the sheer drama of triumph and tragedy and the epic scale of individual stories of unimaginable hardship, awe-inspiring endurance and incredible feats of survival. Or that almost every noteworthy chapter in the history of Antarctic exploration involves the Irish.

Explorers from many nations were engaged in the exploration of Antarctica and it would be foolish to ignore or minimise the memorable actions of men from countries as far as apart as England and New Zealand or Norway and Australia. It would mean disregarding distinguished leaders like Roald Amundsen, James Clark Ross and Robert Scott or the lesser known characters such as Carsten Borchgrevink, Lawrence Oates or Frank Wild.

But Ireland's contribution to Antarctic exploration is notably different because, at almost every stage in a century of discovery, Irishmen were significant and influential characters and the outstanding contributions made by different generations of Irish explorers are indispensable to the overall story. Irish characters grace the story from the very beginning, through the most memorable years and up to the final moments, and it would be impossible to record the enthralling saga of Antarctic exploration without highlighting the significant part played by a series of outstanding Irish voyagers.

The men, some well known and others less so, shared much the same characteristics. They include the enigmatic figure of Edward Bransfield, the charismatic and inspiring leader Ernest Shackleton and unsung heroes like Tom Crean.

They were all men of exceptional courage, with seemingly inexhaustible depths of endurance and unshakeable resolve who, on occasions, touched greatness. But these men also enhanced Antarctic exploration with the distinctive Irish qualities of vibrant good humour, breezy optimism and an occasional song.

The story of Antarctic exploration is surprisingly short, lasting about 100 years. Humans did not set eyes on the frozen wilderness until 1820 and the great age of exploration virtually came to an end a century later in 1922 when focus on the continent moved from the quest of pure discovery to the scientific pursuit of knowledge and understanding.

Antarctica had lived in the imagination of people from ancient times. Greek scholars speculated about the existence of the land well over 2,000 years before the first ships ventured into the frozen seas. The Greeks reasoned that a vast unknown land – *Terra Australis Incognita* – had to be found at the bottom of the earth to 'balance' the lands they knew existed in the northern hemisphere. As the lands of the north lay under the constellation of *Arktos* (Bear), the Greeks identified the undiscovered region as *Antarktikos* – the opposite of *Arktos*.

According to legend, the first voyage towards the unexplored continent was made as long ago as 650 AD by the Polynesian navigator, Ui-te-Rangiora, who reputedly found 'things like rocks' floating in the seas. The first well-documented forays into southern waters, which proved that *Terra Australis Incognita* was not attached to the known world, were made in 1497 when Vasco da Gama sailed around the Cape of Good Hope and when Ferdinand Magellan rounded Cape Horn twenty years later.

Later voyages discovered remote southern island outposts such as the Falklands and the Kerguelen Islands and in 1773 James Cook, the outstanding navigator of the age, crossed the Antarctic Circle for the first time. Although Cook never saw the continent, he ventured as far south as 71° 10' S and described the cold, uninviting region as 'a Country doomed by Nature never once to feel the warmth of the sun but to lie for ever buried under everlasting snow and ice'.

Cook's damning judgement meant that few ships bothered to enter southern waters over the next few decades and interest in the area waned. The only interlopers were occasional whalers and sealers whose sole interest was making money, not exploration. It seems probable that a few intrepid captains made new territorial discoveries in pursuit of their prey, although any new findings were invariably kept a closely guarded secret to ensure that rival skippers did not plunder the hunting grounds.

Edward Bransfield, the navigator and master seaman from Cork, was a key figure when the most important phase of Antarctic exploration began in 1820, sparking a century of historic voyages and discovery. It was Bransfield, a barely recognised character these days, who made the first recorded sighting of the continent.

However, Bransfield's pioneering journey took place at precisely the same time as the Russian Thaddeus von Bellingshausen was exploring waters elsewhere in the Antarctic and his achievement to some extent has been overshadowed by years of impassioned debate about which of the men first sighted the continent. The Russians reported seeing ice formations three days before Bransfield's discovery, but they were unable to confirm the existence of land. Bransfield had no doubts about seeing land and, without realising it, began almost two centuries of bitter dispute.

Two decades after Bransfield led the way, Francis Crozier of Banbridge mapped large chunks of the seas and continental land mass during the greatest voyage of maritime discovery of the nineteenth century. Crozier's voyage with Ross helped to pioneer the route south for the Heroic Age of Exploration of the early twentieth century, the golden age of exploration in which many of the major characters in the story were from Ireland, including Crean and Shackleton.

Regrettably, almost all the Irishmen who made history in the Antarctic from 1820 onwards – with one notable exception – faded into obscurity soon after returning home and were forgotten.

Bransfield and Crozier, even in their own lifetimes, were hardly recognised and drifted to the fringes of history. Bransfield, for example, was a slightly mysterious figure who gave up exploring after only one voyage and quickly disappeared from the public gaze. No portraits or photographic images of Bransfield are thought to have survived, a full account of his life has never been written and there is no statue to the man who set in motion the gripping saga of Antarctic exploration.

Crozier, despite making a remarkable six journeys to the ice during an outstanding naval career stretching for nearly forty years, was another who was easily forgotten. Crozier, a modest, self-effacing man, was engaged in the three great quests of exploration in the nineteenth century – finding the North-West Passage, reaching the North Pole and mapping Antarctica. But his feats were never fully recognised and Crozier had the dubious distinction of being the only leading naval explorer of the age to be denied a knighthood.

The fate of Crean, who made three memorable trips to the Antarctic ice, is typical of how quickly reputations change and individual achievements, regardless of how outstanding, are quietly pushed to the sidelines. Crean, incredibly enough, spent eighty years in the shadows and was almost completely unknown, even in Ireland, until only recently. Crean's Irish companions in the Antarctic – Robert Forde, Patrick Keohane and the McCarthy brothers, Mortimer and Timothy – were equally marginalised and soon forgotten.

The obvious exception, of course, is Ernest Shackleton, who is rightly recognised as one of the great explorers of any age and can be compared with the likes of Columbus, Cook or Marco Polo. Yet even Shackleton was not always the celebrated figure he is today and for many decades he was eclipsed by other explorers, notably the tragic figure of Scott. The renaissance of Shackleton is a comparatively recent phenomenon, which did not materialise until nearly seventy years after his death.

The link between Ireland and Antarctic exploration is more predictable than might be expected. Antarctic exploration, since earliest times, was a job for the navy, and for centuries, Ireland, as a nation of seafarers, was frequently the backbone of the British navy and the country's fleet of merchant ships. The names of Irish sailors can be found in the logbooks of the ships Cook first took across the Antarctic Circle and during the Napoleonic Wars, the era when Britain emerged unchallenged as the world's premier sea power, approximately one in ten Royal Naval seamen came from Ireland.

However, every expedition to the Antarctic in the 102 years from Bransfield in 1820 to Shackleton in 1922, when the age of discovery effectively came to an end, was made while all of Ireland was part of the British Empire. Much of Antarctic exploration was an age of *British* exploration and Britain wrote the history.

To varying degrees, every journey to the ice during this century was dressed up in the mantle of imperial endeavour, partly in reflection of the times and partly for expediency because it was the easiest and most sensible way to guarantee raising money from the government and wealthy benefactors.

It hardly mattered that most Antarctic explorers were not active political figures or buccaneering colonialists. Almost without exception, the expeditions had precious little to do with imperial glory-seeking, even though there was often intense international rivalry between countries. Fridtjof Nansen, the eminent Norwegian explorer, accurately measured the extraordinary feats of individual heroism and discovery against the wider political or commercial interests of nations and concluded: 'It is the man that matters.'

The men, however, were not immune to the greater forces which shape history, and the progression to Irish independence is one reason why the exploits of many Antarctic explorers from the most intense and momentous phase of exploration were overlooked and faded from view. Timing was the key.

The 100 years of Antarctic exploration effectively came to an end on 5 January 1922 with the death of Shackleton and, with striking symmetry, the Anglo-Irish Treaty was ratified by Dáil Éireann two days later. Bransfield and Crozier were already footnotes to history in 1922 and the survivors of the Heroic Age like Crean, Forde and Keohane, who had served a combined total of more than eighty years in the British navy, were compelled to maintain a discreet silence about their exploits. Frank Nugent, the Irish mountaineer and Polar historian, rightly observed that for many years the stories of these men were 'lost in the selective memories of Irish history writers of the 20th century'.

It was easy to forget. Little had been recorded about Bransfield or Crozier. Shackleton aside, no books were written about the explorers when they came back to Ireland from the Heroic Age in the 1920s. Nobody erected statues or celebrated their achievements and few people in Ireland even talked about what these Irishmen had accomplished in the distant wilderness. Some chose to flee the country. The only Irishman of the age to speak freely about his adventures on the ice was the chirpy old sea dog, Mortimer McCarthy, who lived 12,000 miles (19,000 km) from Ireland on the other side of the world.

However, the time is now right to set the record straight and this book pulls together the story of Ireland's special contribution to the great story of Antarctic exploration, with particular emphasis on uncovering the lives of those men – such as Bransfield, Forde and Keohane – who have been half-forgotten or lost in time. They deserve it.

In putting the record straight on the overlooked Irish explorers from the past, this book also provides the first opportunity to chronicle the exploits of the modern-day adventurers from Ireland who have their own remarkable stories to tell. These are the equally gripping accounts of Irish men and women who in recent times have commemorated the pioneers of the past by making their own daring journeys to the Antarctic.

Seen together for the first time, the contemporary stories in honour of the forerunners are an inspiring postscript to the Heroic Age of Antarctic Exploration. They are a collection of equally vivid escapades, which would make early explorers proud of those who have followed so nobly in their footsteps.

Sceptics insist that modern technology and equipment gives 21st-century adventurers a huge advantage over the men from history. But GPS (Global Positioning System) or the latest cold-weather clothing cannot pull a 200 lb (90 kg) sledge in temperatures of -30° F (-34° C) and gale force winds. It is also crucial to emphasise that a few of the modern breed of adventurers, such as Mike Barry, have achieved what even giants such as Shackleton or Crean never quite managed and another – Clare O'Leary – has done what no other Irishwoman has ever achieved – to walk overland to the South Pole.

Taken together, the great stories of early Antarctic discovery and the enthralling adventures of today's travellers represent a powerful and compelling celebration of nearly 200 years of great endeavour by Irish explorers in the most hostile region on earth.

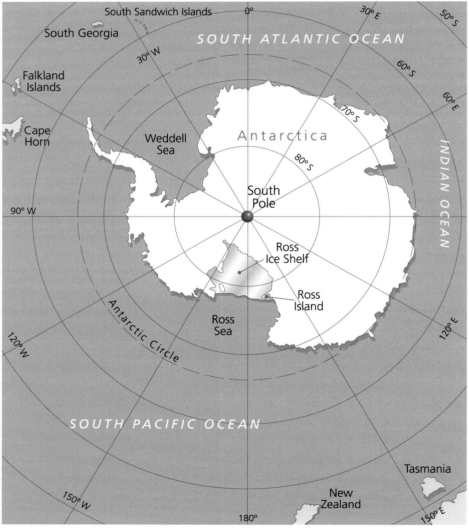

Antarctica

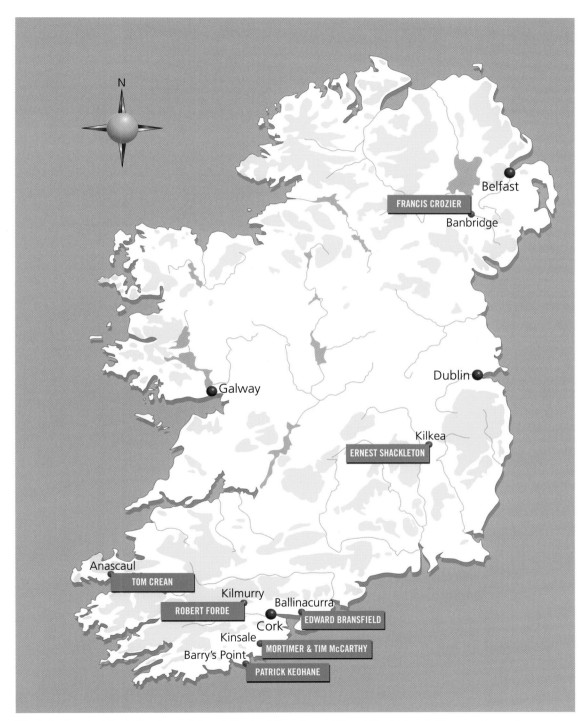

(Clockwise from top) Banbridge, home of Francis Crozier; Kilkea, home of Ernest Shackleton; Ballinacurra, home of Edward Bransfield; Kinsale, home of Mortimer and Tim McCarthy; Barry's Point, home of Patrick Keohane; Kilmurry, home of Robert Forde; Anascaul, home of Tom Crean.

EDWARD BRANSFIELD

1785–1852

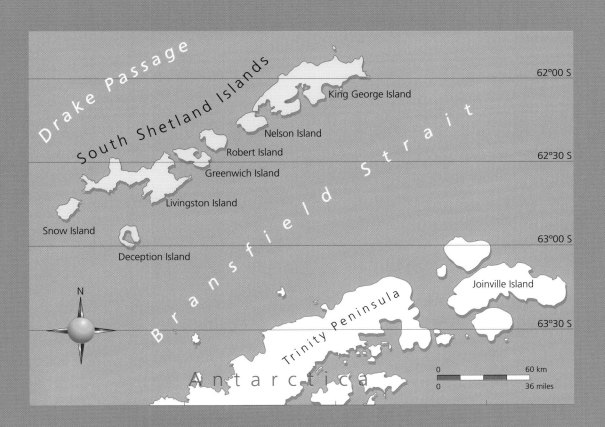

Bransfield Strait, discovered by Edward Bransfield in 1820, separates the
Antarctic Peninsula from the South Shetland Islands.

BALLINACURRA (*Baile na Cora*), the long-established village lying barely a mile from the distillery town of Midleton in County Cork, is a quiet spot, which owes its existence to the water. The village, which can trace its origins back well over 800 years to the earliest Norman settlers, sits at a point where the Owenacurra River meets the most easterly reaches of Cork Harbour. The name *Baile na Cora* was derived from the fish-weir that once crossed the Owenacurra River and the English translation – 'Town of the Weir' – is apt.

For centuries Ballinacurra prospered as the feeder port for Midleton, with a steady stream of barges bringing cargoes of coal, timber and iron, and later flax for the local linen industry. In the more secluded corners of the busy waterways, a few small fishing boats could be found bringing home small catches for local families. It was from this classical seafaring background that the enigmatic figure of Edward Bransfield emerged in the late eighteenth century to leave an indelible mark on the history of exploration.

Bransfield, a man steeped in seafaring, was credited with the outstanding feat of making the first confirmed sighting of the unknown continent of Antarctica and yet, almost two centuries later, he remains a largely unrecognised and shadowy figure whose story is scarcely known. By a strange twist of fate, Bransfield is probably better known for his unintentional role in the lingering controversy about who was first to sight the Antarctic coastline than he is for being a master seaman, accomplished navigator and pioneering explorer.

Edward Bransfield came from one of Ballinacurra's many seagoing families, his father operating a fishing vessel in the local waters. He was born in the heart of Ballinacurra village at 3 Upper Road (sometimes called East Street), a terraced house which remains standing to this day. In keeping with the sketchy details of his background, Bransfield's precise date of birth is uncertain, though the year is generally accepted as 1785.[1]

Little is known about his family or early life, though it is thought that the Bransfields of Ballinacurra were a well-known and respectable Catholic family. The young Edward Bransfield was apparently a bright character who, in contrast to many children of the time, enjoyed a decent basic level of education. It is possible that the family earned enough to pay for a simple education or that he was among those whose learning was scraped together from a 'hedge' school, the improvised solution to the ban on Catholic teachers and enough to pass on a little rudimentary knowledge and a flavour of Irish history and culture. But fate intervened before Bransfield could follow any personal ambitions. In 1803, he was working with his father on a small fishing craft in the waters around Cork Harbour and the nearby port of Youghal when his gentle routine collided with the tumultuous events of the Napoleonic Wars between Britain and France.

Britain had been at war with France for much of the previous decade, but the Treaty of Amiens in March 1802 brought an uneasy peace between the two powers. The harmony did not last long and by early 1803 Britain and France had resumed hostilities.

The house at Ballinacurra where Edward Bransfield was born in 1785. The house, at No 3 Upper Road, Ballinacurra in County Cork, dates back at least 300 years.
MICHAEL SMITH

Britain immediately imposed a blockade on all French ports and Napoleon mustered his armies in preparation for an invasion of England. In the febrile atmosphere, Britain reacted by launching a major mobilisation of its forces, most notably a call to double the number of active seamen and marines to 100,000 strong.

Recruitment in the days before conscription meant sending out the feared thugs from the navy press gangs to round up men, willing and unwilling, to serve the colours. Every major port had a captain or lieutenant in charge of impressment, a crude and arbitrary form of enrolment backed up by the strong arm of the law and brutal enforcement. Dockside ruffians and ruthless hooligans who were anxious to avoid their own impressment – seamen were rarely used to press fellow sailors – were employed as 'gangers' to unearth scores of suitable able-bodied men for service.

In theory, those rounded up needed some seafaring experience to be pressed, but the gangers were not choosy who they recruited from the bars, docksides and whorehouses. Where necessary the press gangs travelled away from the docks and roamed deeper into the countryside and villages to find enough fit men to fill the navy's quotas. Some vague and poorly enforced 'rules' applied to impressments, including one which insisted that the gangs should not take seamen on outward-bound vessels or that those under eighteen or over fifty-five years of age were excused. Merchant shipowners were also promised they could retain some experienced seamen, although the procedure was open to widespread and indiscriminate kidnapping, savage brutality and widespread corruption.

Bransfield, though only around eighteen years of age, was already an experienced seaman and ideal material as the press gangs went to work in the late spring and early summer of 1803 around the waterways of Cork. All the indications are that Bransfield was picked up by the navy tender *Dryad*, which was based at Cork Harbour and regularly combed the coastal waters of Ballinacurra and Youghal in search of men.

By 2 June 1803, Bransfield had been picked off his father's fishing boat and was listed among the many men from around Cork who were 'prest' into service as an ordinary seaman in the Royal Navy. He was soon mustered on board *Ville de Paris*, one of the navy's first-rate warships with a battery of 110 guns under the command of Captain Tristram Ricketts.

Conditions on board naval vessels at the time were truly appalling. Without any prospect of escape or time off, seamen endured a miserable existence of grotesque overcrowding and a vicious and capricious disciplinary regime of flogging and other barbarous punishments which were enforced by bullying, sadistic officers. The risk of death or ghastly injury in sea battles where wooden warships pounded each other to destruction at point-blank range was ever present. Wounded men suffered summary amputation of the limbs without anaesthetic in foul-smelling candlelit holds or were simply thrown overboard if seriously maimed. Diseases such as typhus, cholera and scurvy were rife and despite the often intense close-quarter fighting, seamen of the age were far more likely to die from sickness or disease than a French musket ball or cannon shot. In return for a harrowing and perilous life at sea the newly recruited Bransfield was paid £10 4s 9d a year (equal to about £500 a year today).

Bransfield was thrown into the action only a month after being pressed. In July 1803, *Ville de Paris* was sent across the English Channel to assist with the blockade of Brest, the key port in Brittany and home for a significant portion of the French fleet.

Bransfield shared living quarters on *Ville de Paris* alongside a young midshipman who was also destined to earn his reputation in the Polar regions. William Edward Parry, a twelve-year-old midshipman, joined up a few weeks after Bransfield's impressment and, two decades after serving on *Ville de Paris* with Bransfield, he was the most celebrated Polar explorer alive, having served with great distinction on five expeditions to the Arctic regions. In later life Parry helped oversee the navy's transition from sail to steam-engine-driven ships. However, the contrast between the two young men could hardly have been stronger. While Bransfield had been crudely press-ganged, Parry entered the navy because his father, a well-connected doctor, knew the right people. One of Dr Parry's patients was Elizabeth Cornwallis, the favourite niece of Admiral William Cornwallis, commander-in-chief of the Channel Fleet. After a polite word in Uncle William's ear, Edward Parry joined Bransfield in Plymouth where *Ville de Paris* was being fitted out for war.

Ville de Paris spent three years on dogged sentry duty as the navy ruthlessly enforced the strict blockade of major French ports, which was to prove a significant factor in eventually turning the war in Britain's favour. It was a victory which itself laid the foundations for Britain's economic and military dominance for the next 100 years.

Brest, the main French port serving the Atlantic, was generally policed by a handful of faster-moving navy frigates ordered to monitor shipping and ready to summon the more heavily armed battleships – such as *Ville de Paris* – to attack any French navy or merchant vessels daring to run the blockade. But the French, often outgunned and outnumbered by the far superior Royal Navy fleet, could not break the stranglehold of the blockade and as a result, the threat of Napoleon's armies invading Britain never materialised.

After a three-year stint of enforcing the blockade, *Ville de Paris* was out of commission and by the end of 1806 Bransfield was transferred to another man-of-war, *Royal Sovereign*, a twenty-year-old veteran with the notable pedigree of being the first ship to see action at the Battle of Trafalgar in 1805. *Royal Sovereign*, which also boasted an armoury of 110 guns, sailed into the Mediterranean under Captain Henry Garrett and spent the next six years blockading the strategic French port of Toulon.

Despite the hazards and the severity of conditions on board navy vessels, Bransfield thrived and prospered during his early years at sea. He was a diligent, sober and capable seaman who quickly progressed through the ranks and clearly caught the eye of his superior officers. What impressed most was his skill as a navigator and Bransfield soon gravitated towards the role of ship's Master, the person responsible for navigation. He was promoted to Able Bodied Seaman in 1805 and up to Midshipman and Quartermaster in 1808. His advancement quickly gathered pace, rising to Clerk in 1809 and in late 1812, as Napoleon's disastrous retreat from Moscow was entering its final stages, Bransfield was appointed Acting Master of *Goldfinch* during a further spell blockading Brest.

Bransfield also found time to escape from the rigours of naval routine a year later when he got married for the first time. His bride was 29-year-old Mary Harris. The couple were married on 21 August 1813 at St Andrew's Church, Plymouth, but unfortunately, the union proved short-lived. Mary was dead within a year, though the circumstances remain another of the mysteries surrounding Bransfield's life. Shortly before his wife's death, Bransfield was promoted to the rank of Master. The ranking, which took effect in April 1814 after eleven years of service, was ample recognition of his experience. The rank approximated to that of naval Lieutenant and was granted after the usual examination by Trinity House, the Admiralty's training school, where his superior officers spoke warmly of Bransfield's navigational and piloting skills.

The long war finally came to an end a year later, after Napoleon's crushing defeat at Waterloo in June 1815, leaving Europe to count the cost of between 3 million and 6 million civilian and military dead after more than two decades of bitter fighting. Britain alone lost an estimated 300,000 men, including over 90,000 seamen. Bransfield chose to remain at sea and in 1816 became Master of the *Cyndus*, where he replaced James Weddell, another explorer who would later find fame far below the Antarctic Circle. It was Weddell who in 1823 sailed further south into uncharted Antarctic waters (74° 15' S) than anyone had been before and a century later the Weddell Sea, named after the famed navigator, was the scene of Sir Ernest Shackleton's epic *Endurance* expedition.

Bransfield gained further certificates from Trinity House to serve on larger vessels in 1816 and he was appointed Master of the frigate *Severn*. It was Bransfield's duties on *Severn* which posed a more severe test of his abilities. *Severn*, a 44-gun vessel under the command of Captain Frederick Aylmer, joined a fleet of twenty-seven British and Dutch ships sent to Algiers in the summer of 1816 in a bid to free hundreds of Christian slaves and to curtail slavery in the region. Alongside *Severn* in the fleet heading to North Africa was *Hecla*, a navy mortar bomb vessel which Bransfield's former shipmate Parry took on four expeditions to the Arctic.

The arrival of the Anglo-Dutch fleet in late August provoked a short, brutal engagement, which became known as the Bombardment of Algiers. *Severn*, with Bransfield as Master and navigator, played a key role in the battle. Shortly before 9 a.m. on the morning of 27 August, *Severn* entered the Bay of Algiers alone, flying a flag of truce and carrying a note inviting the Dey of Algiers, the ruler of the city, to surrender peacefully. Crowds of fascinated onlookers flocked to the quays to watch as the fleet lined up behind the *Severn* in an unmistakable declaration of hostile intent.

The offer to surrender was rejected and a few minutes before 3 p.m., a single cannon shot rang out, reputedly fired by the defiant Dey himself. The fleet's batteries immediately responded with a fusillade of cannon fire which one officer reported as 'very terrible and destructive'. In one hazardous manoeuvre, Bransfield took the *Severn* closer to shore, unleashing her guns on the Algerian defences and drawing the fire from the onshore batteries as the larger battleships took up a more effective firing position.

The bloody engagement lasted nine hours and nearly 1,000 seamen – about one in six combatants – were killed or wounded. *Severn* alone unleashed almost 6 tons (5,850 kgs) of powder during the ferocious onslaught and her mast and keel were damaged in the fight. But in spite of the dangerous exercise of drawing the enemy fire, only three of *Severn's* seamen lost their lives. Next day, with the city in flames and most of his ships destroyed, the Dey of Algiers accepted the terms of surrender. Around 3,000 European slaves were freed and the Algerians reluctantly agreed to end slavery, though this reprieve did not last very long.

Bransfield's coolness and navigational abilities under fire during the Bombardment of Algiers were recognised by Captain Aylmer, who reported him 'a very clever and attentive man'. He was awarded a medal for his part in the action. However, cleverness was of little value in the navy during the years following the end of the Napoleonic Wars. The end of hostilities with France left the navy, which was geared for war, not peace, heavily over-staffed and with hundreds of ships of all shapes and sizes suddenly idle.

Thousands of seamen – many recruited by the press gangs – were thrown back on to the streets and quaysides. Although officers were retained, there was precious little activity and hundreds of men were placed on half-pay, waiting for the miracle of a new posting. The peacetime navy at the time could boast around 1,700 Captains or Commanders and more than 4,000 Lieutenants. Significantly for Bransfield, the navy also had nearly 700 qualified Masters, with only a fraction gainfully employed.

Bransfield was not prepared to wait for the call and took matters into his own hands. He took the bold step of approaching the Admiralty to promote his prowess as a navigator, insisting that he could calculate longitude to within half a degree by measuring the angular distance between the sun and moon, using an artificial horizon. Bransfield, a self-confident man, asked for the opportunity to test his theory on 'any vessel going on discovery'. It was his first bid to be an explorer.

While the Admiralty was considering his offer, Bransfield took a new wife, Carolyn Bath, whom he married at St George's-in-the-East, London, on 10 February 1817. Unfortunately, the Admiralty rejected his proposal. However, there was something about Bransfield that attracted the Admiralty bigwigs. In September 1817, Bransfield effectively bypassed scores of other qualified mariners and was appointed Master of *Andromache*, a 44-gun frigate heading into South American waters. Leaving his new wife in London, Bransfield sailed south in December the same year.

Under the command of 33-year-old Captain William Shirreff, the *Andromache* was charged with safeguarding British interests in South America at a time of considerable political upheaval, particularly within Chile where the struggle for independence from Spain was nearing its climax. After a brief stop at Rio de Janeiro, *Andromache* sailed around Cape Horn to the Chilean port of Valparaiso. *Andromache* arrived in May 1818, just three months after Chilean independence, and here Bransfield unexpectedly found his wish for a 'vessel going on discovery'.

His opportunity arose in February 1819 when the *Williams*, a merchant brig, was caught in a storm while taking an assorted cargo of tobacco, clothing and medicines around Cape Horn from Buenos Aires to Valparaiso. Captain William Smith, the skipper and part owner of the *Williams*, drove further south than usual into the Drake Passage in an attempt to find favourable winds and made an unexpected sighting of land that was not on any charts. Despite being lashed by gales and frequent snow showers, Smith managed to place the unknown territory at a latitude of 62° S and longitude 60° W.

Smith, a 28-year-old seafarer who hailed from the North Sea colliery port of Blyth in Northumberland, had gained some experience of the ice after serving on whalers to Greenland seas and decided it was worthwhile waiting for conditions to improve to get a better sight of his discovery. Next day, with the weather a little calmer, Smith pushed slowly south through the ice and caught a clear sight of a bleak headland which he named Williams Point. The headland was the northeastern tip of Livingstone Island, one of the cluster of eleven main islands and a scattering of minor islets which make up the chain of South Shetland Islands, about 500 miles (800 km) south of Cape Horn and 80–100 miles (120–160 km) to the north of the then unknown Antarctic Peninsula. Smith initially called the land New South Britain, though this was later revised to New South Shetlands.

Putting commerce before discovery, Smith wisely withdrew and took his cargo north to Valparaiso, where he dutifully reported news of the sighting to Captain Shirreff of the *Andromache*, the most senior Royal Navy officer in the region. However, business was more important to Smith than new territory for the Crown, particularly as he also reported abundant whales and seals in the area. *Williams* had been blown off course at a time when whalers and sealers, particularly the Americans, were driving further and further south towards the Southern Ocean in search of new hunting grounds. Hunters had already plundered the seas around the Falkland Islands, South Georgia and Patagonia, with seals virtually exterminated on some coasts. Any new finds were like gold dust and Smith, a loyal servant to the King, was anxious to keep foreign vessels from stealing Britain's spoils.

Shirreff, already under pressure because of the volatile political climate, was unsure about Smith's sighting and had more pressing concerns than pursuing vague reports of new land in remote seas. Perhaps feeling that Smith had mistaken icebergs for land, Shirreff decided to take no action.

Smith was unhappy at the rejection, but nevertheless assembled a new cargo for his vessel and prepared to take the *Williams* back around the Horn to the Uruguayan port of Montevideo. Despite initial naval indifference, he also pledged to take *Williams* on a southerly detour to establish clear proof of his earlier discovery. With midwinter fast approaching, the *Williams* endured a terrible battering from gales and strong winds south of Cape Horn. By 15 June – less than a week from midwinter in southern latitudes – parts of the sea were freezing over while Smith struggled in vain to locate the land seen briefly only a few months earlier. He had sailed a little further to the west than on his earlier voyage, but in vain. *Williams* withdrew without ever sighting land, reaching Montevideo where Smith found himself to be the talk of the wharves and quays.

Smith's first sighting of land in February had aroused great excitement in South America, particularly among the eager shipowners salivating at rumours that the waters south of Cape Horn were teeming with whales and seals. Many wanted to send ships south as quickly as possible before news of Smith's discovery became more widespread and attracted the inevitable influx of treasure hunters. One quick-witted American agent had already sent word of the discovery back to Washington and another group of merchants tried to persuade Smith to take *Williams* south on their behalf. But Smith was in no mood to switch allegiance. The war between Britain and America had ended only four years earlier and the loyal Smith politely turned down the offer to sail under a US flag.

Instead, he set about finding a new cargo to take around the Horn and decided once again to take the *Williams* on another search for the mysterious land. *Williams* sailed in late September and by mid-October the vessel had encountered a small snow-capped island – Desolation Island – in the vicinity of his earlier sighting. The waters, he discovered, were stocked with vast quantities of seals, whales and penguins. Next day, 16 October 1819, Smith landed at place he called Venus Bay, taking possession for King George III and the Empire.

After sighting more land in the necklace of New South Shetland islands, Smith promptly headed for Valparaiso with his cargo and the clear message for Shirreff that he had definitely discovered land further south than anyone before. As he spoke, vessels from different parts of the world were already converging on the waters to the south of Cape Horn. Captain Shirreff and the British merchants quickly revised their earlier judgement about Smith's discoveries, buoyed by the commercial prospects of tapping the new-found riches of whale and seal stocks. To many, commerce was more important than the strategic national interest and one keen local businessman, John Miers, proposed chartering *Williams* immediately to beat the Americans to the rich pickings.

Word of Smith's sighting spread quickly. A group of enterprising British merchants across the Andes in Buenos Aires were already putting together their own voyage to hunt for seals and news of the discovery was being relayed back to London. In an unrelated move, Tsar Alexander of Russia had despatched Thaddeus von Bellingshausen, a tough and experienced naval captain, to explore the southern waters, though he was unaware of Smith's discoveries. After his earlier prevarication, Shirreff now moved quickly. He used his authority to take *Williams* on charter and ordered a Royal Navy team to head south to investigate Smith's claims on behalf of the government. His next step was to send for Bransfield. After sixteen years in naval service, it was the first time that Bransfield was posted to take full command of an expedition.

Bransfield was the perfect man for the difficult task. Shirreff had witnessed Bransfield's seafaring skills on the long voyage of *Andromache* to South America and was quick to reassure the Admiralty that the expedition was in safe hands. In a private letter to John Croker, the Admiralty Secretary, Shirreff, wrote of Bransfield that: '. . . from my own observation, I know [him] to be well qualified for the undertaking . . .'[2]

Shirreff's orders to Bransfield were to verify Smith's discoveries, chart any new findings and to observe any wildlife and inhabitants they ran into. Finally, Bransfield was ordered to take possession of any lands for the Empire and commanded not to divulge a word of the discoveries if the *Williams* happened to be driven into any foreign ports. Bransfield was told to 'conceal every discovery that you may have made during your voyage'.

Shirreff's new-found urgency caught Smith on the hop. *Williams*, which was already loaded and ready to take a new cargo back around the Horn, had to be hurriedly unloaded and refitted for the more hazardous voyage to the south. With Bransfield in sole command, Captain Smith was probably reduced to the role of pilot on his own ship.

A recreation of Bransfield's pioneering voyage to the Antarctic in the brig *Williams* in February 1820.
From a painting by Commander G. W. G. Hunt. RICHARD J. CAMPBELL

Williams – the name came from the simple fact that three of its four owners were called William – sailed with a total complement of thirty men. Apart from Bransfield and Smith, the ship also carried three navy midshipmen – Thomas Bone, Patrick Blake and Charles Poynter – and Dr Adam Young, a surgeon from the navy sloop *Slaney*. The *Williams* left Valparaiso on 20 December 1819 flying the British pendant and with fervent hopes that valuable new discoveries were about to be made. The ship took water for ninety days and provisions for twelve months, including four bullocks and other assorted livestock. The day before, the log on Bransfield's old ship, *Andromache*, contained the optimistic entry: '[the expedition] to go on a voyage of discovery towards the South Pole.'[3]

The journey ahead involved sailing more than 2,000 miles (3,200 km) from Valparaiso to the South Shetlands, including a 500-mile crossing of the notoriously difficult seas of the Drake Passage, which separate South America from Antarctica. By any circumstances, the voyage of the *Williams* was a remarkable leap of faith. The small sailing vessel, a wooden two-masted brig of just 216 tons, had not been specially strengthened to withstand the ice of the Southern Ocean and, unlike most other voyages of discovery, the *Williams* was entering mostly unknown seas alone without a support vessel or any means of communicating with the outside world. Bransfield, for all his seafaring skills, was a novice in handling the ice and only Smith among the officers had any recent experience of navigation in icy waters.

Bransfield ran into difficulties almost immediately. It took nine days' battling against unfavourable winds to travel the first 6 miles (10 km) from Valparaiso and, in early January 1820, *Williams* was caught by a sudden heavy squall and her sails were ripped. Soon after, it was discovered that the fresh water barrels had leaked and the daily allowance per man was promptly reduced by a third. Unknown to Bransfield, he was also in danger of being forestalled. Eager British businessmen in Buenos Aires had chartered *Espirito Santo*, a small merchant vessel under Captain Joseph Herring, which landed on Rugged Island, a tiny island adjacent to Smith's Livingstone Island. Herring took a party ashore on Christmas Day 1819, toasted the King with glasses of grog and raised the Union Jack before embarking on a wholesale slaughter of seals.

Fog, a common feature of the Drake Passage in the summer months, was a constant problem as Bransfield struggled to avoid collisions with icebergs or rocks. But on 16 January 1820 the fog lifted to give a clear sight of the rocky shores of Livingstone Island. The austere, forbidding headland was named Cape Shirreff and Bransfield steered *Williams* into the nearby bay, which is now called Barclay Bay. Bransfield wanted to send Smith ashore to find fresh water but the heavy seas and dangerous rocks prevented *Williams* getting close in.

Williams sailed along the northern shore of Livingstone Island and continued gently northwards, running along the ribbon of islands which form a nearly straight line between 62° and 63°. King George Island, the largest of the group, which had been sighted by Smith only a few months earlier, was rounded by 22 January and the ship swung to the south where the expedition came across an inviting-looking bay. Bransfield was anxious to follow protocol by staking a claim for British sovereignty and he took a small party ashore for the ritual of planting the flag on the Empire's most southerly outpost, which was eventually named King George Bay. A toast was held, a gun fired and Bransfield ceremoniously buried a bottle containing several coins. However, the elderly King George III was dead within seven days of the landing and never knew about Bransfield's small addition to the Empire, which lies only around 80 miles (130 km) from the Antarctic Peninsula.

Less than 100 miles (160km) from Bransfield's party, sealers from *Espirito Santo* on Rugged Island were bludgeoning seals by the thousand, completely unaware that anyone else was in the area. Soon afterwards, the hunters in the area were joined by the *San Juan Nepomuceno* from Argentina and the American brig *Hersilia*, whose Second Mate, Nathaniel Palmer, later became embroiled in the controversy about who first discovered the Antarctic continent.

Bransfield turned away from King George Island, first running along the southern shores of the island chain and then heading due south towards Deception Island. But fog

Bransfield Strait, the gateway to the Antarctic, which was discovered by Edward Bransfield in 1820.
Looking south from Livingston Island, the picture shows the Antarctic Peninsula in the distance.

prevented a landing and another flag-raising ceremony. The *Williams* turned south and entered totally unknown seas between the South Shetland Islands and the coast of Antarctica. This deep stretch of water, which is about 200 miles (320 km) long and some 60 miles (100 km) wide, is today called the Bransfield Strait.

More than 1,000 miles away, the Russian Bellingshausen was taking his ships, *Vostok* (East) and *Mirnyi* (Peaceful), below the Antarctic Circle, the first time the meridian had been penetrated since Cook's voyage almost half a century earlier. *Williams* crossed the latitude of 63° and on Sunday 30 January 1820 Midshipman Poynter recorded in his journal: 'At 3 our notice was arrested by three very large icebergs and 20 minutes after we were unexpectedly astonished by the discovery of land . . .'[4]

Shortly after, the haze cleared and they found themselves 'half encompassed with islands'. The land appeared to be 'immense mountains, rude crags and barren ridges covered with snow', which one observer said presented a 'most dreary and dismal aspect.' Poynter wondered whether they had found 'the long-contested existence of a Southern Continent'.[5] Bransfield rounded the small Tower Island and observed a rocky chunk of the northwestern Antarctic Peninsula which was named Trinity Land. The land, his charts recorded, was 'partly covered with snow'.

Williams sailed along the coast in stormy weather but it was impossible to get too close to shore because the entrance was blocked by a cluster of thirty-one icebergs, which were lined up in regimental fashion to form an insurmountable barrier. Fog soon obliterated the landscape and Bransfield withdrew, not realising how close he was to becoming the first man to set foot on the Antarctic continent. In squally winds and dense fog, the experienced navigator was acutely aware that *Williams* was risking a potentially fatal collision with rocks or an iceberg. He had little choice but to withdraw further. As he sailed away, Bransfield could clearly pick out a fine snow-capped peak in the distance, which gave a final view of the new discovered land. Today the peak, which climbs to 2,500 ft (760 m), is called Mount Bransfield.

Events which sparked two centuries of controversy were unfolding 1,500 miles (2,400 km) away across the Southern Ocean where Bellingshausen's *Vostok* and *Mirnyi* were closing in on the Antarctic coastline. On 27 January, three days before Bransfield's sighting, Bellingshausen reached 69° 21' S where he observed 'continuous ice' and 'ice mountains' stretching out before them. Bellingshausen's position placed him near the ice shelves of Kronprinsesse Martha Kyst and Prinsesse Ragnhild Kyst, little more than 20 miles from the coast of today's Dronning Maud Land. But he did not realise how close he was sailing to the continental land mass.

Crucially, he made no record of seeing land, perhaps because he did not fully appreciate that almost every inch of the Antarctic continent is covered in ice and snow, and because he expected land to look quite literally like land. Mikhail Lazarev, commander of the *Mirnyi*, reported an 'ice shore of extreme height' but he, too, did not distinguish ice from land. The dispute about whether it was Bransfield or Bellingshausen who first saw the Antarctic continent continues to this day. Bransfield was convinced he had discovered new land and in true efficient naval style recorded his discovery, whereas Bellingshausen was unable – or unwilling – to state for certain that he had encountered land. Bellingshausen reported what he saw and did not make any judgement, whereas Bransfield had a clear view of the distinctly rocky shoreline and mapped his discovery according to the orders he received before sailing.

Nathaniel Palmer, the American sealer, added to the controversy by later claiming that his sloop *Hero* had made a definite sighting of the Peninsula in November 1820 – precisely ten months after the voyages of Bransfield and Bellingshausen. Fanciful though Palmer's claim sounds, the lack of conclusive evidence over the years has merely fuelled the controversy. Bellingshausen's inconclusive reports and the curiously indifferent reception he received on returning to Russia meant that his claims were largely ignored for over a century. His account of the voyage was not translated into English until 1945.

More mysterious was the disappearance of Bransfield's log of the *Williams*, the crucial evidence which would have added weight to the legitimacy of his claim to be the first to sight Antarctica. Initially, support for Bransfield's claim relied on the charts he drew at the time or the flimsier evidence of a few articles in some publications of the day. But his case was greatly strengthened in the 1990s by the discovery of the private journal of Midshipman Poynter, the only known original account of the voyage.[6] In addition, more recent examination of the surviving charts indicate that the positions plotted by Bransfield are very close to those accurately established by modern cartography.

Bransfield was totally unaware of the controversy which would later surround his voyage as he turned *Williams* north in February 1820. Rocked by gales and a heavy fog, the ship occasionally sailed blind and once the crew mistakenly thought they glimpsed a new chunk of land. *Williams* sailed between Gibbs and O'Brien Islands and eased around the north shore of Elephant Island, a grimly inhospitable dot in the Southern Ocean where, 100 years later, men from Shackleton's *Endurance* would be marooned. A brief landing was made at Cape Bowles on nearby Clarence Island to plant the Union Jack, but the weather was atrocious and Bransfield did not linger.

Despite the high winds and squally seas, he decided there was sufficient time in the season for a little more exploration. He sailed east for a further ten days, occasionally turning south into the outer reaches of the infamous Weddell Sea and along the eastern side of the Antarctic Peninsula where it was hoped to spot new land. But thick ice shaped an impassable barrier and on 23 February, at a 'furthest south' of 64° 56' S, the expedition turned north.

The doughty *Williams* sailed into Valparaiso on 14 April after an outstanding voyage into the largely uncharted and most hazardous waters on earth. The ship, which was poorly equipped and pitifully unsuited to the immense challenges of the Southern Ocean, survived because of Bransfield's highly accomplished seamanship and not a man was lost on the four-month expedition.

One curiosity is that Bransfield gave names to a host of newly discovered geographical features, the first time that parts of the continent of Antarctica had been authoritatively mapped. However, the modest Bransfield did not follow custom and name any places after himself. An even bigger mystery is what happened to Bransfield's documents of the expedition. Bransfield handed his log, charts and sketches of the new land to Captain Thomas Searle of the frigate *Hyperion*, the most senior officer available. On the assumption that he had fulfilled his duties, Bransfield rejoined *Andromache* in May 1820. Searle forwarded the documents, including the logbook of the *Williams*, to London. It was never seen again.

Bransfield was aware that his voyage had only scratched the surface of the region and was anxious to return to the south at the earliest opportunity. In handing over his expedition records, Bransfield told Captain Searle: 'I beg leave to offer my services to finish it [the exploration] the next season, being of the opinion there is a great deal more to be done . . .'[7] Searle, adhering to naval procedure, insisted that Bransfield not talk to a soul about his voyage, which in the fevered climate only added fuel to the rumours about the expedition. But, crucially, Searle did not ask Bransfield to make a second voyage south.

By contrast, Smith, whose initial discovery had prompted the navy to send Bransfield south, quickly provisioned the *Williams* and embarked on a mission to plunder the new hunting grounds. Eager American hunters also joined the pursuit and within a year the seal population on the South Shetland Islands had been virtually exterminated.

Bransfield returned to England on the *Andromache* a year later and slipped quietly into obscurity. He was paid off from *Andromache* in September 1821 and never sailed on a Royal Navy vessel again. He picked up a modest payment for his voyage of discovery and remained on half-pay for the rest of his life. But he never enlisted on a Royal Navy ship again and, for reasons which are still unclear, instead turned his considerable energies to the merchant service.

Bransfield's motives for leaving the navy after eighteen years' service may never be known. But events at the Admiralty in London and the curious lack of official interest shown in his discovery must have been bewildering and probably influenced his decision. He returned to London with news of his Antarctic discovery at a time when the two most influential men at the Admiralty – Irishman John Croker and John Barrow – had their attention fixed on the other end of the globe.

Croker and Barrow, the Admiralty's most important power brokers, were almost totally preoccupied with the Arctic, principally the quest to find the elusive North-West Passage with Parry. John Croker, who was born in Galway, came from a background of influence and privilege. His father was Surveyor General of Customs and Excise in Ireland and Croker did not waste the opportunity fate had bestowed upon him. He was friends with the Duke of Wellington, served as an MP for twenty-six years and held the lofty position of Admiralty Secretary for twenty-one years. Loathed and feared in equal measure, Croker was an energetic political animal who formed a formidable partnership to direct key naval policy with John Barrow, the powerful civil servant and Admiralty Second Secretary for over forty years.

Barrow and Croker decided that, with ships and men idle at the end of the war with France, the country should embark on a sustained programme of exploration – especially to find the North-West Passage. Both men had staked considerable political capital in a successful campaign to locate the Passage and it is possible they regarded Bransfield's Antarctic discovery as an irritating sideshow to the main event. The prevailing opinion in London, first espoused by Captain Cook fifty years earlier, was that the frozen Antarctic was worthless.

Bransfield's timing was also unfortunate. As word of the Antarctic discovery reached England in the autumn of 1820, Parry was returning in triumph from a highly successful voyage to the Arctic in which he had penetrated halfway to the Bering Strait, sailed further west than anyone else and charted thousands of miles of new coastline. In the face of official apathy, Bransfield slipped off the Admiralty radar over the remaining years of his life. While many of the men who had pursued the ambition of Barrow and Croker in the Arctic were given knighthoods for their endeavours, Bransfield was overlooked for honours and soon forgotten. William Smith, whose sighting of the South Shetlands prompted Bransfield's trip, died poor and ignored in 1847 at the age of fifty-six. The *Williams* outlasted almost everyone, finally serving as a colliery vessel before being broken up in 1882.

Few details of Bransfield's later life have survived, although it is known that he sailed on numerous merchant vessels on the busy trading routes to the Mediterranean and South America and is thought to have earned a decent living. There is some speculation that on his regular visits to South America Bransfield occasionally returned to Antarctic waters. He was nearing his sixties when he married for the third time, though none of his marriages produced any children. His new bride was Anne, a woman seven years his junior. In 1848, when Bransfield was 63, the couple settled in Brighton on the south coast of England, one of the country's earliest seaside resorts, which was enjoying a boom from the influx of day trippers pouring into the town for a dip in the sea. The Bransfields lived quietly at 11 Clifton Road, only a short walk to the fashionable seafront. A couple of years later, the pair moved to 61 London Road, near the newly built railway station.

Edward Bransfield died on 31 October 1852 of what was called 'organic disease of the stomach', which was probably cancer. He was aged sixty-seven and had outlived Bellingshausen, his rival for the accolade of discovering the Antarctic continent, by just ten months. He left Anne a yearly pension of £50, which she continued to receive until her death in December 1865, aged seventy-three. Bransfield asked that, after Anne's death,

25

Bransfield's penultimate home. The property at Clifton Road, Brighton, where Edward Bransfield lived with his wife Anne during his final years. The couple lived at Clifton Road from 1848 and moved to the nearby London Road shortly before his death in 1852.
ROB STEPHENSON

any possessions should be given to the children of his brother, William Bransfield, in Midleton, County Cork. A few other items were donated to an old colleague from the *Andromache* days, Thomas Porter. Without children to perpetuate his memory or official naval recognition to commemorate his feats, Bransfield disappeared from view. Equally, Antarctica itself was as soon forgotten as Bransfield in the mid-Victorian age.

Interest in the Antarctic virtually disappeared after 1850. Even the voracious whalers took their bloody trade elsewhere and it was not until the early 1890s that curiosity in the continent was revived, first by renewed visits from the whaling fleets and then by teams

The last resting place of Edward Bransfield. He is buried at the Extra-Mural Cemetery on the outskirts of Brighton and the inscription, which celebrates his great voyage of discovery, reads: "The First Man to See Mainland Antarctica in January 1820." MICHAEL SMITH

of explorers. The first recorded landing on the Antarctic mainland was made at Cape Adare in January 1895 and in 1898, the *Belgica* crossed the Bransfield Strait to the Antarctic Peninsula before becoming the first expedition to overwinter in Antarctica. *Belgica*'s Second Mate was Roald Amundsen, who, a decade later, would be first to set foot at the South Pole.

Recognition for Bransfield did not materialise until well into the twentieth century when several geographic features were finally named after the man from Ballinacurra. The Bransfield Strait, the stretch of water between the South Shetlands and the

Antarctic Peninsula, which was first penetrated by Bransfield in 1820, had originally been named by Weddell in 1825. But more than 100 years after his death there followed the 2,500 ft (760 m) Mount Bransfield (63° 17' S, 57° 6' W) and Bransfield Island (63° 11' S, 56° 37' W) at the northeast tip of the Antarctic Peninsula. Sir Vivian Fuchs, who in the mid–1950s made the first ever coast-to-coast crossing of the Antarctic, recommended that the British Antarctic Survey's supply vessel should be named RRS *Bransfield* in his honour.

A different type of recognition came 150 years after his death when Sheila Bransfield, a distant descendant of the seafarer, raised funds to renovate Bransfield's grave at the Extra-Mural Cemetery in Brighton as a more fitting monument to his achievements. The ceremony in 1999 was attended by many representatives of modern Polar institutions – including the British Antarctic Survey, Royal Navy and Scott Polar Research Institute – who are indebted to the skill and courage of Bransfield in helping to open the pathway to the continent nearly two centuries before. The refurbished tomb is unequivocal about Bransfield's achievements and confidently avoids any debate about who was the first to sight the Antarctic continent. The simple inscription reads: 'The First Man to See Mainland Antarctica in January 1820'.

In keeping with his enigmatic character, no portrait or photograph of Edward Bransfield has yet been discovered and the man who made the first definite sighting of the Antarctic continent died without history ever being able to recognise him fully. All that remains is the unambiguous statement from the grave.

FRANCIS CROZIER

1795–*c.* 1848

Francis Crozier, captured by an unknown artist in the early 1820s, around the time when he made his first voyage to the Arctic with Parry.

NOTHING IN THE LONG and rich history of the Crozier family gave even the slightest clue that the most famous Crozier of all – Francis Crozier – would become one of the nineteenth century's most accomplished and prolific explorers. Or that his remarkable exploits, which included six voyages of discovery to the Arctic and Antarctic during the era of sailing ships, would slip largely unnoticed into the half-forgotten corners of history.

Francis Crozier was a member of an old-established and prosperous family from Banbridge, County Down, with a history that can be traced back almost 1,000 years to the Norman invasion of the British Isles. The name Crozier stems from the French *croisé* (crusader) and the earliest known members of the family landed in England with the Norman armies of William the Conqueror in 1066. Later generations settled in the north of England, Scotland and eventually in Ireland. For generations, the Croziers were to be found among the ranks of professional soldiers, affluent landowners, respectable lawyers and clergymen.

The first to settle in Ireland was Captain John Crozier, a cavalry officer who came across from England in the 1630s and was stationed at Dublin Castle guarding Sir Thomas Wentworth, the ruthless Lord Deputy of Ireland. Captain Crozier remained behind in Ireland after Wentworth's departure and subsequently put down roots in County Down among newly transplanted Protestant and Presbyterian communities.

The Crozier dynasty in Ireland became firmly established in Down over the following years, acquiring sizeable measures of land and slowly climbing the social ladder through a series of well-selected marriages into other prominent landowning families. George Crozier, the father of Francis Crozier, was an enterprising solicitor who married Jane Graham in the late eighteenth century and raised thirteen children. He built a highly successful law firm in the rapidly developing town of Banbridge on the banks of the River Bann, which was enjoying the benefits of Down's fast-growing linen industry. But the key to George Crozier's own prosperity was a close business and personal association with the Marquis of Downshire and Lord Moira, two of Ireland's most powerful landlords.

The house in Banbridge where Francis Crozier was born in 1796. It was built in 1791 and is today known as Crozier House. MICHAEL SMITH

In recognition of the strong ties between the families, the fifth son of George and Jane Crozier was named Francis Rawdon Moira Crozier after Francis Rawdon, the Earl of Moira.

Francis Rawdon Moira Crozier was born on 16 September 1796 and enjoyed a comfortable upbringing in the family home of Avonmore House (now called Crozier House) in the heart of Banbridge, which was an impressive and unmistakable symbol of the family's elevated status. But young Francis did not remain in Banbridge to enjoy the benefits of the family's prominence, nor did he follow the path taken by his brothers into the law or the church.

Instead George Crozier used his impeccable connections to send thirteen-year-old Francis Crozier into the Royal Navy. In June 1810, three months before his fourteenth birthday, Francis Crozier travelled from Banbridge to Cork, enlisted in the navy and was posted to the frigate *Hamadryad*. Crozier's appointment was the start of nearly forty years of outstanding naval service which, in adult life, would involve him with the three great endeavours of nineteenth-century exploration – navigating the North-West Passage, reaching the North Pole and mapping the unknown continent of Antarctica.

The contrast between teenage Crozier's cosy life in Banbridge and the brutality of the navy in 1810 was stark and immediate. Britain's war with Napoleonic France was reaching a new intensity in 1810 when Crozier joined up, with the critically important Peninsula Campaign in Spain and Portugal at its height. Crozier, in training to become an officer, had little time to adjust to the grim reality and constant dangers of the wartime navy. His first voyages on *Hamadryad* were to escort merchant ships across the Atlantic and bring fresh troops to the battlefields of Portugal. He was also given an early demonstration of the navy's strict disciplinary regime when two deserters were given 150 lashes apiece.

Despite the abrupt change in lifestyle, Crozier adapted well and began to flourish. By 1812, with the tide of the war turning against Napoleon, Crozier had completed his initial training and was appointed Midshipman on board *Briton*, a 44-gun frigate under the command of Sir Thomas Staines which was in the direct line of fire patrolling the Bay of Biscay to enforce the blockade of France. Soon after joining *Briton*, Crozier made his first voyage of discovery.

In 1814, Staines was ordered to pursue the American frigate *Essex*, which was harassing British vessels off the coast of South America and had escaped into the Pacific to evade capture. The orders meant taking *Briton* around Cape Horn alone in midwinter. More than 100 sailors were incapacitated as *Briton* battled high winds, heavy waves and strong currents, and the ship eventually reached Valparaiso in Chile to learn that *Essex* had already been captured. *Briton* was ordered to pursue another American ship towards the remote Marquesas Islands, but became lost in the vast expanses of the Pacific and stumbled across a small uncharted island. On landing, the party were astonished to be greeted by friendly inhabitants speaking English and discovered that the unmapped island was Pitcairn, the tiny outpost where John Adams, the last surviving mutineer from the *Bounty*, was living in blissful exile. Only one other vessel had ever reached Pitcairn before.

After another alarming trip around Cape Horn, Crozier returned to England in the summer of 1815, shortly after Napoleon's defeat at Waterloo, which brought an end to the long war. By chance, a later posting to the sloop *Dotterel* took Crozier to St Helena, the isolated tropical island in the South Atlantic where Napoleon was exiled.

However, Crozier, like so many aspiring young officers, found that life in the navy had changed dramatically with the end of the Napoleonic Wars. Dozens of warships were suddenly idle, thousands of press-ganged sailors were summarily dismissed and nine in every ten officers were left unemployed and anxiously waiting for a posting which, in all probability, would never come. Crozier, at barely twenty years of age, faced limited prospects. A new posting was remote and promotion was improbable in a navy in which commissions were granted on the basis of age. Some admirals were still serving into their eighties and the Admiralty had thousands of capable officers on its books should a vacancy suddenly occur.

One ray of hope was a decision by the Admiralty to employ a few redundant ships and men on a new programme of exploration to areas of the world considered important to the Empire. Britain, an unrivalled power in the world after the defeat of France, had turned the peace into a golden opportunity to expand the Empire and develop profitable new sources of commercial trade. Top of the agenda was to discover a navigable route through the North-West Passage – a sea route linking the Atlantic and the Pacific across the top of North America.

The search for the North-West Passage had defied navigators for almost 300 years and the Admiralty's two most influential figures of the day – John Croker and John Barrow – believed that Britain needed to find the elusive pathway before other foreign powers stole the country's thunder. Barrow set the jingoistic tone by insisting it would be 'little short of national suicide' if an upstart foreigner beat the might of the Royal Navy to the accolade.

Over the next thirty years the Admiralty sent a volley of ships to the Arctic ice and created a generation of famous explorers, including Edward Parry, John Franklin and the uncle-and-nephew pair of John and James Clark Ross. Lieutenant Francis Crozier from Banbridge was twenty-five years old when he joined the illustrious line.

The opportunity arose in 1821 when Crozier volunteered to join an expedition under Parry to find the Passage. Parry was the most celebrated explorer of the day who had earlier sailed his ships further west into Lancaster Sound, the gateway to the Passage, than anyone before. After being thwarted by a wall of ice in Lancaster Sound, Parry now intended to take *Fury* and *Hecla*, the specially strengthened ice ships, into the largely unknown Foxe Basin, which lies between Hudson's Bay and Baffin Island. The two modified navy mortar bomb ships sailed in May 1821 and were gone for over two years. It was a voyage which confirmed that the mysterious Passage did not exist around Hudson's

Bay, although the expedition did discover the more promising Fury and Hecla Strait high above the Arctic Circle. Hopes were high that the narrow channel might solve the riddle of the Passage. But another insurmountable barrier of ice prevented the ships penetrating very far and it was not until 1948 – some 126 years after the visit of *Fury* and *Hecla* – that a modern icebreaker managed to smash a way through the ice.

Crozier, who served on *Fury*, impressed Parry with his cool head and strong sense of duty during the two-year voyage. He was loyal, hard-working and showed a particular ability with the maritime sciences of the day, astronomy, collating magnetic data and tidal observations.

However, Parry sometimes wondered whether Crozier took his job too seriously. On one occasion Parry became concerned when Crozier failed to return to the ship on schedule after a visit ashore in appalling weather to measure tidal flows. Parry led a search party to the windswept beach where they found a diligent Crozier sheltering behind a rock and calmly logging tidal readings, apparently oblivious to the raging storm or the concern of his captain.

Crozier was again recruited in 1824 when Parry led a fresh attempt to find the Passage by once more driving into Lancaster Sound and exploring Prince Regent Inlet to the south. But atrocious weather checked progress and *Hecla* and *Fury* were forced to spend ten months holed up in a bleak cove more than 300 miles (480 km) above the Arctic Circle.

Thick ice and high winds continued to torture the ships after their release in July 1825 and a month later *Fury* was driven ashore in a gale and had to be abandoned. *Hecla*, with 120 men and supplies crammed on board, limped home alone in late 1825. With the North-West Passage seemingly beyond his grasp, Parry's attention was drawn to the North Pole. Once again he asked Crozier to go with him.

The expedition, timed for the summer of 1827, planned to take *Hecla* to Spitsbergen in the Svalbard archipelago and despatch two teams of seamen, supplemented by the auxiliary power of Scandinavian reindeer, to drag boats on a 700-mile (1,100-km) trek across the ice and open seas to the Pole. The dependable Crozier was given responsibility for remaining in charge of *Hecla*, ensuring the ship did not become ice-bound and to lay down food depots for the sledging parties to pick up on the way back from the Pole.

It was a hopelessly optimistic venture. Parry aimed to travel 15 miles (24 km) a day, but the reindeer were totally ineffective and, with each boat weighing 1,800 lb (850 kgs), the pulling was impossibly hard. To compound the misery, the currents and drift drove them south almost as fast they trudged north. During an exhausting five-week trek, the men covered 668 miles (1,070 km) but advanced only 172 miles (275 km) towards the Pole because of the contrary winds and currents. Five days' punishing work at one stage carried them only 1 mile (1.6 km) north and the slog was halted soon after. But the record 'furthest north' of 82° 45' N – about 500 miles (800 km) from the North Pole – would stand for almost half a century. The disappointed expedition returned to London in October 1827 to discover there had been a change of political mood at the Admiralty and, after a decade of endeavour, Arctic exploration was no longer a priority.

There was, however, some consolation in defeat for Crozier. In 1827, during the time *Hecla* was berthed at Spitsbergen, Crozier's keen eye as an astronomer was recognised at the most senior levels and he was elected a Fellow of the esteemed Royal Astronomical Society.

Another idle period followed before his appointment in 1831 to the frigate *Stag*, which was sent to Portuguese waters to protect British interests during a local civil war. But Crozier was back in the ice towards the end of 1835 when he was summoned to help locate eleven whaling ships that had gone missing in the Davis Strait off western Greenland. The search mission was led by James Clark Ross, Crozier's former shipmate on the Parry expeditions and by now a close friend. The Admiralty asked Ross to pick his own team and take the whaler *Cove* in search of the missing ships. From the deep ranks of unemployed naval officers, Ross selected the reliable and experienced Crozier to be his deputy. *Cove* spent many weeks in the icy waters and managed to account for ten of the eleven ships, though one whaler and her entire crew were never found.

A far grander mission awaited Crozier and Ross in 1839 when the Admiralty finally turned away from the Arctic and decided to send a major expedition under Ross to explore the almost completely unknown Antarctic and improve scientific understanding of the region. Ross, with almost the entire navy to choose from, once again picked Crozier to sail as his deputy. Antarctica was a radical departure following the Admiralty's long obsession with the North-West Passage. Few ships had been south after the voyages of Bransfield and Bellingshausen in 1820 and little of the continent had been mapped. Only eager whalers and sealers, in search of new hunting grounds, bothered to venture into the unwelcoming seas but their interest was to make money, not to map the continent or improve scientific knowledge.

Although the expedition was directed by the Admiralty, the motivating force came from three of Ireland's most distinguished scientists – Humphrey Lloyd, Edward Sabine and Francis Beaufort – who wanted to compile an accurate magnetic chart of the globe, valuable data which would help determine the effects of the earth's magnetic field on compasses and hence aid navigation. The scientific community, led by Lloyd and Sabine, persuaded the Admiralty to equip an expedition to locate the Magnetic South Pole and fill in the gaps in their magnetic data. Some called it the 'Magnetic Crusade'.

One of the driving forces behind the crusade was Sir Francis Beaufort, the son of a Church of Ireland cleric from Navan, County Meath, who was among the most renowned nautical scientists of the age. Although largely self-educated, he developed the Beaufort Scale of measuring wind speed at sea and as Head of Hydrography at the Admiralty created the world's finest surveying and charting body. Some of Beaufort's charts are still in use today.

Beaufort was ably supported by Lloyd, an outstanding scientist from Dublin and among the leading authorities on terrestrial magnetism who, while still in his thirties, advised governments and devised his own instruments. The third leading 'Crusader' was Sabine, another Dubliner who explored the Arctic with Parry as a young man and later propelled the national campaign for improved magnetic research with single-minded determination. It was Sabine who successfully connected scientific theory with the practice of navigation and together with Lloyd and Ross was responsible for the first magnetic survey of the British Isles.

Francis Crozier and James Clark Ross were an ideal team to undertake the lengthy mission to the Antarctic. They had amassed great experience of the ice and were among the leading practitioners of the naval sciences, astronomy and magnetism. Ross, a dashing, charismatic figure who joined the navy a few days before his twelfth birthday, had journeyed on seven voyages of discovery and was the first to locate the Magnetic North Pole. He was suitably matched by the dependability and experienced seamanship of Crozier, a 43-year-old veteran of four voyages to the ice who had been at sea for over thirty years. Shortly before sailing, Crozier was promoted to the rank of Commander.

The pair had first met in 1821 on Parry's North-West Passage expedition and it is a fair indication of Ross's high regard that the major task of fitting out and provisioning the expedition ships, *Erebus* and *Terror*, was left entirely in the capable hands of Crozier. Ross would command 372-ton *Erebus* and Crozier, in his first posting in charge of an expedition ship, would take 326-ton *Terror*.

The expedition, the last of its type made entirely under sail, eventually lasted for four years and is regarded as the nineteenth century's greatest voyage of maritime discovery. Between 1839 and 1843, the expedition achieved the first penetration of the Antarctic pack ice in the Ross Sea area, charted thousands of miles of new seas and coastline and gave names to many of the Antarctic's most prominent landmarks which became familiar seventy years later during the Heroic Age of Exploration.

Notable discoveries included the Ross Sea, Ross Island and Mount Erebus, the earth's most southerly volcano. Victoria Land was named after the newly crowned Queen and a further discovery was the Great Icy Barrier, later called the Ice Barrier and formally renamed the Ross Ice Shelf in the 1950s. McMurdo Sound, the inlet near Ross Island where Scott and Shackleton would establish their base camps in the early twentieth century, was named after Archibald McMurdo, the 27-year-old naval Lieutenant on *Terror*. Cape Crozier, the desolate and windswept point on the east side of Ross Island, was commemorated eighty years later in *The Worst Journey in the World*, Apsley Cherry-Garrard's acclaimed book about Scott's last expedition.

Erebus and *Terror*, three-masted bomb vessels, were originally reinforced to withstand the powerful recoil of 3-ton mortars. But before encountering the Southern Ocean, each deck was doubled-planked and oak beams were fitted to reinforce the hull, which was also

Erebus and *Terror* battling the ice during the expedition to the Antarctic made by Crozier and Ross from 1839 to 1843. Crozier captained *Terror* and never lost a man during the four-year journey.

sheathed in a double layer of copper as extra insurance against the crushing power of the ice. Each ship carried sixty-four men and the large holds were stocked with supplies and equipment for a journey lasting at least three years, including tons of tinned meat and vegetables, barrels of lemon juice to stave off scurvy and a crude form of central heating pipes which sent hot water coursing through the living quarters from the ships' stoves.

Erebus and *Terror* sailed down the River Thames in late September 1839 and ran into the first of many gales after only three days. The first port of call was St Helena, where an observatory was erected close to the house once occupied by Napoleon during his exile. This was followed by an uncomfortable two-month sojourn on the remote and windswept Kerguelen Islands in the Indian Ocean where hurricanes and violent storms raged for forty-five of the sixty-eight days of their stay.

Gales next carried the ships to Hobart, the penal colony on Van Diemen's Land (renamed Tasmania in 1855) where the island's Governor was Sir John Franklin, the old Arctic explorer and friend of both Ross and Crozier. Under Franklin's scrutiny a squad of 200 convicts built a new observatory called Rossbank. A painting of the observatory, made by a former convict, showed Crozier, Ross and Franklin standing outside the building and was later sent as a gift to Sabine.

While at Hobart, Crozier fell deeply in love. The focus of his affections was Sophy Cracroft, the attractive niece of Franklin and companion to his wife, Lady Jane Franklin.

Unfortunately, the flirtatious Cracroft was attracted to Ross and she politely rejected Crozier's advances. The epic voyage south began in November 1840, with Crozier and Ross each carrying a pot of jam made by Jane Franklin and Crozier convinced he had found his true love. He resolved to seek Sophy's hand in marriage on his return from the ice.

The aim was to stick closely to the 170° meridian to avoid areas where rival expeditions from France and America might be operating. The Antarctic Circle was crossed for the first time on New Year's Day 1841 and extra clothing was given to the men as the temperatures dropped. A few days later *Erebus* and *Terror* ran into the dense pack ice which encircles the Antarctic continent at anything between 350 and 1,800 miles (560–2,880 km) in width.

Erebus and *Terror* edged forward, sometimes probing delicately and sometimes using brute force to bludgeon a route through the ice. Swirling fog hampered progress and this was quickly followed by driving gales, which increased the risk of collision with the surrounding mass of icebergs that frequently towered above the ships' masts. Moving slowly through the maze it was soon apparent that any hope of retreat was futile as the ice closed together behind *Erebus* and *Terror*. Muskets were fired and bells rung as the vessels occasionally became separated in the foggy gloom. But the spirit of the party was unshakeable and in spite of the risks, Crozier and Ross calmly went on board each other's ship to celebrate Twelfth Night with a glass of cherry brandy.

Skilful seamanship and a decent slice of good luck carried the ships southwards and by 9 January a welcome strong breeze had shifted the fog. At noon the weather cleared and Crozier and Ross unexpectedly found themselves in open, ice-free waters. Using only sail, Crozier and Ross had penetrated the pack of the Ross Sea area for the first time, an incredible feat of seamanship to rank alongside the achievements of the great navigators such as Vasco da Gama, Ferdinand Magellan and James Cook.

Later explorers also saluted the triumph of Crozier and Ross. Roald Amundsen, who was first to navigate the North-West Passage and stand at the South Pole, once paid a glowing tribute to the voyage of *Erebus* and *Terror*. In his book about the South Pole, Amundsen wrote: 'Few people of the present day are capable of rightly appreciating this heroic deed, this brilliant proof of human courage and energy. With two ponderous craft – regular "tubs" according to our ideas – these men sailed right into the heart of the pack, which all previous Polar explorers had regarded as certain death. It is not merely difficult to grasp this; it is impossible – to us, who with a motion of the hand can set the screw going and wriggle out of the first difficulty we encounter. These men were heroes – heroes in the highest sense of the word.'[1]

In a mood of euphoria Crozier and Ross pushed south, hoping that the open seas would permit *Erebus* and *Terror* to sail unhindered to the Magnetic South Pole or even to the South Pole itself. Two days later the cry of 'Land' shattered the illusions. Mountains and snow-covered land came into sight as they sailed deeper into what is now called the

The first sighting of Mount Erebus, the world's most southerly volcano, in 1841.

Ross Sea. Although thick ice and heavy seas made it impossible to get a shore party onto the mainland, the expedition managed the next best thing with the customary ritual of claiming the territory for the Empire. On 12 January 1841 Ross and Crozier stepped onto a small island about 5 miles (8 km) off the coast of Victoria Land for a modest and hastily arranged ceremony. It was the first new possession of the Victorian age and the inauspicious frozen speck of land – the island is 2 miles (3 km) long – was awarded the appropriate name of Possession Island. Watched by countless thousands of indifferent penguins, Crozier and Ross stood knee-deep in bird droppings to toast their discovery with an 'excellent sherry' and hurriedly left the most remote outpost of the Empire after just twenty-five minutes.

A few days later it was calculated that the ships had beaten the 'Furthest South' of James Weddell (74° 15' S) in 1823 and extra grog was dished out in celebration. An imposing new island soon came into view as the ships pressed further south. It was initially called High Island, although more than sixty years later Captain Scott renamed it Ross Island and it became the launching place for the twentieth century's Heroic Age of Exploration.

High Island's most extraordinary feature was an active volcano, the 12,450 ft (3,795 m) smoking beacon, which is the most southerly volcano on earth and which was named Mount Erebus. A nearby extinct volcano was named Mount Terror after Crozier's ship.

An even more spectacular sight greeted the party as the ships sailed eastwards and came across a vast perpendicular wall of ice which towered over their mastheads at heights of up to 200 ft (60 m). Ross initially named it the Great Ice Barrier because it blocked any hope of *Erebus* and *Terror* sailing direct to the Magnetic South Pole. 'We might with equal chance of success try to sail through the Cliffs of Dover,' Ross said.

The Magnetic Pole, it was reckoned, was probably situated about 160 miles deeper into the interior of Victoria Land and well beyond their reach. It was not until 1909 that men from Shackleton's *Nimrod* expedition – Edgeworth David, Alastair Mackay and Douglas Mawson – became the first to stand at the Magnetic South Pole, where they discovered that the constantly moving 'wandering pole' was about 230 miles (370 km) further north than calculated by Crozier and Ross in 1841.

Erebus and *Terror* sailed further east alongside the mighty Barrier, still hoping the ice shelf would eventually come to an end and allow them to plot a route to the south. After travelling 250 miles (400 km) to 78° 4' S, their 'furthest south' of the season, there was no sign of an end to the wall of ice.

By early February, with winter fast approaching, the ships turned back to Ross Island and were greeted by a sudden eruption of fireworks from Mount Erebus. After a brief consultation, Crozier and Ross turned *Erebus* and *Terror* north and headed back to the comfort of Van Diemen's Land. The ships reached Hobart in April 1841, where Crozier tried again to begin a romance with Sophy Cracroft, but she turned down his proposal of marriage.

After a few months of rest and refitting the ships, *Erebus* and *Terror* sailed south again on 23 November 1841, with Crozier and Ross hoping to follow up the successes of the first year. But the encircling pack ice was a more troublesome barrier on the second leg of the voyage and the ships were trapped for forty-seven days, under constant assault from gale-force winds and persistent fog. Crozier was forced to flood *Terror* to a depth of 2 ft when a potentially disastrous fire broke out below decks and on another occasion hurricane-force winds ripped the rudders from both ships.

The weather was noticeably colder and one diarist noted that the build-up of ice saw the 1½ inch (3.80 cms) ropes swell to 12 inches (30 cms) in diameter. A fish, wrenched from the sea by a crashing wave, was instantly frozen against the side of *Terror* but the ship's cat moved quickest and snatched the prize before the ship's naturalist could examine the specimen.

It was a frustrating time and the ships did not manage to escape the grip of the ice until mid-February, leaving barely any sailing time that season. The Barrier was finally reached towards the end of the month and a new 'furthest south' of 78° 10' S was attained as *Erebus* and *Terror* continued the search for a break in the ice formation. But the fortification was impenetrable and when the ships ran across a new belt of pack ice in late February, it was decided to retreat before winter closed in. The destination was the Falkland Islands.

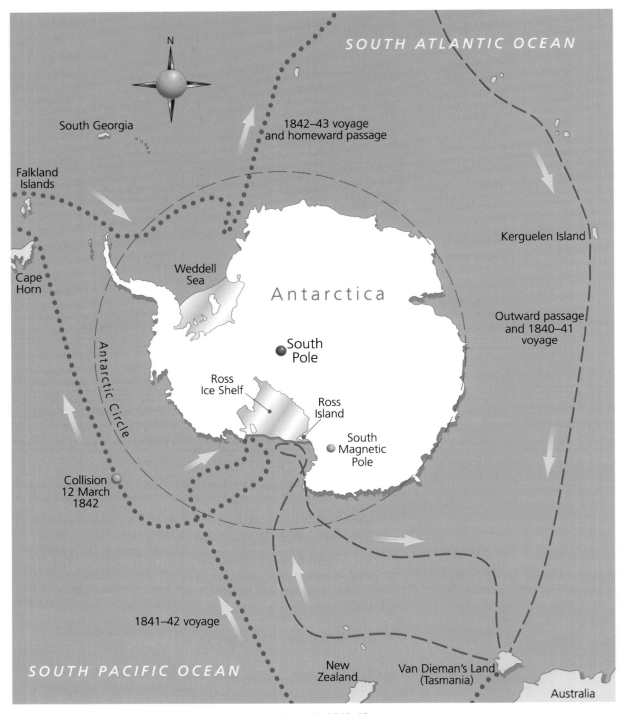

The pioneering voyages of *Erebus* and *Terror* to the Antarctic, 1840–43.

The run north was uneventful until the night of 12 March when a flotilla of bulky icebergs suddenly loomed out of the darkness and threatened to collide with the ships. One berg was estimated to be standing 200 ft (60 m) out of the water as Ross, fearing a collision, hastily ordered *Erebus* to slow down by taking in topsails. But Crozier in *Terror* was still running on full sail in the total darkness and not aware of the looming danger. Ross turned away sharply and ran directly into the path of the faster-moving *Terror*. The ships collided with a juddering crunch, knocking everyone off their feet and the two riggings became entangled. *Erebus* suffered badly, with the bowsprit, foretopmast and other smaller spars ripped away in the crash. In heavy rolling seas, *Terror*'s keel was exposed as the vessel was carried to the top of a huge wave and threatened to smash into the stricken *Erebus*. Somehow the knot of riggings worked free in the wild seas and Crozier, seizing his moment, saw his chance to escape. Two icebergs stood directly ahead but Crozier had spotted a narrow gap between the mountains of ice and gambled that he could steer *Terror* through the opening like threading a needle.

In darkness and pounded by heavy seas, Crozier calmly guided *Terror* between the two icebergs as many of the crew watched, paralysed with fear. The slender gap, one officer commented, was 'not twice the breadth of the ship' and Crozier later confessed that he had no idea how *Terror* had avoided a collision. Once through the opening, a relieved Crozier lit a blue lamp as a beacon for Ross, who with the same skill and calm assurance brought the wounded *Erebus* through the gap an hour later.

A few hasty running repairs allowed the ships to reach the Falklands by early April 1842, where the news was mixed. Crozier learned that after thirty-two years of dedicated service, he had finally been promoted to the rank of Captain. But the mood of celebration was tempered by news that the Falklands were in a state of anarchy, with barely enough food to feed the handful of islanders and law and order close to breaking down. Organised farming had virtually collapsed after Britain had annexed the islands a few years earlier and, instead of replenishing their own provisions, Crozier and Ross had to dip into their own modest supplies of food to feed the pitiful inhabitants.

The five months spent on the Falkland Islands was the expedition's low point. Many on board felt that, after three years away, the expedition had been forgotten and morale sank further when it was discovered that the mail from home had not arrived. Officers quarrelled among themselves and drunkenness among the seamen was rife, while relations between the expedition and Richard Moody, the island's inexperienced young governor, deteriorated badly.

However, the expedition left a lasting legacy: a new capital for the islands. The Falklands, which lie 8,000 miles (12,000 km) from Britain, were totally dependent on shipping for survival and Moody asked the experienced seafarers, Crozier and Ross, to help locate a suitable new harbour and lifeline to the outside world. The choice fell between Port William in Jackson Harbour, where the deep water was more favourable,

The terrifying moment in March 1842 when *Erebus* and *Terror* collided during a heavy storm in the Southern Ocean.

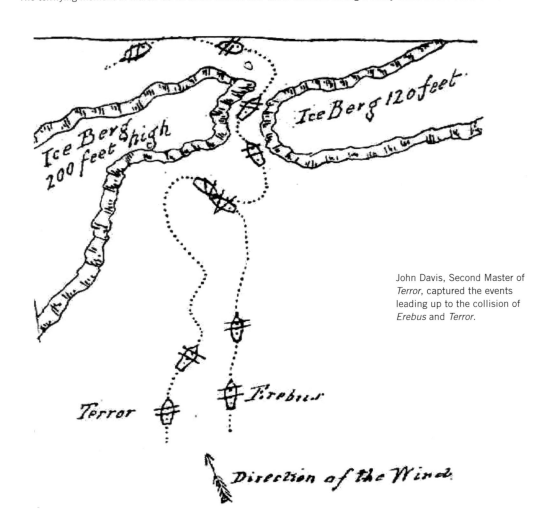

John Davis, Second Master of *Terror*, captured the events leading up to the collision of *Erebus* and *Terror*.

or the existing site in Port Louis. Ross and Crozier, with a lifetime's experience of the sea, chose Port William, which was later renamed Port Stanley. Today two streets running alongside Stanley Harbour bear the names Crozier Place and Ross Road, in recognition of the two men who were instrumental in creating the island's new capital.

Erebus and *Terror* left the Falklands in September 1842 with few regrets, heading for Cape Horn and a third voyage south. The new target was to sail as far south as possible down the 55th meridian and add to the discoveries of James Weddell twenty years earlier in the treacherous waters of what is now the Weddell Sea. Christmas was celebrated amidst the string of South Shetland Islands and the ships ran along the Antarctic Peninsula where Bransfield had sailed two decades before. Amid a flurry of new place names, the expedition named Snow Hill Island and Paulet Island, two islands which seventy years later would became a focus for the marooned men of Shackleton's *Endurance* expedition. In another territorial ritual, Crozier and Ross went ashore on the tiny 1-mile (1.6-km) wide Cockburn Island and planted the flag for the Empire.

The ships turned into the Weddell Sea, where they immediately ran into ice far more densely packed than any they had experienced in the Ross Sea. One officer described the seas as 'repellent' and *Erebus* and *Terror* were quickly surrounded on all sides by thick, choking ice.

For almost six weeks the ships dodged and weaved in a constant battle with the ice, always hoping to find an open lane to the south. The pack finally released the vessels on 4 February at the disappointing latitude of only 65° 15' S, which was almost 10° further north – over 700 miles (1,120 km) – than Weddell had managed. It had been a perilous, highly demanding leg of the expedition. One officer said it was a journey of 'constant gales, fog and snow storms'. The relentless barricade of thick ice stood firmly in the way of venturing further south and on 5 March 1843 *Erebus* and *Terror* came to a standstill at 71° 30' S. It was the end of the great journey. Only about 50 miles (80 km) across the horizon – unknown to Ross and Crozier – was the coastline of Dronning Maud Land, an area on the Antarctic mainland that would remain undiscovered for another ninety years.

Erebus and *Terror* turned north, crossing the Antarctic Circle for the last time during the second week of March, bound for the South African port of Simon's Town. But the ships ran into another ferocious storm, the worst they had experienced during the entire voyage, as the Antarctic bade a fulsome farewell to *Erebus* and *Terror*. Men were forced to remain on deck throughout the night on constant alert for ice. The surgeon on *Erebus* wrote: 'They were nights of grog and hot coffee, for the orders to splice the main brace were many and imperative if the crew were to be kept up to the strain on their nerves and muscles'.[2]

Simon's Town was eventually reached on 4 April 1843 where the party, drained by the long stretch at sea, began to recover from their ordeal. But the strain of the four-year journey was readily apparent. One woman observed that Crozier and Ross's hands

trembled so much they could hardly hold a glass. 'One night in the Antarctic did this for both of us,' Ross explained.[3] Other men found it hard to cope with the heat of South Africa after such a long time in a colder climate.

The party enjoyed a month recuperating and refitting the ships for the final leg of the voyage. The only alarm was caused by a wild rumour that the expedition was heading south again, though this proved false and the *Erebus* and *Terror* left South Africa as scheduled on 30 April. By early September the ships were anchored off the Kentish port of Folkestone. The expedition, the last great voyage of discovery conducted entirely under sail, formally drew to a close on 23 September 1843 – almost four years to the day that *Erebus* and *Terror* had left England.

It was a comprehensive triumph of navigation, discovery and scientific enterprise, which made the first successful navigation of the pack in the Ross Sea area, found vast tracts of new territory and produced a mass of data on the region's waters, geology, botany and magnetism. Only the Magnetic South Pole remained beyond grasp, but so much analytical information was collected that the expedition's final papers were not published for twenty-five years. Another triumph was the remarkably low casualty rate among the 128 men who began the journey in 1839, a rarity on lengthy sea voyages of the time. Crozier did not lose a single man on *Terror*, though two officers were invalided home. Ross, by contrast, suffered the loss of three sailors from *Erebus*.

Antarctica was left largely untouched for fifty years after the departure of *Erebus* and *Terror* in 1843. *Pagoda* under Lt Thomas Moore made a brief incursion into southerly waters in 1845 and in 1874 *Challenger* under Captain George Nares became the first steamship to cross the Antarctic Circle. The first recorded landing outside the Peninsula was made in 1895 when a party from the *Antarctic* came ashore at Cape Adare, the headland in Victoria Land discovered by Crozier and Ross in 1841 and named after the Irish peer, Lord Adare. Despite its many achievements, the voyage of *Erebus* and *Terror* to the Antarctic did not capture the public's imagination in the way that Parry had popularised Arctic exploration two decades earlier. Four years away from home was too long and the desolate, ice-bound territory offered little prospect of trade or commercial rewards for the country.

Crozier tried to slip back into a normal routine, with mixed results. He was best man at Ross's wedding six weeks after returning from the Antarctic. But he failed to renew his relationship with Sophy Cracroft who, once again, rejected his proposal of marriage. Cracroft, now twenty-eight years of age and still unmarried, liked Crozier well enough but had no intention of marrying a sea captain. Jane Franklin once called Cracroft a 'sad flirt' and when asked why she would not marry Crozier, replied: 'The pity is, Sophy liked the man but not the sailor.'[4]

The one consolation for Crozier was official recognition of his outstanding work on five voyages of discovery. In December 1843, three months after returning from the

Facing page: Through the eye of a needle. Crozier's cool head and great seamanship managed to steer *Terror* between two giant icebergs after the dramatic collision with *Erebus* in the Southern Ocean.

Antarctic, he was elected a Fellow of the prestigious Royal Society. It was a great honour and given added significance by the prominent men of the day who gladly sponsored his election to the much respected institution. They included John Barrow from the Admiralty, the acclaimed astronomer Sir John Herschel and the much admired Beaufort.

Unfortunately, the honour did nothing to help Crozier's growing despair. Unhappy, out of work and approaching his fifties with limited prospects, Crozier drifted into a deepening depression, partly because of the strain of the Antarctic expedition and partly because of his lost love. 'I feel adrift wherever I am,' he wrote to Ross. 'I could go anywhere being so much alone as I have been.'

Unknown to Crozier, Barrow was putting together an ambitious new plan to find the North-West Passage with the tried and tested Polar ships, *Erebus* and *Terror*. Fearing that Russia or another power was near to stealing British glory, Barrow called for one last push to finish centuries of work in pursuit of the Passage.

Inexplicably, the man picked to lead the expedition was 59-year-old Sir John Franklin, who had not taken a ship into the Arctic seas for twenty-seven years. With Ross and Parry retired, the obvious candidate to lead the expedition was the battle-hardened, reliable Crozier. Lord Haddington, the First Secretary at the Admiralty, thought Crozier was the best man for the job. But the affable Franklin was a more popular figure at the Admiralty and Haddington allowed sentiment to blur his judgement. Franklin was asked to take command, with Crozier as his deputy.

Crozier was unsure about the expedition and it is possible that Haddington, too, realised that he was struggling and possibly in no fit state for another arduous voyage. Crozier, still suffering from depression, told Ross in late 1844: 'In truth, I sincerely feel that I am not equal to the hardship.' Yet he somehow stifled his misgivings and agreed to serve alongside Franklin. The inevitable speculation was that Crozier sailed in the faint hopes of impressing Sophy Cracroft to change her mind about marriage.

The North-West Passage venture, the largest and best-equipped expedition ever to leave Britain, sailed on 19 May 1845. Crozier, once again captain of *Terror*, cut a disconsolate figure, mourning the loss of Sophy Cracroft and still nursing grave reservations about the expedition itself. His mood was further soured by the decision to hand over many of the key responsibilities – the selection of officers and crew and collecting important magnetic data – to James Fitzjames, a naval officer who had never been to the ice before but was blessed with friends in high places. It was a massive snub to Crozier, a vastly more experienced naval officer who had fitted out the successful *Erebus* and *Terror* voyage to the Antarctic and whose impressive work on magnetism led to his election to the Royal Society.

Crozier's other concern was Franklin's casual style of leadership. He reported 'everything in confusion' on Franklin's vessel, *Erebus*, and added the damning view that

Francis Rawdon Moira Crozier. The only known photograph of Crozier, taken in 1845 shortly before he departed on the disastrous Franklin expedition to discover the North-West Passage.

'[Franklin] has not good judgement'. After four major journeys to the Arctic, Crozier was also worried the ships had sailed north too late in season and that *Erebus* and *Terror* would not have enough time to make significant headway into Lancaster Sound that year.

All his anxieties and fears were summed up in Crozier's last letter, a sad and melancholic note written to his old friend Ross. The letter, dated 9 July 1845, includes the telling remarks: 'All goes smoothly but, James dear, I am sadly alone, not a soul have I in either ship that I can go and talk to. I feel that I am not in the spirits of writing but in truth I am sadly lonely . . .'[5]

Erebus and *Terror* were last seen by whaling ships in late July, shortly before crossing Baffin Bay and entering Lancaster Sound. The whalers, who carried back their last letters, reported that the crews of both ships were in 'excellent health and spirits.' The two ships, with 129 men on board, vanished and were never seen again.

Over the following years, about fifty ships were sent north in a frantic hunt for the lost expedition. Search parties combed thousands of miles of the Arctic landscapes and seaways, looking everywhere but the right place for the clues to the fate of the expedition. Ross briefly came out of retirement for one last fruitless search to find his friend but returned without even a hint of the expedition's whereabouts. One ship sent north to look for the expedition carried a letter from Sophy Cracroft to Franklin which asked her uncle to 'remember me kindly to Captain Crozier'. The letter was returned unopened. Sophy Cracroft, who went blind in later life, died in 1892 at the age of seventy-seven. She never married.

Crozier's desperate attempt to lead over 100 men to safety from the Arctic wilderness in 1847 was depicted fifty years later in this painting by explorer Julius Payer. Crozier is shown at the top clutching a gun and ready to repel an assault by a polar bear. All 129 men on the expedition perished.

CZECH GEOPHYSICAL INSTITUTE OF THE ACADEMY OF SCIENCES/NATIONAL GALLERY OF PRAGUE

An outline of the tragedy has been pieced together by the testimonies of local Inuit and the discovery of a few relics, including the skeletons of the dead and a single piece of paper revealing the ships' fate. But, in truth, the whole story of what happened may never be fully told and the final days of the Franklin expedition, the worst disaster in the history of Polar exploration, will remain a subject of intense investigation, speculation and guesswork.

The note, first discovered in 1859 by an expedition under the command of the Dundalk-born Leopold McClintock, revealed that Franklin was dead by 1847 and *Erebus* and *Terror* irretrievably trapped in the ice off the coast of King William Island. Crozier, for the first time in his life, was in charge of an expedition and had the impossible task of leading over 100 survivors in a desperate attempt to escape by marching overland to the hunting grounds in the south. None survived. Only a few bones and scattered relics were ever found. The Inuit, who had learned the bitter realities of surviving in the harsh environment, were forced to abandon the starving sailors to their fate because the meagre hunting grounds could not support a large band of hungry men for any length of time. Men fell down and died in their tracks. According to some accounts and more recent studies, some desperate men even resorted to cannibalism.

The precise date of Crozier's death remains unknown, though some oral accounts by the Inuit indicate that he was among the last survivors. Some say he lived in the wilds for many years, though this is highly improbable. More likely is that Crozier, along with most of the survivors, died in the winter of 1848 or 1849. But Crozier's long march towards escape probably took him to the Simpson Strait, the channel at the south end of King William Island which was the final missing piece of the North-West Passage jigsaw. Although the honour of navigating the Passage went to Amundsen over half a century later, Crozier actually saw the key stretch of water over fifty years before the Norwegian sailed through the Passage for the first time.

Crozier, a modest and unassuming man, never gained popular support at the Admiralty or among the general public for almost forty years of dedicated service to the cause of exploration and science on six voyages of discovery. Alone among the acclaimed explorers of the age – Back, Franklin, Parry, Richardson, and James and John Ross – Crozier never received a knighthood for his prodigious efforts. While Franklin was feted as a national hero who died serving his country, Crozier was quietly forgotten. However, he was highly respected by his fellow explorers, the men who knew him best. McClintock said Crozier had earned the 'highest professional reputation' and Ross readily praised a man of 'such high reputation'.

More than 100 years passed before Crozier received proper recognition for his admirable contribution to exploration, with the naming of Crozier Crater on the Moon. The crater, some 240,000 miles (approximately 380,000 km) from earth at 13.5° S, 50.8° E in Mare Fecunditatas, is among a cluster of features named after the most distinguished Polar explorers, including Cook, Parry, Ross, Nansen, Amundsen, Scott and Shackleton. Crozier, at last, stands shoulder to shoulder with his peers.

Although no headstone marks the last resting place of Francis Rawdon Moira Crozier, his memory is preserved in a variety of places around the earth. There are eight places on the globe named after Crozier, including Cape Crozier on Ross Island in the Antarctic. But perhaps the finest memorial is the commanding statue of Crozier, which stands

The commanding Crozier Memorial in the centre of Banbridge, which was built with money donated by local people and unveiled in 1862.
MICHAEL SMITH

opposite the family home in the centre of Banbridge. It is a measure of the respect for Francis Crozier among those who knew him that money for the memorial, which was unveiled in 1862, was raised entirely by donations given by local people in the Banbridge area.

SIR ERNEST SHACKLETON

1874–1922

Shackleton's grave today, with the granite headstone which replaced the original cross in 1928.
CON COLLINS

SIR VIVIAN FUCHS, the first man to cross the Antarctic continent from coast to coast, once remarked that every child is an explorer at birth. He may well have been thinking of Shackleton, the Irishman who was captivated by tales of great explorers from an early age and fantasised of travelling to unknown parts of the globe where no one had stood before. As a man, Shackleton lived the dream.

Shackleton was the last of the great Edwardian adventurers, a man whose remarkable exploits on four expeditions to the Antarctic a century ago marked him out as one of the finest explorers of any age. Shackleton, the boy who dreamt of matching the feats of men like Marco Polo, Columbus or James Cook, today ranks alongside the greatest voyagers in history. He was a larger-than-life character who, it was said, lived life like a 'mighty rushing wind'. Roald Amundsen, the most accomplished of all Polar explorers, once said: 'Sir Ernest Shackleton's name will for evermore be engraved with letters of fire in the history of Antarctic exploration.'

Ernest Shackleton, aged eleven. As a child he often dreamed of being an explorer.

Ernest Henry Shackleton was born on 15 February 1874 at Kilkea House, a substantial farmhouse near the hamlet of Kilkea and a short distance from the old market town of Athy on the edge of the Pale in County Kildare. The Shackletons of Kilkea were descended from a mixture of English Quakers and wealthy Irish landowners. Originally from Harden in Yorkshire, the Shackletons came to Ireland in the early eighteenth century and in 1726 established a Quaker school at Ballitore, Kildare. Among the first pupils at Ballitore were the statesman Edmund Burke and the revolutionary James Napper Tandy. The family had gravitated to the Anglican Church by 1872 when Henry Shackleton, Ernest's father, married Henrietta Gavan of Carlow, whose family boasted a strong Irish heritage dating back at least 800 years. Henrietta was linked to the ancient Fitzmaurice family of Kerry and the old-established Gavans whose roots were in the church. Together Henry and Henrietta would raise a family of ten children.

Kildare, with its rich farming land, had long been among Ireland's more affluent counties and a popular retreat for Ireland's landed gentry. Kilkea House, a typically imposing Georgian property, was rented from the Duke of Leinster, and the large Shackleton family was among the last to be raised under the protective cloak of the Protestant ascendancy in Kildare.

But change was coming to Kildare as young Ernest grew up. The ascendancy was in decline, the clamour for land reform in Ireland was intensifying and the life of a farmer did not suit a studious man like Henry Shackleton. In 1880, at age of thirty-three, Henry Shackleton suddenly uprooted the family from Kilkea House and moved to Marlborough Road, Dublin, to study medicine at Trinity College. After qualifying in 1884, he shifted the family to London where he eventually set up in practice in Sydenham, a respectable suburb to the south of city.

Henry Shackleton quickly built a thriving practice as a local family doctor and was hoping to steer Ernest into a similarly sound upright career. In pursuit of Henry's ambitions, the youngster was sent to nearby Dulwich College, a bastion of English middle-class schooling and a traditional training ground for generations of bankers and merchants who oiled the wheels of the Empire and the civil servants and diplomats who administered it all. But Ernest showed no flair for a classical education and was soon inconsolably bored. He shared a birthday with Galileo Galilei and doubtless would have sympathised with the great Italian's philosophy: 'You cannot teach a man anything; you can only help him find it within himself'.

Shackleton, a restless dreamer, did little work at Dulwich and struggled to keep up. With his distinctive Irish accent, he also stood out among the sons of well-off English financiers and civil servants and was frequently drawn into playground scraps. Caught between the cross-currents of his rural Irish upbringing and the genteel customs of suburban England, Shackleton searched for an escape route.

For Shackleton the route out was the sea. The sea had always held a particular fascination for the young man, who was drawn to the historic exploits of daredevil explorers and buccaneering colonialists. A tree trunk in the garden at Kilkea House was his 'ship' and *Twenty Thousand Leagues Under the Sea*, the classic Jules Verne story, was his favourite book. Like many children, he talked about running away from home and on one occasion he tried to enlist on a ship moored in the Pool of London. It was said that his last act before leaving Kilkea House was to climb into his tree-trunk 'ship'.

Bored with school, Shackleton pestered his father to let him leave and his persistence eventually won the day. In April 1890, shortly after his sixteenth birthday, Shackleton left Dulwich College and enlisted as a ship's boy on *Hoghton Tower*, a square-rigged clipper in the White Star Line. His first voyage, which chimed with the dreams of childhood, was the tempestuous baptism of sailing a clipper around Cape Horn to Valparaiso, Chile.

Life as a merchant seaman on board the 1,600-ton *Hoghton Tower* was hard and dirty work and a world apart from the leafy suburbs of Sydenham and subdued cloisters of Dulwich College. Shackleton, however, was in his element and spent the next ten years at sea, travelling the world. Shackleton advanced steadily through the ranks and by 1898 the 24-year-old had qualified as Master and was able to take command of any ship on the high seas. He was an engaging, easy-going and popular character who, despite his dislike of school, had developed a passion for poetry. But he was a restless man and within a few years was looking for a new challenge. To complicate matters, he had fallen in love with Emily Dorman, a friend of his sister from a prosperous family of solicitors, who shared his fondness for poetry.

The opportunity Shackleton was seeking emerged in the final days of the nineteenth century with the news that Britain was putting together a major expedition to explore the Antarctic, the last unexplored continent on earth. Shackleton, eagerly looking for new horizons, was determined to join the quest. His chance came in 1900 during a voyage carrying troops to South Africa for the Boer War. He struck up a friendship with Cedric Longstaff, whose

Shackleton, aged sixteen, starting his apprenticeship at sea.

father, Llewellyn Longstaff, was the largest individual donor to the planned National Antarctic Expedition. Longstaff was suitably impressed with the eager young merchant navy officer and persuaded the Royal Geographical Society, who were coordinating the expedition, to take Shackleton as Third Officer. He was the only officer to join the expedition without the formality of an interview.

The expedition, the largest, best-equipped undertaking ever sent to explore the Antarctic interior, was led by an untried Royal Navy commander, Robert Scott. *Discovery*, a specialist ice-strengthened ship, was specially built in Dundee and, buoyed by a rising tide of national optimism, the party of naval officers, seamen and scientists carried high hopes of venturing as far as the South Pole itself.

It was a huge challenge. The Antarctic continent was almost completely unknown as *Discovery* left London in July 1901. The first landing outside the Peninsula had been made only six years earlier in 1895 and almost nothing was known about conditions in the interior of the continent. Only three of *Discovery*'s 48-man party had any experience of the ice and hardly anyone on board knew how to use skis or drive teams of dogs. Basic survival skills were pitifully inadequate and Scott himself admitted that 'our ignorance was deplorable'.

Shackleton was belatedly put in charge of training dog teams to pull sledges, but he had no experience of handling animals and had little patience with the task. In the event, little

Officers and scientists assembled on board *Discovery* in 1901, before the expedition sailed to the Antarctic. Shackleton is second from left and also pictured are his companions who achieved a record 'furthest south' in 1902, Wilson (first on left) and Scott (seventh from left).

was achieved and the animals, though the most efficient form of travelling across the ice, were relegated to a minor role. Instead, Scott fell back on man-hauling sledges, a grindingly hard regime which had failed miserably decades earlier in the Arctic.

After a difficult voyage in the slow-moving *Discovery*, the expedition made a last port of call at Lyttelton, New Zealand, before finally departing for the ice on Christmas Eve, 1901. *Discovery* crossed the Antarctic Circle for the first time in early January and reached the mainland, last seen by Crozier and Ross, at the end of the month.

The expedition began in almost calamitous fashion. Scott had been persuaded to use a hydrogen-filled balloon to get better views of the uncharted landscape facing the explorers. He went up first and was nearly killed when he mistakenly threw out the sand-bag weights, sending the balloon shooting skywards. Undeterred by Scott's narrow escape, Shackleton jumped into the basket next and soared to 800 ft (240 m), where he took the first ever aerial photographs of the Antarctic's interior spread out before him. But Shackleton was very lucky to survive. On descending the balloon was discovered to have developed serious leaks and was never used again.

A suitable spot was found in McMurdo Sound, the inlet on Ross Island discovered by Ross and Crozier in the 1840s. Scott decided that the party would spend the next two years packed together on board the ice-bound *Discovery*, although a small wooden hut was

Southern Party, November 1902 (l–r): Shackleton, Scott and Wilson at the start of the sledge journey which penetrated deeper into the unknown interior of Antarctica than ever before.

erected on the frozen Hut Point Peninsula. After surviving their first winter, the expedition's spring offensive was to send a small party inland to get as close as possible to the South Pole.

Scott initially intended to take only his friend, Edward 'Bill' Wilson, on the trip, but Wilson, an accomplished naturalist and qualified doctor, wisely insisted that a third person was necessary, in case one of the team broke down. After further consideration, Scott accepted Wilson's advice and added Shackleton to the party. The three men, backed up by a support party carrying additional supplies and nineteen unenthusiastic dogs, set off on 2 November 1902, pulling more than three-quarters of a ton (approximately 800 kg) of food and equipment for a round trip of three months.

It was an exhausting ordeal from the start, partly because the men struggled to cope with skis and partly because conditions were far worse than anyone expected as soon as they ventured inland. Travelling was very difficult and temperatures dropped sharply as the party stepped on to the Ice Barrier, the flat plain of ice stretching south from Ross Island

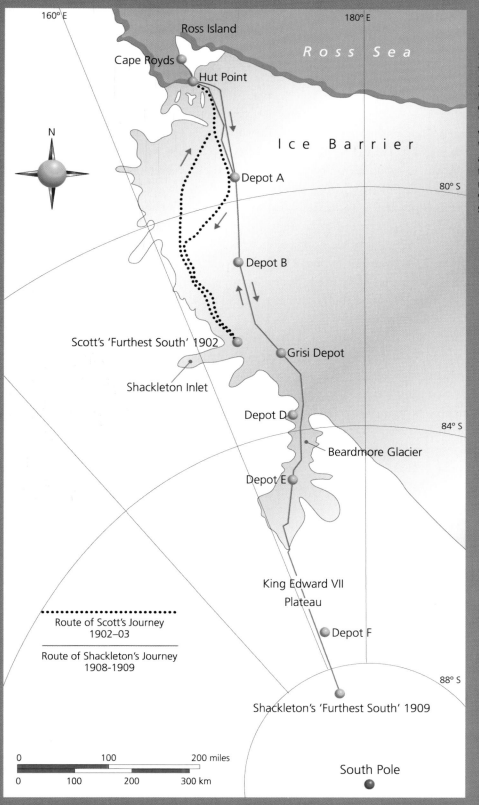

160° E

180° E

Ross Island

Cape Royds

Hut Point

Ross Sea

Ice Barrier

N

80° S

Depot A

Depot B

Scott's 'Furthest South' 1902

Grisi Depot

Shackleton Inlet

Depot D

84° S

Beardmore Glacier

Depot E

King Edward VII
Plateau

Depot F

••••••••••••••• Route of Scott's Journey
                 1902–03

───────────── Route of Shackleton's Journey
                 1908-1909

88° S

Shackleton's 'Furthest South' 1909

0   100   200 miles

0   100   200   300 km

South Pole

Shackleton made
two long sledging
journeys into the
unknown interior
of Antarctica, the
'furthest south'
with Scott and
Wilson in 1902–03
and his 1908–09
trek when he
marched to within
97 miles of the
South Pole.

which was discovered by Crozier and Ross sixty years earlier and is now called the Ross Ice Shelf. Progress slowed to a trickle when the support party turned back after a fortnight. One day's heavy pulling saw the three men advance only 2½ miles (4 km) south, while the ineffective dogs ambled alongside and the redundant skis were dumped on the sledges to be dragged along with everything else. After a month of slog, Shackleton reported that travelling was 'awful' and the men were unable to pull the full weight of their sledges. The only option was to relay, taking one sledge forward and returning for the other, which meant marching 3 miles (5 km) for every 1 mile (1.6 km) advanced south. Hunger increased with the extra workload. The daily diet, which relied largely on pemmican, barely filled their stomachs and each night the men climbed into their sleeping bags still hungry. The first of the dogs died soon after.

Shackleton, too, was struggling. He had developed an irritating cough days after leaving the ship and relations with Scott, a moody, quick-tempered and introverted character, had deteriorated under the strain of the march. It needed all the calming influence of Wilson to keep the peace.

Mountains appeared in the distance and Christmas was celebrated with a minor feast which included a Christmas pudding Shackleton had kept hidden in a spare sock. But neither a full stomach nor a mountain range on the horizon could obscure the reality that, after nearly two months on the march, the starving men were getting weaker and the trek was coming to an end. A little later Wilson later found the men displaying early signs of scurvy, the killer ailment caused by a lack of vitamin C. Without a decent intake of the vitamin C found in fresh meat or vegetables, scurvy develops quickly and the small quantity of seal meat carried on the sledge was not enough to stave off the sickness. Shackleton was the weakest, struggling badly with the hacking cough, swollen legs and blackened gums, the unmistakable signs of scurvy. He was often short of breath, always hungry and frequently irritated by Scott's leadership.

The three men made their last camp at 82° 15' S on 30 December 1902, impressed by crossing the 82nd parallel for the first time and the sight of land which no human eyes had ever seen before. But the Pole was still about 550 miles (880 km) to the south. Scott was determined to press ahead to extend his record for the 'furthest south' but decided that Shackleton would not share in the honour. For reasons which remain unclear, Scott ordered Shackleton to remain behind in the tent while he took Wilson on a few miles to 82° 17' S, further south than anyone before. It was a snub Shackleton would never forget.

The drained and hungry men turned northwards on the last day of 1902, with the remaining five dogs close to collapse and chain of food depots left on the outward march their only hope of survival. Despite the lighter loads, the men found the going very hard and after a terrible struggle they stumbled into the first depot a fortnight later. A full meal helped restore some vigour, but it was only temporary relief. Soon after, the last two dogs were killed, though Scott chose not to cut up the animals for extra food.

Picking out the small depot flag in the ocean of whiteness was critical and Shackleton's decline continued. By mid-January he was short of breath and coughing up blood, driven forward each day solely by his incredible willpower. Scott reported Shackleton's condition on 15 January 1903 as 'highly alarming'. After a few more days Shackleton broke down, unable to take his place in the harness and leaving Scott and Wilson, who were also feeling the strain of the march, to haul a load of more than 500 lb (230 kg). A few slices of seal meat helped revive a little of Shackleton's strength and towards the end of January he was able to resume pulling. Three days later the three men reached the last food depot, about 60 miles (100 km) from the ship, where they gorged themselves on soup and sardines.

However, even with safety in sight Shackleton's condition took a turn for the worse. He was gasping for breath, suffering from chest pains and barely able to walk. One night he overheard Wilson warning Scott that he did not expect Shackleton to survive until morning. The remark galvanised Shackleton and next day he summoned almost superhuman powers of endurance to resume the march.

The final few miles were torturous, with all three in a very weak condition and Shackleton in particular being driven solely by his strength of will. On 2 February, Scott wrote in his diary: 'We are as near spent as three persons can well be.' Although Shackleton had shown some signs of recovery, Scott was not convinced and added the warning: 'If Shackleton has shown temporary improvement, we know by experience how little confidence we can place in it, and how near he has been and still is to a total collapse.'[1]

Rising the next day, the three plodded slowly ahead and were astonished to see two dark specks suddenly appear ahead. At first they thought they were penguins but the shapes quickly materialised into the profiles of two companions from *Discovery*. The three men had been on the march for 93 days and travelled well over 900 miles (1,400 km) – after allowing for the extra mileage of relaying – on the longest-ever journey into the interior of the Antarctic. Shackleton, Scott and Wilson had charted around 300 miles (480 km) of previously unknown territory and discovered that the Ice Barrier was the pathway to the South Pole.

However, *Discovery* was still trapped in the ice and the relief ship, *Morning*, had arrived in McMurdo Sound with fresh supplies and a mission to bring home the men who were regarded as unfit or unsuited to the demands of the Antarctic. One of these men was Shackleton. After his near collapse on the southern journey, Scott decided that Shackleton was 'unequal to the rigours of the Polar climate' and he was ordered home on *Morning*. A bitterly disappointed Shackleton sailed north on 2 March 1903, reaching New Zealand three weeks later. By June Shackleton was back in London, still smarting from the humiliation of being invalided out of the expedition. But he was already planning his return to the ice.

Shackleton also had other pressing matters on his mind. In April 1904 he married Emily Dorman in London and began settling into family life and forging a new career away from the sea. It was no easy task. He spent a couple of years embroiled in a variety of speculative money-spinning schemes or in unfulfilling jobs, including an unhappy spell as Secretary of the Royal Scottish Geographical Society in Edinburgh. He had joined the secret society of Freemasons before the *Discovery* expedition in the hope of finding a short cut to suitable moneymaking opportunities, though all his forays into business were hopeless failures.

Nor was he any more successful in a brief encounter with the idiosyncratic world of mainstream politics. In search of new horizons, he was persuaded to join the Liberal Unionist Party in 1904 but suffered an embarrassingly heavy defeat in his attempt to become MP for Dundee, the city where *Discovery* had been built. The election campaign placed Shackleton in a delicate position since the Liberal Unionist Party was created by hard-line Empire loyalists and implacable opponents of Home Rule in Ireland. Shackleton was very proud of his Irish heritage and invariably gave his nationality as Irish, rather than British. However, Shackleton came fourth of five candidates in the Dundee election and his political nous was never fully tested again because he abandoned politics forever after the thumping defeat.

Shackleton was on a roller-coaster in the years after *Discovery*. He celebrated the birth of his first two children – Raymond in 1905 and Cecily in 1906 – yet drifted into a series of romantic affairs, and a succession of promising business ventures all descended into spectacular flops. Shackleton grew restless and turned his attention to a new expedition. The South Pole was still unconquered and amid growing speculation that parties from France and Belgium were planning to go south, he resolved to mount his own attempt. With a mixture of charm and lavish promises, he managed to raise enough funds to launch the British Antarctic Expedition, the first private undertaking with the specific aim of reaching the South Pole. The expedition was cobbled together in little more than six months, often in haphazard fashion, and was founded on the unconvincing framework of hefty borrowings and questionable promises.

While Shackleton was a charismatic and well-liked character who inspired enormous loyalty from his men, his financial affairs were invariably a shambles. Money slipped through his fingers like water, he was haunted by debts throughout his life and was often reduced to relying on the kindness of friends to pay his

Shackleton, aged thirty-three, before the *Nimrod* expedition, 1907.

bills. It was said with some vigour that his men could trust Shackleton with their lives but not with their money.

Taking *Nimrod*, a 41-year-old sealer, the expedition sailed from London in July 1907 and reached McMurdo Sound in February 1908. A base was established at Cape Royds on Ross Island, only a few miles from where *Discovery* had been berthed. It was a highly contentious decision which re-opened old wounds with Scott. Improbably enough, Scott claimed to have exclusive rights to the McMurdo Sound area and that Shackleton had given a written agreement to look elsewhere to establish base camp for his shore party. However, circumstances drove *Nimrod* into McMurdo Sound and relations with Scott subsequently suffered an irrevocable breakdown.

Although the later *Endurance* expedition is regarded as Shackleton's greatest triumph, *Nimrod* was his tour de force. It was on *Nimrod* that he made his most exceptional feats of discovery and demonstrated for the first time that he possessed outstanding skills as a leader of men in the most demanding conditions. Shackleton first touched greatness on *Nimrod* and the incredible story of *Endurance* might have been very different without the experience gained on *Nimrod*.

In little more than a year, Shackleton's expedition made the longest sledge journey ever undertaken in the Antarctic, pioneered a route through the Transantarctic Mountains by climbing the Beardmore Glacier on to the unexplored Polar Plateau and came within touching distance of reaching the South Pole. The expedition also completed the first ascent of the 12,450 ft (3,795 m) Mount Erebus, located the Magnetic South Pole and brought several innovations to the Antarctic, including the first motor car and the first printing press. Nor was a single life lost.

Shackleton, on his first voyage in command, was revitalised by the challenge. All the debts and pressures of family life were left behind and to most people he seemed a different man from the person they knew at home. He developed strong bonds with his men, largely because he always placed their welfare above all else. To the men, Shackleton was known simply as 'The Boss'.

The South Pole journey, the main focus of the expedition, began on 29 October 1908. It started optimistically, prompting Shackleton to write that everything pointed to an 'auspicious beginning'. There were hopes that the Barrier, which he had partly crossed with Scott and Wilson only six years earlier, ran unbroken all the way to the Pole. But all optimism quickly evaporated as the four-man party – Shackleton, Frank Wild, Jameson Boyd Adams and Dr Eric Marshall – ran into severe difficulties soon after leaving Cape Royds.

The fate of the expedition relied heavily on Shackleton's decision to take Manchurian ponies instead of dogs to haul sledges across the flat Barrier. Shackleton had failed to master dogs on *Discovery* and he believed that horses would provide the extra pulling power. It was an error of judgement which, ultimately, may have cost Shackleton the honour of being the first to reach the South Pole. Horses struggle in the soft snow, are far less efficient than dogs on the ice and need huge quantities of food which itself has to be hauled on sledges.

Shackleton provisioned the expedition for a round trip of some 1,720 statute miles (2,767 km) in 91 days, which set the daunting target of averaging nearly 19 miles (30 km) a day over hundreds of miles of largely unknown terrain. By the second week, with the men travelling at less than 7 miles (11 km) a day, Shackleton was already calculating how, with 'careful management', the party could extend their journey to 110 days by eating a little less at each mealtime. A supporting party from Cape Royds turned for home on 7 November, leaving the four men each leading a pony pulling around 600 lb (270 kg). Without the extra manpower, the best daily march achieved, of 14½ miles (23 km), was far behind schedule and on 21 November the first pony was shot.

Shackleton passed Scott's 'furthest south' of 82° 17' S on 26 November. Significantly, the four-man *Nimrod* party men had covered the same distance in twenty-nine days, half the time taken by Scott, Wilson and Shackleton in 1902. But the achievement was overshadowed by the worsening condition of the ponies and two days later another animal was put down.

Moving slowly forward, the men came closer to the chain of mountains first seen six years earlier. But it soon became apparent the mountains turned to the east, blocking their path and ending all hopes that the Barrier extended to the Pole. December arrived with the men picking a path through the notoriously broken ground where the immense natural force of the Barrier collides with the Transantarctic Mountains. Crevasses, steep pressure ridges and soft snow slowed the pace and intensified the misery for the two remaining ponies. The third was shot, leaving a single animal to haul one sledge, with Shackleton, Wild, Adams and Marshall dragging the other. Despite some welcome slices of horseflesh for dinner, hunger was already gnawing at their bodies. Less than five weeks after starting out and with only one quarter of the journey completed, Shackleton wrote: 'We are very hungry these days and we know that we are likely to be for another three months.'

A route had to be found up the mountains and the party came across a vast glacier which sliced through the towering peaks in a south-to-north direction. The glacier, although a daunting prospect, offered the best path through the mountains to the Pole and Shackleton named the highway after his principal sponsor, the Scottish industrialist, Sir William Beardmore. The Beardmore is among the world's largest glaciers, some 25 miles (40 km) wide and extending for about 125 miles (200 km). The ascent began on 5 December in surprisingly warm weather, but the going was very hard for men who had spent weeks pounding out the repetitive rhythm of man-hauling on the flat Barrier. Treading uphill was notably harder and Shackleton stashed some supplies in a depot to reduce weight for the gruelling slog.

Shackleton bids to reach the South Pole. The four-man team of Shackleton, Wild, Adams and Marshall setting off for the Pole in October 1908.

The task ahead was formidable, especially for men who were already growing increasingly hungry. The remaining journey to the Pole and back to Cape Royds was roughly 1,300 miles (2,100 km) and the glacier, the most difficult and draining leg of the trek, started with a new disaster when the last surviving pony crashed through the ice and disappeared into an abyss.

Pulling almost half a ton uphill, one day's colossal effort advanced the party just 3 miles (4.8 km) and, after assessing the remaining supplies, Shackleton ordered a further cut in the daily rations. The men, labouring hard all day, were probably consuming little more than 3,000 calories a day, less than half they needed. By contrast, the modern-day adventurer, Sir Ranulph Fiennes, consumed 7,000 calories a day on his 1993 Antarctic trek and still lost over 44 lb (20 kg) in weight. Christmas Day brought some minor relief as they camped at about 9,500 ft (2,850 m) on the Polar Plateau and indulged in the welcome luxury of a spoonful of crème de menthe and a cigar. The Pole was about 280 miles (450 km) away but Marshall, the doctor, was shocked when he examined the condition of the men. Their body temperatures, he found, were 2 °F below the normal 98.4 °F (36.9 °C).

Once again, it was decided to cut back on food, spreading one week's rations to ten days. Another depot was laid and, even with a lighter sledge, it was calculated that the party needed to cover 14 miles (22.5 km) per day to reach the Pole and get back to the cache. The schedule left little or no margin for safety and over a month had passed since they last travelled 14 miles in a day. More significantly, the return journey from the Pole would see the four men caught on the windy Plateau, almost 2 miles (3 km) above sea level, as the colder autumn season closed in.

A biting southerly wind blew into their faces as they edged forward in sub-zero temperatures. On 29 December body temperatures registered between 3 ° and 4 ° below normal and the higher altitude – they were over 10,000 ft (3,000 m) above sea level – inflicted annoying nosebleeds and piercing headaches on some of the party. Although they were pulling equal to 150 lb (68 kg) per man, the growing fatigue meant it felt like at least 250 lb (115 kg) and Shackleton conceded: 'The Pole is hard to get.'

Good distances were gained during the opening days of 1909, but their worsening physical condition had reduced the men to walking skeletons. Marshall's thermometer, which only measured down to 94 °F (34 °C), did not pick up a reading for three of the four during one inspection. 'All nearly paralysed with cold,' Marshall's diary reported.

Shackleton by now realised that the Pole was beyond reach and he faced a critical decision of when to halt the march and turn for home. With the Pole about 175 miles (280 km) away, he set a new target of marching to within 100 geographic miles (115 statute miles or 185 km) of the Pole. 'We are not travelling fast enough to make our food spin out and get back to our depot in time,' he said. 'I must look at the matter sensibly and consider the lives of those who are with me.'[2] Dredging up reserves of strength, the party staggered forward with one tent and ten days of half rations. But even the lighter sledge – about 70 lb (31 kg) a man – was a terrible struggle for the drained men.

A blizzard struck on 7 January and raged unbroken for sixty hours, with Shackleton recording between 60 °F and 70 °F of frost and winds touching 70 to 80 mph. 'We are so short of food and at this high altitude, 11,600 ft, it is hard to keep any warmth in our bodies between scanty meals,' Shackleton wrote on 8 January, '. . . too cold to write much in the diary.'[3] Next day, the blizzard passed and the men pushed on. They stuffed their pockets with a few biscuits and a little chocolate and decided to make a quick dash south. Without the burden of a sledge, they stumbled forward – 'half walking and half running', said Shackleton – for five hours. At nine o'clock in the morning of 9 January 1909, the group stopped at 88° 23' S, some 97 geographic miles from the Pole. In statute miles they were 111½ miles (179 km) from the most southerly point on the globe. 'We have shot our bolt,' Shackleton wrote.[4]

A piercing wind cut them to the bone as they lingered on the Polar Plateau long enough to plant the Union Jack and claim possession of the icy wilderness for the King, bury a cylinder of stamps and take two photographs. 'We stayed only a few minutes,' Shackleton said.

Furthest south (l–r): Adams, Wild and Shackleton standing 97 geographic miles (111.5 statute miles or 179 km) from the South Pole, 9 January 1909.

Shackleton's decision to halt the march was a masterstroke of judgement and arguably the most courageous decision by any explorer so close to his ultimate goal. He put the safety of his men above personal glory and had the guts to turn back with the Pole perhaps ten days' march to the south for fit men. But the margin between success and failure was so narrow that Adams later calculated another hour's march southwards would have killed all four men.

The return journey of 840 miles (1,350 km) to Cape Royds was a race against death, delicately balancing the dwindling provisions against the urgent need to cover ground before the food ran out. Hugh Robert Mill, Shackleton's first biographer, wrote in the 1920s that the men turned for home with '. . . Death on his pale horse, the blizzard, following close.'[5] Relying mostly on the outward tracks as a guide and with strong wind at their backs, the men made astonishingly good progress in the first few days. One day produced a 29-mile (46-km) march by using the floor cloth of the tent as a sail; two men had to act as 'brake' because the wind was driving so hard.

But encouraging distances of the early days could not disguise the worsening condition of the men. All were permanently cold and hungry and suffering painful injuries, notably Shackleton whose heels were split and suppurating. They marched from seven o'clock in the morning until nine o'clock at night in a desperate attempt to gain miles on the punishing descent of the Beardmore Glacier, with only brief stops for a quick drink of tea or cocoa. Only scraps of food remained in late January as the men came closer to the depot at the bottom of the Beardmore. The terrain was riddled with crevasses and ice ridges and they all suffered bad falls. In his diary one night, Shackleton scribbled: 'I cannot describe adequately the mental and physical strain of the last 48 hours.'[6]

Three of the party – Shackleton, Wild and Adams – were on the brink of total collapse as the party staggered towards the next depot. Only a little tea and cocoa were left in the food bag and Marshall, the only one still capable, bravely left his three shattered companions in the tent and struck out alone to find the precious depot. He managed to survive three falls before stumbling across the precious cache and rushed back to his colleagues with a little pony meat, cheese and biscuits. It was the first solid meal they had eaten in forty hours.

Shackleton's willpower and resolve were extraordinary. Despite his own poor condition and intense hunger, he drove the party forward and inspired his companions to feats of endurance which most thought were beyond them. Never once was defeat even considered.

A fresh crisis emerged when Wild, who was battling with severe dysentery, could not keep down his pemmican or pony meat. Dry biscuits, his only source of food, had run out and Wild's outlook was bleak. In an exceptional act of generosity, Shackleton gave Wild his last biscuit. 'I do not suppose that anyone else in the world can thoroughly realise how much generosity and sympathy was shown by this,' Wild wrote. 'But I DO and BY GOD I shall never forget. Thousands of pounds would not have bought that one biscuit.'[7]

Each day was a monumental struggle and on 30 January it needed 10 hours of hard slog to cover 13 miles (21 km). Shackleton's brief diary entry summed up the grim situation: 'Short of food, down to 20 ounces [560 grams] a day. Very tired.'[8] A few days later all four were struck down with acute dysentery and Shackleton recorded: 'Terrible day. No march possible; outlook serious.'[9]

Digging deep into reserves, the men managed 8 miles (12 km) next day but finished utterly spent. 'Great anxiety', Shackleton wrote. Helped by a strong following wind, they chalked up an incredible 20 miles (32 km) on 10 February, with food being the sole topic of conversation. Shackleton celebrated his birthday on 15 February with a single cigarette. 'It was delicious,' the 35-year-old declared. It was a similar pattern as the four men pushed themselves to the limit each day, always focused on reaching the next depot. Only the sight of familiar mountain peaks on Ross Island helped raise morale. In temperatures of –20 °F (–29 °C), with the food bag completely empty, they trekked 14 miles (22 km) on 20 February and reached the cache, the penultimate depot.

The men ate heartily for the first time in almost three months, but now an even bigger worry surfaced as Shackleton calculated that the party might miss the return of *Nimrod*. Shackleton had left Cape Royds months before with the clear message that *Nimrod* should sail north to avoid getting trapped in McMurdo Sound if the Polar party had not returned by 1 March. The well-provisioned Bluff Depot was the key, enabling the party to grab enough food and supplies to make the final sprint before the ship sailed. But the march to the depot began with mixed results. Somehow they managed to cover 20 miles (32 km) but were badly shaken when a blizzard suddenly blew up and temperatures plunged to –35 °F (–37 °C). In normal circumstances, the men would have camped but Shackleton pushed on, saying it was now 'neck or nothing' if they wanted to catch the ship. 'Our food lies ahead and death stalks us from behind,' he wrote in his diary.[10]

The sight of ski tracks in the snow raised hopes that the depot was not far away. In one last desperate gamble, the party camped about 12 miles (18 km) from the depot and Shackleton ordered them to eat all their remaining food and to race as fast as possible to the cache. 'If we do not pick up the depot, there will be absolutely no hope for us,' he said.[11] The men staggered forward on the morning of 23 February, straining their eyes to see the depot flag. Wild caught a brief sight of the flag in late morning and they finally arrived at the depot after more than nine hours of marching. After months of starvation, the little group found food fit for the gods.

Helped by the restorative powers of a huge meal of sausage, eggs and porridge, the men launched themselves on the final trek of 50 miles (80 km) to catch *Nimrod* before she sailed. But another debilitating bout of diarrhoea struck and a blizzard penned them in the tent for a day. Then Marshall, once the strongest, collapsed and was unable to take another step.

On 27 February – less than forty-eight hours before *Nimrod* was due to sail – Shackleton took another crucial decision. Leaving Adams to nurse Marshall, Shackleton decided to take Wild and make a run for the old *Discovery* hut at Hut Point from where he could signal to *Nimrod* in McMurdo Sound. Flogging their emaciated bodies for one last time, Shackleton and Wild trekked almost uninterrupted for thirty-six hours, travelling over 30 miles (48 km) to Hut Point where, to their utter dismay, they found a note indicating that *Nimrod* had sailed on 26 February – two days earlier than expected.

Shackleton and Wild could see no sign of *Nimrod*. They tried in vain to start a fire and raise a flag to signal the ship. But the wood was too damp and their fingers too cold to tie a knot in the flag. The next morning – 1 March – they were able to raise the flag and were stunned when, almost to schedule, *Nimrod* suddenly emerged into view. 'No happier sight ever met the eyes of man,' Wild remembered.

Safe. Shackleton's Southern Party on board *Nimrod*, 4 March 1909, showing the effects of the harrowing return journey. (L–r) Wild, Shackleton, Marshall and Adams marched for a total of 1,755 statute miles (2,800 km).

The men at Cape Royds and on *Nimrod* had virtually given up all hope for Shackleton, Wild, Adams and Marshall. This was hardly surprising since they were provisioned for only 91 days and *Nimrod* picked them up from Hut Point after 120 days. On reduced rations for over four months, the four men had travelled 1,755 statute miles (2,800 km), mostly over unbroken ground.

Nimrod sailed from Cape Royds a few days later and Shackleton returned to London in June 1909, where he was greeted as a national hero. He was subsequently rewarded with a knighthood and the welcome gift of a substantial government grant, which helped settle at least some of the expedition's many unpaid bills. But while he generously gave money to charity, some men were still waiting anxiously to be paid for their part in the expedition.

Nimrod was nevertheless the most successful Polar expedition of the age, establishing both the route to the Pole and a new record 'furthest south'. But more sober reflection centred on Shackleton's wisdom of taking ponies on the southern journey, rather than more effective teams of dogs. It was a decision which probably cost Shackleton the distinction of being the first to the Pole. Amundsen, whose expertise with dog teams was a critical factor in winning the race to the Pole, once wrote: 'A little more experience . . . would have crowned their work with success.'

However, Shackleton's outstanding achievements on *Nimrod* were soon pushed into the background by momentous events elsewhere. Only a few months after his return from the Antarctic, Frederick Cook and Robert Peary each claimed have reached the North Pole and by early 1912 it was revealed that Amundsen's Norwegian team had reached the South Pole. By February 1913, when Shackleton was looking for a new challenge, word reached the outside world that Scott and four companions had perished on the way back from the Pole.

The 'loss' of the two Poles left Shackleton's ambitions in limbo. Once more, he struggled to cope with the daily routine and the discomforting demands of making a straightforward living. A further series of dubious business ventures failed, he drifted into new romantic affairs and was drawn into a scandal surrounding his brother, Frank Shackleton, a shady character who was sent to prison for defrauding an elderly woman. The urge to get away was never stronger.

By 1913 Shackleton had produced an ambitious proposal to make the first coast-to-coast crossing of Antarctica, a bold scheme which reflected the grand scale of his ambitions. Despite Shackleton's personal popularity, many thought the idea was highly impractical and far too dangerous.

The expedition involved two ships, over fifty men and substantial sums of money, which he did not possess. The influential Royal Geographical Society was flatly opposed to the idea and even his friends were worried that, for once, Shackleton had bitten off more than he could chew. Like all his ventures, the grandly titled Imperial Trans-Antarctic Expedition was put together in a hurry, was very thin on detail and badly funded. One senior Royal Geographical Society figure spoke of the 'impossibility of getting any clear answers' from Shackleton about the precise details of the expedition and even Marshall, his companion in 1909, said the chances of crossing the Antarctica plateau were 'too remote to be considered seriously'.

The bare bones of the plan were to take one ship – *Endurance* – into the treacherous waters of the Weddell Sea, establish a base at Vahsel Bay and for Shackleton to lead a party of six men across completely unknown ground to the South Pole. From the Pole, Shackleton would retrace the steps of Scott back to McMurdo Sound, picking up food supplies deposited on the ice a year earlier by groups of men from the expedition's second ship – *Aurora* – who would operate from Scott's old hut at Cape Evans.

A supremely optimistic Shackleton calculated that the 1,800-mile (2,880-km) overland journey could be accomplished in just 100 days by using teams of dogs to haul sledges. This would be an astonishing feat, particularly for men with precious little experience or known aptitude with dogs. Amundsen, by contrast, had made a round trip of 1,800 miles (2,880 km) to the Pole and back in ninety-nine days, but the Norwegians were expert dog handlers and one of the team was a Nordic ski champion.

Sir Ernest Shackleton in October 1914 before embarking on the epic *Endurance* expedition. He is photographed with the geologist James Wordie a few weeks before *Endurance* sailed into the Antarctic ice.

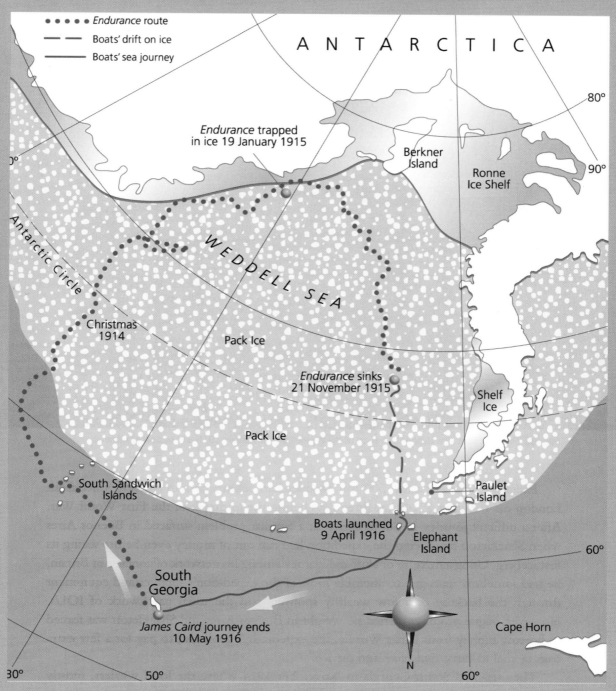

The epic voyage of the *Endurance* expedition, 1914–16. After becoming trapped in the Weddell Sea, *Endurance* sank and the twenty-eight men drifted on the ice before sailing their small boats to Elephant Island.

Trapped. *Endurance* became trapped in the ice of the Weddell Sea in January 1915 and was never released.

Endurance, a three-masted, 300-ton, wooden barquentine built in Norway, sailed from London on 1 August 1914, just three days before the outbreak of the First World War. After a difficult journey to South America, a familiar problem surfaced in Buenos Aires when Shackleton discovered the expedition had run out of money even before seeing its first iceberg. Using a mixture of bluff and blarney among his network of contacts in Britain, he had somehow managed to assemble most of the expedition's supplies and equipment through the backing of a few wealthy sponsors and the usual patchwork of IOUs. However, vague promises carried no weight in Buenos Aires and Shackleton was forced to borrow money from James Wordie, the expedition's geologist, to pay for a few extra bags of coal to carry *Endurance* into the ice.

They reached South Georgia in November 1914 where the local whalers, mostly Norwegian sailors, warned Shackleton that the ice of the Weddell Sea was particularly severe that season and that the ship was in danger of becoming trapped. But Shackleton was in no mood to retreat and resolutely headed into the Weddell.

The Weddell Sea is a huge basin of mostly impenetrable ice, surrounded on three sides by the land mass of the Antarctic. Currents from the east drive the waters in a clockwise direction, first southwards and then north up the long Antarctic Peninsula. It is a graveyard for ships.

The Norwegians' warnings were painfully correct and by 19 January 1915 *Endurance*, with twenty-eight men on board, was irredeemably trapped. The nearest human settlement was about 1,500 miles (2,400 km) away and without proper radio communications, there was no hope of ships coming to their rescue. Caught by the currents, *Endurance* drifted slowly southwards past the intended landing spot of Vahsel Bay and was carried to the north. At first, few on board were unduly concerned, most assuming that the ship would be freed when they entered the

Pressure from the ice slowly crushed *Endurance* and the ship finally sank in November 1915.

warmer waters in the northern reaches of the Weddell. They were wrong.

The party, a mixture of Polar veterans like Tom Crean and Frank Wild, young scientists like Wordie and a clutch of hardbitten sailors, settled down for the winter. Weeks turned into months, the ice refused to release the ship and Shackleton's hopes of making the coast-to-coast crossing of the continent began to seep away. By the middle of 1915, the ship was in mortal danger. The continual movement of the ice began to grind and crush *Endurance*. Timbers began to buckle and snap under the intense pressure and Shackleton ordered provisions, equipment, the three lifeboats and the party's sixty dogs to be placed on the ice. On 21 November 1915 *Endurance* sank.

Shackleton appeared to grow in stature as the crisis deepened. Even with the responsibility of twenty-eight lives, he radiated confidence and slowly instilled the belief

After the loss of *Endurance*, Shackleton tried to lead the party of twenty-eight men to safety by dragging their boats towards open water. Despite enormous effort, the task was beyond them and the castaways camped on the ever-moving ice for over six months.

that, despite the overwhelming odds, they would all escape. He made sure the men were kept busy, maintained morale by ensuring everyone was well fed and had the happy knack of apparently finding time for any individual who was struggling to cope with the fear and isolation. Shackleton, with the minimum of fuss and absolute conviction, simply told the anxious castaways: 'So now we'll go home.'

The *Endurance* party had drifted over 1,000 miles (1,600 km) on the ice since the ship became trapped and at one stage Shackleton proposed hauling the lifeboats to Snow Hill Island, about 350 miles (560 km) away at the tip of the Antarctic Peninsula. It was part of his scheme to keep the men occupied but it was a hopeless exercise, requiring a colossal effort to advance a pitifully short distance. The march was abandoned after just two days.

A second attempt was made soon after but the gruelling work lasted only a few days before this trek, too, was also abandoned.

The drift of the ice continued to carry the men northwards, often at rapid pace. Once a gale drove the floe about 100 miles (160 km) in a week and on 21 January 1916 – almost exactly a year to the day since *Endurance* first became trapped – the castaways re-crossed the Antarctic Circle. The weeks passed slowly, with little to do and little to see. The last of the dogs were shot and new calculations showed that the drift had carried them beyond the Antarctic Peninsula. In early April the snow-capped mountains of Elephant and Clarence Islands could be seen on the distant horizon and for the first time in over a year the swell of the sea was felt beneath their feet. Small lanes of open water appeared as the ice began to break up.

Since entrapment, the expedition had drifted approximately 2,000 miles (3,200 km) in a giant semicircle around the Weddell Sea and Shackleton knew that, both physically and mentally, it was time

Launching the *James Caird* from Elephant Island on the perilous journey to South Georgia, April 1916.

to strike out for dry land. The three small boats – *James Caird*, *Dudley Docker* and *Stancomb Wills* – were launched from the ice on 9 April. Shackleton, in the *Caird*, led the way through the scattered chunks of ice and heavy seas, hoping to reach one of the many small islands around the Antarctic Peninsula or one of the outposts in the chain of South Shetlands. Three days after setting out a calculation showed that the powerful running currents pouring out of the Bransfield Strait had carried the boats miles away from the initial target of the Peninsula and Shackleton was forced to alter course on several occasions before finally settling on the target of Elephant Island. The appalling journey, which lasted seven days, ended on 15 April when Shackleton engineered a landing at Cape Valentine on the island. At least a third of the party were close to collapse. After only a brief rest, the boats were taken along the coast to a new haven, which was named Cape Wild.

Elephant Island, a windy, desolate dot in the ocean, is no place to be marooned. The island lies far away from the main shipping routes and no one was coming to their rescue. With no prospect of relief, Shackleton again rose to the challenge with an audacious plan. He proposed leaving twenty-two men on Elephant Island and sailing 800 miles (1,200 km) to the whaling stations on South Georgia in the largest lifeboat, the 22 ft (7 m) *James Caird*. Leading from the front, Shackleton took charge of the vessel and was joined by Frank Worsley, Tom Crean, Tim McCarthy, Henry 'Chippy' McNish and John Vincent. *James Caird* left Elephant Island on 24 April 1916, watched by the twenty-two hopeful men on the beach under the command of Wild. As the little craft disappeared behind the mountainous waves, one of the castaways wrote: 'The *Caird* is our only hope.'

Shackleton's astute and inspirational leadership was a critical factor on the journey. He maintained the discipline shown on the ice by ensuring the men were well fed and properly rested whenever circumstances allowed and found time to offer a few encouraging words to anyone seen to be struggling. Appropriately, Shackleton was perched at the bow of the boat as *James Caird* was brought ashore at King Haakon Bay, South Georgia on 10 May. All six men had survived an incredible feat of endurance and managed to locate the isolated island of South Georgia by taking just four sightings of the sun in seventeen days at sea.

However, the ordeal was far from over. The *Caird*'s rudder had disappeared in the landing and the only prospect of reaching the whaling stations on the north side of the island was to trek across the mountains and glaciers. He chose Crean and Worsley to make the journey, leaving McCarthy in King Haakon Bay to look after the exhausted pair of McNish and Vincent. He calculated that speed was essential and decided to travel light. All they carried was a small stove, three days' food, a carpenter's adze and a length of rope. To provide a modest amount of grip on the icy slopes, screws were pulled from the sides of the *Caird* and hammered through the soles of their boots.

The crossing of South Georgia began in the early hours of 19 May, guided by the soft glow of moonlight. For two hours the men climbed an icy slope, but thick fog hampered

This is believed to be the ice slope which Shackleton, Crean and Worsley descended during the crossing of South Georgia in May 1916. After being caught in the open with night falling, the trio fashioned a makeshift toboggan from a length of rope and rode down the slope.
CON COLLINS

their view of the land directly ahead and in the haze the men stumbled close to the edge of a crevasse before Shackleton ensured that all three were roped together for safety. Shackleton led the way, plodding forward in the gloom. When the fog lifted the men found themselves walking out to sea across frozen lump of ocean. It was the first of many setbacks which forced them to retrace their steps as they battled to find a pathway through the mountains.

Towards nightfall, the men found themselves up at a height of 4,500 ft (1,500 m) with temperatures dropping fast. Shackleton feared they would freeze to death in the darkness and ordered a hasty retreat by tobogganing down the icy slope. Coiling the rope into three circles, the three men sat down and launched themselves down the slope.

Shackleton took the lead, sitting in front with Worsley behind and Crean taking up the rear. Locked together the men kicked off and careered downhill at breakneck speed, yelling at the tops of their voices as the rough and ready toboggan plunged into the unknown. After what seemed an eternity, the crazy downhill slide came to an abrupt halt when the trio ran into a soft bank of snow, leaving them dazed and shaken but unhurt.

The men marched forward, stopping only occasionally for a hot drink or a quick bite to eat. A little later the sight of Stromness Bay in the distance gave the first clear hint that the journey's end was within reach. Hopes rose further when Shackleton thought he heard a sound. Knowing that the factory whistle of the whaling stations called the men to work at 7 a.m., Shackleton, Crean and Worsley huddled together expectantly looking at their watches. On cue at 7 a.m. the blast of a factory whistle rang out, the first sound they had heard from the outside world for nearly eighteen months.

The men, dishevelled worn-out wrecks, walked slowly towards the whaling station and ran into two small boys, who turned and fled. A more compassionate whaler took

Shackleton (right) with Tom Crean after crossing the interior of South Georgia, May 1916.

them to the station manager, one of the men who had warned against taking *Endurance* into the Weddell Sea in December 1914. The hardened whalers were amazed at what Shackleton, Crean and Worsley had done, first on the open boat journey and then crossing the interior of South Georgia. 'These are men,' one exclaimed. Some forty years later the explorer, Duncan Carse, retraced the traverse of South Georgia and admitted: 'I do not know how they did it, except that they had to.'

After lifting McCarthy, McNish and Vincent from King Haakon Bay, Shackleton's next task was to rescue the twenty-two men marooned on Elephant Island. It was a tortuously difficult and frustrating task which took four months. Three attempts were made to penetrate the ice surrounding the island and each time they were repulsed. On one occasion a vessel came within sight of the island before being driven back by the ice. The strain was intense, particularly as the men on Elephant Island had been marooned throughout the bleak and windswept Antarctic winter. At one point Shackleton scribbled a poem in the visitor's book of a house at Punta Arenas in Chile, which gave a hint of his anxiety. He wrote:

Rescuing the twenty-two castaways from Elephant Island, 30 August 1916.

We were the fools who could not rest
In the dull earth we left behind
But burned with passion for the South
And drank strange frenzy from its wind
The world where wise men sit at ease
Fades from our unregretful eyes
And thus across uncharted seas
We stagger on our enterprise.

By late August, Shackleton's legendary powers of persuasion enabled him to borrow a ship from the government of Chile and launch the fourth attempt to reach Elephant Island. The ship – a rusty 120 ft (36 m) steam tug with a top speed of 10 knots called *Yelcho* – had seen better days and was now reduced to the mundane task of supplying nearby lighthouses. Shackleton was given *Yelcho* on condition that the ship would not be taken into the ice, an impossible feat if he was ever to reach Elephant Island.

Yelcho sailed from Punta Arenas on 25 August and after dense fog cleared, Elephant Island was sighted on 30 August. Shackleton decided to ride his luck. He hurried ashore and lifted the men off the island in little more than an hour. *Yelcho* beat a hasty retreat from the island with all twenty-two castaways safe and sound. But it was a close-run thing. After more than four months' isolation living under the upturned lifeboats, many feared the *Caird* had sunk on the journey to South Georgia and the men on the beach were desperate. One man had undergone an operation to amputate his frostbitten toes, food was running out and some were at the end of their tether.

Shackleton emerged from the dramatic *Endurance* expedition with the reputation of being the finest leader of men and the legend that he never lost a man. Like most legends it was not strictly accurate.

The *Aurora* party, the sister expedition to *Endurance* on the opposite side of the Antarctic, had suffered appallingly after being marooned at Cape Evans without proper supplies for over two years. As promised, the ten men of *Aurora* laid a line of supply depots for Shackleton's transcontinental party who, in the event, never managed to set foot on the mainland. Three men died during the sledging trips and Shackleton later had to defend himself against charges of sloppy preparation and neglect of his men. Symbolically enough, the depot-laying journey of the *Aurora* party, which covered around 1,500 miles (2,400 km), was the last major sledging expedition of the Heroic Age of Polar Exploration.

Aurora returned to New Zealand in February 1917 with the remnants of the expedition and Shackleton was back in England by the end of May to find the war in Europe still raging. At home for the first time in nearly three years he found his three children had grown – a third child, Edward was born in 1914 – but there was also the customary pile of unpaid bills and anxious creditors. Before long he was grappling with the familiar restlessness of life at home.

Aside from making a little money, Shackleton was also keen to find a suitable role in the war effort. But he was not suited to routine work or soldiering and the next few years were another frustrating cycle of unfulfilled promises, vague get-rich-quick schemes and precious little reward. One job offered the dim prospect of travelling above the Arctic Circle to help keep Russia in the war but it never materialised and a few other woolly business deals vanished into thin air without ever making a penny. A diplomatic mission to South America brought Shackleton under the stewardship of Edward Carson, the government minister and Unionist MP. But Shackleton was no diplomat and the initiative quickly fizzled out.

Shackleton returned to London in April 1918 to discover that a few considerate friends were paying family bills, such as school fees for the children. By the summer he was recruited to join another venture on the Russian front, but the war mercifully came to an end in November 1918 without Shackleton ever seeing action. Even a proposed business venture in the Russian port of Murmansk after the war came to nothing when the region fell into the hands of Bolsheviks.

With debts from *Endurance* and *Aurora* still piled up, Shackleton embarked on a series of public lectures to generate a little money. His prospects appeared to take a turn for better at the end of 1918 when *South*, his ghostwritten book on the expedition, was published to decent acclaim. Sadly Shackleton never saw a profit from book sales because all rights were signed over to creditors to help settle old debts.

By 1920 Shackleton was a restive forty-six years old and had heart trouble. Once again he was drifting aimlessly, bored with the lecture circuit and unable to find a suitable niche for his talents. Inevitably, he turned back to exploration and began to piece together plans for a fourth voyage into the ice, his first to the Arctic. This new proposal was to travel into

Shackleton's last journey. *Quest* sails down the River Thames and past the Tower of London at the start of Shackleton's final expedition, September 1921.

the mostly unmapped Beaufort Sea in the Canadian Arctic during the summer of 1921 and from there to strike out for the North Pole. But the Canadian authorities were unsure about the proposal and frustrating delays in the negotiations meant little time was left to take advantage of the 1921 Arctic sailing season. An impatient Shackleton abruptly switched hemispheres.

Instead of going north, he swung his attention to the south and came up with an alternative idea to circumnavigate the Antarctic continent and locate a series of supposedly 'lost' islands in the Southern Ocean. He also speculated about making a detour to South Trinidad (now Trindade) to unearth the buried treasure of seventeenth-century pirate Captain Kidd. The overall journey, plus or minus the hunt for buried treasure, was estimated at over 30,000 miles (48,000 km).

A benevolent old school friend from Dulwich helped finance the expedition and a ramshackle wooden sealer was bought from Norway and renamed *Quest*. In the hopes of rekindling the past, Shackleton turned to the old guard from the Antarctic, including Worsley, Wild and Crean. In the event, Crean turned down Shackleton's request to join up again, but *Quest* could still boast eight old Antarctic hands like Wild and Worsley. *Quest* sailed from London on 18 September 1921 with twenty-one men cramped on board the dilapidated little vessel. Observers noticed that Shackleton looked slightly frail and older than his forty-seven years.

The ship, heavily weighed down with supplies and equipment, was a sluggish traveller and laboured across the Atlantic to Rio de Janeiro where it was discovered that major repairs were needed. Shackleton was also struggling. During the four-week stay at Rio, he suffered a major heart attack. Against all medical advice, Shackleton drove himself on. The patched-up *Quest* headed towards South Georgia in the final days of 1921, with

Quest moored at Grytviken Harbour, South Georgia, shortly before Shackleton's death on 4 January 1922.

Facing page: One of the last photographs of Shackleton, taken on board Quest in late 1921 heading towards South Georgia.

Old comrades gather at the little cemetery in Grytviken, South Georgia, to say farewell to Shackleton, the man they called 'The Boss'. Frank Wild, Shackleton's most loyal lieutenant, stands second from left.

Shackleton remaining on the bridge every night during a four-day storm, in spite of his faltering health. He continued to push himself to the limit. One night he took Worsley's watch in addition to his own and when his bunk became sodden in the squalls, slept on a wardroom bench to ensure that none of his men was disturbed.

But Shackleton was not his old self. He was melancholic and unsettled, almost as though he sensed some imminent catastrophe. In a diary entry on 2 January, he wrote: 'Ah me! The years that have gone since in the pride of young manhood I first went forth to the fight. I grow old and tired, but must always lead on.' *Quest* reached South Georgia on 4 January, with Shackleton scanning the familiar mountains and glaciers through binoculars and guiding the vessel into the harbour at Grytviken which he remembered so well. He briefly came alive when chatting about crossing the island six years earlier, but he was unusually subdued.

Shackleton was impatient to get away quickly but admitted to his diary: '. . . the prospect is not too bright'. Almost as an afterthought, he added the lines: 'In the darkening twilight I saw a lone star hover Gem-like above the bay.' They were the last words he ever wrote. Ernest Henry Shackleton, aged forty-seven, died of a heart attack at 3.30 a.m. on 5 January 1922. Although her husband's body began the journey back to England, Emily Shackleton decided it was appropriate for him to be laid to rest in South Georgia. Shackleton was finally buried in the Norwegian cemetery at Grytviken on 5 March 1922. It was where he had been happiest.

Among the deluge of tributes paid to Shackleton over the years, none was more eloquent and astute than that made by Raymond Priestley, a colleague from the *Nimrod* expedition and a member of Scott's *Terra Nova* party. He wrote: 'Scott for scientific method, Amundsen for speed and efficiency but when disaster strikes and all hope is gone, get down on your knees and pray for Shackleton.'

THOMAS CREAN

1877–1938

The earliest known photograph of Tom Crean, taken in 1901 shortly before he joined the *Discovery* expedition to the Antarctic in 1901. CREAN FAMILY

NO ONE MAN typifies the great age of exploration to the Antarctic more than Tom Crean. He was the down-to-earth farmer's son from the pastures of Kerry who ran away from home at fifteen, was an outstanding figure on three major expeditions to the ice and outlived almost all of his famous contemporaries, such as Scott and Shackleton. Crean was a good-humoured, resolute and indestructible survivor who wrote his own name across Antarctic history, but circumstances dictated that he was never able to speak openly about his incredible exploits and he died half-forgotten. He epitomised the ordinary man from the ranks, rising from a humble background to become a crucial figure on historic voyages of discovery and yet was never fully recognised for his feats until long after his death.

The farmhouse near Anascaul, County Kerry, where Tom Crean was born in 1877. MICHAEL SMITH

Thomas Crean came from a typically large Kerry family in the last decades of the nineteenth century. His parents, Patrick and Catherine Crean, were simple farmers who produced a flock of ten children and scratched a living from an isolated smallholding at Gurtachrane (*Gort an Corráin*), outside the village of Anascaul (*Abhainn an Scáil*) on the Dingle Peninsula in Kerry. Tom Crean (*Tomás Ó Croidheáin*) was born on 20 July 1877 and brought up speaking both Irish and English. Hardship was a way of life for the Crean children – six boys and four girls – and their early days were characterised by a prevailing climate of widespread poverty, a meagre education at the local school in Anascaul and limited prospects. However, Kerry folk are traditionally proud, determined and adaptable people with a formidable sense of survival. Tom Crean was a classic Kerry survivor.

Crean, like so many of his generation, was among the legions of youngsters forced to leave home to find a better life. It was a depressingly familiar trend in Kerry, which had the unhappy distinction in the post-Famine era of exporting more of its own than any other Irish county. Tom Crean joined the exodus in 1893 when he was just fifteen years of age.

Although tradition was probably far from his mind at the time, Crean was joining a long line of adventurers and travellers from Kerry. It is a lineage which can be traced back to Brendan the Navigator, the monk from near Fenit in Kerry who reportedly reached the Americas almost 1,000 years before Columbus. Crean's farm was barely a dozen miles (18 km) across the hills from Brandon Creek, the site from where Brendan began his journey in the Middle Ages. Crean himself proudly carried the tradition of great Kerry voyagers into the twentieth century and it was maintained into the modern era when Mike Barry from Tralee became the first Irishman to walk overland to the South Pole in 2004.

Tom Crean's adventure began unobtrusively a few days before his sixteenth birthday in the summer of 1893 when he walked the few miles from the family farm to Minard, the coastguard station which then overlooked Dingle Bay, to enlist in the Royal Navy. Crean was sent to the Queenstown (now Cobh) naval base and officially enrolled on 10 July 1893.

Crean, who stood only 5 foot 7¾ inches tall at the time, was an adaptable young man who shaped up to the new routine on board *Impregnable*, the old wooden training ship at Devonport, Plymouth. After two years of intensive training, Crean passed his examinations and was appointed to the rank of Ordinary Seaman. Clearly at home in the navy, in 1895 Crean signed on for a further twelve years of service. The following years were spent as a typical navy 'bluejacket' serving on a variety of warships, honing his seafaring abilities and developing new skills at various gunnery and torpedo training schools. By 1900 Crean had advanced through the ranks to reach Petty Officer 2nd Class and was posted to *Ringarooma*, a warship operating in Pacific waters. It was an appointment which changed his life.

Ringarooma, a P-Class torpedo vessel of 6,400 tons, was in New Zealand in November 1901 when *Discovery*, Captain Robert Scott's expedition ship, sailed into the port of Lyttelton en route to the Antarctic. Captain Frederick Rich of *Ringarooma* was asked to help Scott with his final preparations before the expedition headed south and groups of sailors, including Crean, were sent across the harbour to lend a hand. However, *Discovery* was not a happy ship. Heavy drinking was rife among the crew at Lyttelton and one officer admitted on the eve of sailing that there was 'not a single sober man' on board. Scott struggled to restore discipline but Harry Baker, a troublesome seaman, struck a Petty Officer in a drunken quarrel and deserted. Scott turned to Captain Rich for a replacement and Crean volunteered to join *Discovery* for a journey into the unknown.

Polar explorer. The first picture of Tom Crean (front, far right) in the Antarctic. He was twenty-five years old and is photographed with crew members of *Discovery* in 1902.

Tom Crean's first major sledging expedition. Pictured in October 1902 with the twelve-man group preparing to embark on a 250-mile (400-km) round trip to lay supply depots for Scott's bid to reach the South Pole. Crean is second from left in the back row, his face partially covered against the biting cold.

Crean, who was twenty-four years old, was appointed to the officially named British National Antarctic Expedition on 10 December 1901 and joined the 48-man party jammed on board the heavily laden *Discovery* as the expedition left New Zealand on Christmas Eve. Crean crossed the Antarctic Circle for the first time in his life on 3 January 1902, following the track set by Ross and Crozier sixty years earlier.

The ship was moored in McMurdo Sound alongside a neck of land on Ross Island, called Hut Point Peninsula. Initially it was planned that *Discovery* would land a small overwintering party and retreat north before the ice closed in. But Scott changed his mind in the belief that McMurdo Sound, though choked with ice, would be a safe winter harbour and he ordered the entire party to be quartered on the ship for the duration of the expedition.

Men had never wintered that far south before and Crean, an eager and adaptable member of the crew, was called into action from the first moment of arrival. On 3 February 1902 he travelled on the expedition's first sledging trip into the interior of the Antarctic, a brief overnight incursion to the ice for a party of six men which immediately demonstrated their inexperience. In the rush to get under way the novice travellers took only a single small tent and one unfortunate scientist was forced to spend the night in the open while five bulky seamen were packed into a single tent designed for three. No one had worked out how to operate the portable stove, which meant the food had to be eaten cold in sub-zero temperatures.

The *Discovery* expedition was the largest-ever group up until then to overwinter in the Antarctic. But initially it proved particularly painful for Crean, who was struck down by a mysterious illness in the depths of winter which resulted in his losing almost 20 lb (9 kg) in weight and threatened his participation in the spring sledging programme. Crean's legs became badly swollen with symptoms of oedema – excessive fluid retention then known as dropsy – and Scott feared the traditional naval curse of scurvy. However, Crean's condition improved and by mid-July a relieved Scott was able to report: 'He is now quite recovered and the doctors are quite reassured that it was not scurvy but due to some obstruction which they cannot at present place – they think however that he ought not to go sledging, which is a loss for our parties.'

Scott's judgement was a little pessimistic, since Crean made a full recovery and was able to take part in the centrepiece of the expedition, Scott's ambitious attempt to penetrate deeper into the interior of Antarctica and even strike out for the South Pole itself. Crean was a member of the support group, led by Lieutenant Michael Barne, which was asked to back up the three-man party of Scott, Edward Wilson and Ernest Shackleton on the first leg of the great march south.

Cheered on by their enthusiastic shipmates, the supporting party strode out on 30 October 1902 pulling five sledges on to the Great Ice Barrier. Crean, Barne noted in his diary, flew an Irish flag as the march began. Lt Barne, the 25-year-old son of a wealthy MP, had made only one brief journey on to the ice before and was taking charge of a sledging party for the first time. All hands were comparative beginners and inevitably they found the going very tough. A blizzard slowed up the march and the group was forced to trek through the night to catch up with Scott.

Within a fortnight, the group had travelled beyond the 'furthest south' of 78° 55' S recorded by Carsten Borchgrevink a few years earlier and in mid-November Crean was among the small band of men to establish the new record southerly latitude of 79° 15' S. Soon after, Barne's support party halted the march and turned north.

Scott, Wilson and Shackleton waved farewell to Barne's party on 13 November and drove deeper on to the Barrier. With prodigious effort, they reached a 'furthest south' of 82° 17' S at the end of 30 December but called a halt some 550 miles (880 km) from the Pole. The three men, ravaged by hunger and the growing effects of scurvy, only narrowly survived a desperately hard return journey to *Discovery*. Crean arrived back to *Discovery* with the support party in late November after completing a round trip of over 200 miles (320 km) in a little over three weeks. After a short rest, the group was on the move again on 12 December, making a six-week trek to the southwest.

Pulling the equivalent of more than 140 lb (65 kg) per man, the group discovered a new line of mountains running alongside the western extremities of the Barrier. But a frustrating mixture of blizzards and fog obscured the view and with supplies running low, Barne turned for home, reaching *Discovery* on 30 January 1903, a few days before Scott's return. *Discovery* remained firmly trapped in the ice of McMurdo Sound and the expedition settled down for a second winter and another round of sledging trips the following spring. But the eagerness to get back on to the ice brought added risk and Crean was fortunate to survive one of the second season's first journeys, a depot-laying trip on to the Barrier where they encountered over 100 °F of frost.

The outing in mid-September 1903 was very early in the season when conditions were poor and temperatures still very low. The thermometer was down to -40 °F (-40 °C) near the coastline, but the six-man party was shocked as they stepped on to the Barrier and discovered that temperatures had plunged to -67 °F (-55 °C). One man's toes became severely frostbitten and it was feared that he faced amputation. Huddled together for warmth, Crean and his colleagues improvised brilliantly and took turns in placing the man's frozen foot on their bare stomachs for a few minutes at a time to restore his circulation. Each man could stand the cold torture for only a few minutes and the frozen foot was quickly moved to the next warm stomach. It was an inspired remedy which ultimately saved the man's foot from the surgeon's knife.

Less than three weeks after returning from the hazardous spring journey, Crean embarked on another arduous ten-week sledging trip to the new area of mountainous land to the southwest tentatively explored the previous year. Led by Barne, the southwest journey across the Barrier began on 6 October and was the longest sledging trip made by Crean during the *Discovery* expedition. It was also the most difficult. Hauling the sledges for up to eight hours a day, the six-man party struggled into a strong headwind and, once, a blizzard pinned them in the tent for four days. Soon after, force 6 winds (up to 30 mph) made travel very difficult and it took almost ten days to cover the first 73 miles (117 km).

The men had to be roped together as they neared 80° S, the broken, crevasse-riddled ground at the western edges of the Ice Barrier which runs into the peaks and glaciers of the Transantarctic Mountains. In better weather than a year earlier, the group's discoveries included the Barne Inlet and the striking 15-mile (24-km) wide Byrd Glacier which pours more ice on to the Barrier than any other ice stream.

Barne's party turned for the ship in early December and made a further valuable discovery on the way back. As they pulled towards a food depot established the previous year it was discovered that the cache of supplies had moved. On taking bearings, it was found that the depot had travelled 608 yards (665 m) in a year, which was the first time anyone had measured the speed at which the Barrier – now called the Ross Ice Shelf – was moving towards the Ross Sea.

The southwestern party returned to *Discovery* on 13 December, having been on the march for sixty-eight days and covered around 400 miles (640 km). According to one doctor, Barne looked 'a perfect wreck' with a hint of scurvy, and the swollen faces of all the men were a mess of 'scabs and sores'. None of the party made another major sledging trip on the expedition. Barne was the last surviving member of *Discovery* when he died in 1961, aged eighty-three.

Two relief ships – *Terra Nova* and *Morning* – reached McMurdo Sound in January 1904 with blunt orders to abandon *Discovery* unless the ship, which had been ice-bound for two years, was freed within a matter of weeks. Frantic efforts were made to hack and saw a path out of the ice, though the ship was only released a month later by using dynamite to blast the ice apart. *Discovery* eventually left the Antarctic on 19 February 1904 and reached London on 15 September 1904 after a voyage lasting over three years.

Crean's Antarctic apprenticeship had been an unqualified success. He was a popular, dependable member of the team who made five major sledging journeys and totted up a

Icebound. *Discovery* (on left) was trapped in the ice of McMurdo Sound for two years and the relief ships, *Morning* and *Terra Nova* arrived in 1904 with orders to abandon the ship unless the ice released the vessel. Helped by dynamite blasts, *Discovery* was eventually released on 16 February 1904.

total of 149 days in the harness. Only seven others could claim to have spent longer sledging.[1] Both Scott and Sir Clements Markham, President of the Royal Geographical Society and the main driving force behind the expedition, were among those who saluted Crean's contribution. Scott recommended his promotion to Chief Petty Officer and Markham wrote that Crean was: 'An excellent man, tall with a profile like the Duke of Wellington and universally liked.'[2]

Although the expedition had travelled deeper into the continent than any previous one and mapped hundreds of miles of unexplored territory, the vast proportion of the Antarctic remained undiscovered and the Pole was far beyond reach. However, Scott was determined to go back to finish the job and Crean, having proved himself on *Discovery*, was among the first men he selected to accompany him south again.

Scott's ambition to reach the Pole was reinforced in 1909 when Shackleton, his great rival, marched to within 97 geographic miles (111½ statute miles or 179 km) of the Pole. Scott and Crean were together on a train when they caught sight of a newspaper headline proclaiming Shackleton's great achievement and Scott turned to Crean and said: 'I think we'd better have a shot next.'

Crean, now thirty-two years old, was appointed to the British Antarctic Expedition in March 1910 and was among the hand-picked band of robust, experienced naval Petty

Officers that Scott saw as the engine room of the expedition who would drive his party to the Pole. Despite evidence that dogs were the most efficient way to travel on the ice, Scott planned to rely on a combination of Manchurian and Siberian ponies to drag the heaviest sledges on the first leg of the journey and turn to man-hauling sledges on the longest and most demanding stage. Much of the responsibility for the hard work fell on the broad shoulders of men like Tom Crean. Crean, loyal, adaptable and resourceful, was the ideal man for Scott's plans. 'Crean is perfectly happy, ready to do anything and go anywhere, the harder the work the better,' he once wrote.[3]

Terra Nova, an old whaling ship purchased to carry the expedition to the ice, left London on 1 June 1910 and took 4½ months to reach the Australian port of Melbourne, where Scott first learned that Roald Amundsen, the highly accomplished Norwegian explorer, was planning to race the British to the Pole. From there, the party sailed to McMurdo Sound in January 1911 and set up base camp at Cape Evans, about 15 miles (24 km) from where *Discovery* had been berthed. Crean's experience from *Discovery* was invaluable in the early days of the *Terra Nova* expedition. He was among only a handful of men who had been south before and for two of the party on their first trip to the Antarctic, Crean's know-how and raw courage were the difference between life and death.

Two months after landing at Cape Evans, Crean was asked to help Lieutenant Henry 'Birdie' Bowers and Apsley Cherry-Garrard bring four of the expedition's ponies back to Hut Point Peninsula, the site of the *Discovery* hut. The short journey of a few miles was the first time that Bowers, a wholehearted marine officer, had taken charge of men in the south and the three men immediately ran into trouble.

The ice was breaking up in the unstable area near Hut Point Peninsula where the sea ice joined the shelf ice of the Barrier. Crean, sensing the danger, urged Bowers to make a detour and move on to firmer ice with the animals and four well-stocked sledges. But Bowers was determined to follow Scott's orders to get the ponies back quickly by crossing the sea ice.

As night approached, Bowers decided to rest the tired animals and camp on a floe. Although the motion of the sea could be felt beneath their feet, Bowers naively believed it was safe to camp on the gently moving ice. The men were woken at 4.30 a.m. to find that the ice floe had split in two and one pony had disappeared into the black water. In semi-darkness and bitterly cold temperatures, the three men were slowly drifting out to sea on a 30 ft (10 m) wide ice floe. Cherry-Garrard said it was a 'quite hopeless' situation.

The men leapt from floe to floe in a desperate bid to find more stable ice, dragging the sledges and enticing the three surviving ponies to jump across leads of open water. As they jumped, menacing killer whales poked their black and yellow heads above the water. Moving apprehensively, the men spent six hours trying to find a stable chunk of ice, keep the ponies alive and avoid the killer whales. A sizeable floe was eventually found close to the Barrier, but it was impossible to lift sledges and ponies up the sheer 20 ft (6 m) cliff face.

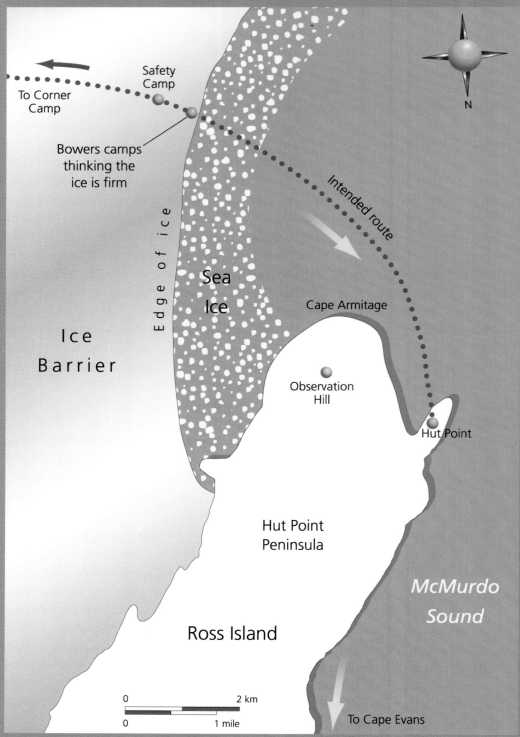

To Corner Camp

Safety Camp

Bowers camps
thinking the
ice is firm

N

Intended route

Edge of ice

Sea
Ice

Cape Armitage

Ice
Barrier

Observation
Hill

Hut Point

Hut Point
Peninsula

McMurdo
Sound

Ross Island

0   2 km

0   1 mile

To Cape Evans

Crean saved the lives of Bowers and Cherry-Garrard in 1911 when the three men were drifting out to sea on a floe, surrounded by killer whales.

At the darkest moment, Crean calmly and bravely volunteered to go for help. Stuffing his pockets with a little food and a note for Scott, he took off on his own, jumping from floe to floe, watched by killer whales and his anxious companions. One slip would have been fatal. It took several hours of frantic effort to find a suitable floe which offered any chance of climbing on to the Barrier. Bowers said Crean behaved 'as if he had done this thing often before'. Using a ski stick to dig foot-holes, Crean clambered up the cliff face and on to the Barrier. Bowers admitted that Crean had managed the climb at 'great risk to himself'.

Although worn out from his efforts, Crean hurried southwards looking for Scott's party. Tryggve Gran, the Norwegian, saw a shape approaching in the distance and skied out to find Crean 'tired and done in' from the incident. According to Scott, Crean was 'exhausted and a little incoherent' after his escape. 'The sea was like a cauldron at the time,' Scott reported. 'It was a desperate venture, but luckily successful.'

Bowers and Cherry-Garrard were quickly rescued from the drifting ice floe, although the unfortunate ponies were beyond saving. Yet Crean was typically modest about his heroism in saving Bowers and Cherry-Garrard and the story was among several episodes involving Crean which were overshadowed by subsequent events and quickly forgotten. His only comment about the dramatic incident was in a brief remark to Cherry-Garrard: 'I was pretty lively and there were lots of penguins and seals and killers knocking around that day. It was a terrible place, but I thought it [climbing the Barrier face] was the only chance.'[4]

While Crean's courage in rescuing Bowers and Cherry-Garrard was widely applauded, the strict navy protocol of the time produced a curious twist to the story. Segregation between officers and men in the hut at Cape Evans was such that Crean was not permitted to eat at the same table as the men whose lives he had saved.

His physical strength, cool head and all-round capability made Crean an essential member of Scott's party which began the march to the South Pole in October and November 1911. Taking a mixture of ponies, dog teams, two motorised tractors and man-hauling parties, the Polar journey began with sixteen men, though only four were scheduled to make the final group striking out for the Pole itself. For those in the final group, the round trip to the Pole and back was a journey of almost 1,800 miles (2,880 km). The experimental motor tractors cracked first and were discarded after only a few miles while Scott, for the second time in the Antarctic, had mistakenly underestimated the value of dogs. But the ponies, wading up to their bellies in the soft snow, also struggled and the burden of transporting heavy sledges inevitably fell to the man-hauling teams.

After marching the first 400 miles (640 km) across the Barrier, the last of the ponies was shot in early December and, soon after, the under-used dog teams were sent back. This left the remaining twelve men to climb the daunting Beardmore Glacier, the route through the Transantarctic Mountains and on to the Polar Plateau discovered by Shackleton three years earlier.

It was an exhausting uphill climb of about 125 miles (200 km) across treacherous crevasses and in soft yielding snow, with each man dragging the equivalent of around 200 lb (90 kg). Each day was a demanding slog and, unknown to the men, Amundsen's group reached the South Pole on 14 December 1911 when Scott was barely halfway up the Beardmore Glacier. Scott's group faced another 450 miles (800 km) to the Pole and after six weeks of hard work, some were showing clear signs of fatigue. A few days later the party camped at 85° S and Scott pared his group down to a final eight when he sent back the First Supporting Party of man-haulers, Atkinson, Keohane, Cherry-Garrard and Wright.

With around 325 miles (520 km) to go, Scott's next decision was to choose the final four men for the Pole. Scott's verdict, which he announced on 3 January 1912 as they stood about 150 geographic miles (about 172 statute miles or 240 km) from the Pole, came as a shock to everyone. At the expedition's eleventh hour he decided to add an extra man to the final party and take five to the Pole, leaving three to make the long trek back to Cape Evans.

Tom Crean, to his enormous disappointment, would not be the first Irishman to stand at the South Pole. At 87° 32' S he was perhaps only two weeks from the most southerly point on the globe and Crean was devastated by the news. He was particularly offended that Scott, who was anxious to avoid an uncomfortable encounter with his loyal companion, could not give him the bad news face to face.

Scott, who did not like confrontation, scratched around for a suitable excuse and found it in Crean's lifelong habit of smoking a pipe. Scott entered the tent to break the news and heard Crean clearing his throat. Scott seized his opportunity and said: 'You've got a bad cold, Crean.' But the canny Crean saw through Scott's attempt to tiptoe around the truth and fired back his own incisive response: 'I understand a half-sung song, sir.'[5]

A disappointed Crean was in tears on 4 January 1912 as the team returning to Cape Evans – Crean, Bill Lashly and Lt Teddy Evans – bade farewell to the Polar party of Scott, Wilson, Oates, Bowers and 'Taff' Evans. Temperatures were hovering around -17 °F (-27 °C) and biting winds whipped up loose snow as the trio gave three hearty cheers for their companions continuing the march south.

The long journey of the Last Supporting Party, a perilous 750-mile (1,200-km) march of between six or seven weeks, was fraught with risk. Only Lt Evans could navigate, locating the supply depots spaced out along the route was critical and any illness or injury among any of the men would endanger the survival of all three. To add to the concerns, both Evans and Lashly's strength was already severely depleted after man-hauling sledges for over two months, far longer than Crean.

As he watched the men head north, Scott casually observed that Evans and Lashly were a 'bit stale' but reckoned the group's sledge was 'a mere nothing to them'. They would, he forecast, make a 'quick journey' back to Cape Evans.[6] Initially, the men had to

Eve of Polar march. Scott's party assembles in October 1911 before setting out to reach the South Pole. Crean (front row, far right) is the only man smiling. Also shown are Scott (back row, eighth from left), Robert Forde (back row, second from right) and Lt Teddy Evans (back row, fifth from left), whose life was saved by Crean.

travel about 230 miles (370 km) across the windy, bitterly cold Polar Plateau and then scramble down the Beardmore, a descent of around 125 miles (200 km) through hazardous ice falls and hidden crevasses. The final haul was some 400 miles (640 km) over the flat featureless Barrier at a stage when their strength would be fading fast and the sharply lower temperatures of the autumn season would start to bite.

Although Lt Evans was in charge, the men were heavily reliant on each other to pull through. Evans rightly saw the journey as a 'fight for life' and reasoned it would be necessary to haul their load of around 400 lb (180 kg) for up to thirteen hours a day to cover the distances between each supply depot.

A few days after leaving Scott, the group ran into a three-day blizzard but there was no time to spare and the men were forced to grope forward in very poor visibility. 'The blizzard blinded and baffled us, forcing us always to turn our faces from it,' Evans said. 'The stinging wind cut and slashed our cheeks like the constant jab of a thousand frozen needle points.'

Unknown to the men, the blizzard had driven them miles off course in the region above the treacherous Shackleton Ice Falls which lead to the Beardmore Glacier. Evans calculated that, without food to spare, a detour would cost several days they could not afford to lose. In desperation, Evans proposed tobogganing down the Ice Falls on board the sledge.

Crean and his pony, Bones, at the start of the march to the Pole. Crean coaxed the animal for 400 miles (640 km) across the ice before man-hauling his sledge.

Perched at the top of the falls, the three men huddled together on the sledge and kicked off downhill. The sledge careered down the slope at gathering speed, the men yelling at the tops of their voices in exhilaration as they shot across gaping crevasses. Somehow, the do-it-yourself toboggan avoided colliding with rocks and came to a shuddering halt at the bottom of the slope, rolling over and over and throwing the men to the ground like rag dolls. Luckily it was a soft landing on a mound of snow and no one suffered any injury, though Crean's windproof trousers were badly torn. 'How we ever escaped entirely uninjured is beyond me to explain,' Evans remembered. 'It makes me sweat, even now, when I think of it.'[7]

By 21 January the trio had safely navigated the descent of the Beardmore, despite repeated threats from crevasses and agonising attacks of snow blindness. Although the men were drained by the ordeal, Evans said Crean and Lashly had 'hearts of lions'. But hopes of getting through were shattered as the men stepped on to the Barrier. After almost fourteen weeks on the march, Evans had developed the first symptoms of scurvy. What began as stiffness in the knees for Evans soon progressed to blackened gums, growing fatigue and chronic diarrhoea. 'As day followed day, my condition became worse,' he wrote. A few days later Evans began passing blood and was unable to pull the sledge.

Travelling across the horizontal Barrier surface is like being at sea and only Evans could navigate. Without his crucial ability, the party risked being lost in the white wilderness. The only reassuring fact was that Lashly, a tough 43-year-old naval stoker, was mercifully free of scurvy even though he had been man-hauling for as long as Evans. But he was inevitably growing increasingly tired. The extra burden and responsibility fell to the redoubtable and endlessly optimistic Crean. Evans and Lashly both kept records of the journey and commented on Crean's continued cheerfulness, regardless of the overwhelming odds. After a strenuous day's march, Crean could be heard around the nightly camp quietly singing or cracking jokes as though the three men did not have a care in the world.

The reality was entirely the opposite. Evans was in free-fall as they drove themselves forward and all surplus gear was dumped to lighten the sledge load. Evans collapsed altogether about 100 miles (160 km) from Hut Point, the nearest spot where help would be found. Crean, barely able to control his emotions, thought he was dead and Evans remembered: 'His hot tears fell on my face as I came to and I gave him a weak kind of laugh.'[8] Evans was placed on the sledge, adding to the weight.

Without a navigator, Crean and Lashly were totally reliant on picking up the tracks of the outward march to guide them back and despite growing fatigue managed to cover up to 12 miles (18 km) a day. But they were fighting a losing battle. A desperately ill Evans was conscious enough to realise that he might not survive and weakly ordered Crean and Lashly to leave him behind to save themselves. In defiance of the navy's customary code of blind obedience, Crean and Lashly flatly ignored the order. It was, said Evans, the only time in his long naval career that anyone had disobeyed an order.

Crean and Lashly pushed themselves to the limit and were cheered when some familiar landmarks around Hut Point could be seen in the distance. But they were not travelling fast enough and to extend the marches, it was necessary to cut the daily ration by half. Although their hunger was acute, they reasoned that a few extra days would be the difference between life and death for Evans.

By mid-February, six weeks after leaving Scott, the men came across one of the broken-down motor tractors abandoned at the start of the Polar march. A frantic search for any scraps of food uncovered only a few stale biscuits tainted by paraffin. Crean and Lashly, weak and ravenous, camped about 40 miles (64 km) from Hut Point on the night of 17 February. After dragging the dying Evans for around 100 miles (160 km), the men had little stamina left. 'I don't think we have got the go in us we had,' Lashly admitted, 'but we must try and push on.'

Evans, emaciated and near to death, collapsed next morning and the last drop of brandy was poured into his mouth. Crean and Lashly, fighting their own exhaustion and hunger, staggered forward in one last supreme effort. But the men were running on empty and Evans recalled: 'I could see them from the sledge by raising my head — how slowly their

Crean showing the effects of nearly four months on the ice. He was photographed in February 1912 after returning from a 1,500-mile (2,400-km) trek towards the Pole and saving the life of Lt Evans by walking the final 35 miles (56 km) alone to fetch help.

legs seemed to move, wearily but nobly they fought on. Their strength was spent, and great though their hearts were, they now had to give up. In vain, they tried to move the sledge with my wasted weight upon it – it was hopeless.'9 Crean and Lashly stumbled to a halt about 35 miles (56 km) from the safe haven of the *Discovery* hut at Hut Point Peninsula. Only one day's food remained and it would take four or five days of gruelling struggle at the present deathly slow pace to reach the hut.

Faced with the certain knowledge that all three would perish, Crean courageously volunteered to set out alone to fetch help from Hut Point, leaving Lashly to nurse Evans. A fit, nourished person might expect to walk 35 miles in ten to twelve hours. But Crean was drained and starving after a four-month slog of 1,500 miles (2,400 km). He reckoned that speed was essential and decided to travel without any baggage. He left his sleeping bag behind and had no means of making a hot drink. His only food was three biscuits and two sticks of chocolate. He set off at 10 a.m. on Sunday 18 February 1912. 'He strode out nobly and finely,' Evans recalled. 'I wondered if I should ever see him again.'

The path towards Hut Point was a highly dangerous obstacle course of broken ground littered with crevasses. Any injury from a bad fall would be fatal. Crean hiked for about 16 miles (25 km) through soft snow and undulating ice formations before stopping for a breather. He ate the chocolate and two of the three biscuits and his only drink was a handful of snow. Crean placed the last precious biscuit back into his pocket – for emergencies! It was around midnight when Crean came to Barrier's edge. Hut Point was about 6 miles (10 km) away and the surface was punctured with half-hidden crevasses and the type of unstable sea ice which he encountered a year before in saving Bowers and Cherry-Garrard. To his horror, Crean could see the weather was breaking up and a blizzard was approaching in the distance. Without shelter, Crean had no hope of surviving an Antarctic blizzard.

Fighting back the fatigue, Crean steered away from the treacherous sea ice and climbed up Observation Hill, the 750 ft (250 m) knoll which overlooks the Hut Point. From that vantage point, he could plainly see the deadly blizzard powering towards the Peninsula. Crean, utterly exhausted and close to collapse, managed to summon enough strength to scramble down the other side of Observation Hill where, to his profound relief, he ran into a few dogs milling around which indicated that the camp was occupied. Over his shoulder the blizzard was getting closer.

Hurrying over the final few steps, Crean finally staggered into the hut at around 3.30 a.m. on Monday 19 February and collapsed semi-conscious on the floor. He had been on the march, virtually without a break, for nearly eighteen hours and was revived by Atkinson, by chance the only doctor within 400 miles (640 km). Minutes later the blizzard smashed into Hut Point.

Revived by a shot of brandy, Crean gave Atkinson the news of Evans and Lashly out on the Barrier and bravely volunteered to go back out with the rescuers. Atkinson sensibly refused his offer and instead took a team of fast-moving dogs to pick up the two men. Evans survived by a whisker and never forgot the extraordinary courage and endurance of Tom Crean, the man who saved his life.

Crean's account of the trek was typically brief and modestly understated. In a letter to a friend, Crean merely revealed: 'My long legs did the trick.' He gave only a fleeting glimpse of the drama in private conversations with Cherry-Garrard, author of *The Worst Journey in the World*, the famous book on the expedition. However, the story was subsequently overshadowed by the tragic death of Scott's party on the way back from the Pole and Crean's remarkable act of single-handed bravery to save the lives of Evans and Lashly was quickly forgotten.

All hopes for Scott evaporated in late March and Crean was among the depleted group of thirteen men who settled down to spend a second winter at Cape Evans. By October, the survivors went back on to the Barrier in search of the dead party. The searchers, who were provisioned for a journey of 500 miles (800 km) across the Barrier and up the Beardmore Glacier, left Cape Evans on 29 October 1912 and came across a tent on 12 November, just 11 miles (18 km) from the well-stocked One Ton supply depot. Inside were the bodies of Scott, Wilson and Bowers and notes revealing that 'Taff' Evans and Oates had died elsewhere on the return from the Pole.

Crean was moved to tears by the sight of the frozen corpses and any resentment at the exclusion from the Polar party was forgotten as he bent down and kissed Scott's forehead. Moments later the tent was collapsed and a 12 ft (4 m) cairn of snow built over the three men.

The expedition finally left Antarctica in early 1913 and by June *Terra Nova* was berthed in Cardiff, the Welsh capital which had contributed generously to the expedition's funds. Among the visitors to the ship were Scott's widow, Kathleen, and her three-year-old son, Peter. The highlight of the day for the youngster, who grew up to become the famous naturalist Sir Peter Scott, was being carried up to *Terra Nova*'s crow's nest in the muscular arms of Tom Crean.

Members of the expedition were reunited a few weeks later at Buckingham Palace where King George V presented Crean and Lashly with the Albert Medal, the highest award for gallantry, for saving the life of Evans. Evans never forgot the selfless courage of Crean and Lashly. He once told a meeting at the Royal Geographical Society that 'No tribute could be too great'. Kathleen Scott said Crean and Lashly were 'magnificent fellows' and Herbert Ponting, the expedition's photographer, described Crean's 35-mile solo march as 'one of the finest feats in an adventure that is an epic of splendid episodes'.

Crean, by now thirty-six, returned to Anascaul in the autumn of 1913 and was evidently planning for his retirement from the navy. While in Kerry, Crean bought a run-down pub in the village for the liquor licence and laid the foundations for leaving the navy and starting a new career as a publican. But his plans to settle down were interrupted a few months later when Shackleton reappeared and invited the Kerryman to serve on a new expedition. Crean, never one to shirk a challenge, readily agreed to join the Imperial Trans-Antarctic Expedition.

Crean was a key member of the expedition, a highly ambitious scheme to make the first-ever coast-to-coast crossing of the continent. Crean, the dependable and stalwart veteran of *Discovery* and *Terra Nova*, was among the six men Shackleton wanted to make the overland journey, a trip of around 1,800 miles (2,880 km). The expedition, with Crean serving as Second Officer, left London on 1 August 1914 and sailed to South Georgia, where the news was very discouraging. Local whaling captains warned that *Endurance* risked getting trapped in the dangerous waters of the Weddell Sea even before reaching the Antarctic mainland but Shackleton was impatient and the ship sailed to the Antarctic on 5 December 1914. Six weeks later *Endurance* was trapped and never released.

Encased in solid ice, *Endurance* drifted around the Weddell Sea and by July 1915 the currents had carried the party hundreds of miles. But the growing pressure from the ice was slowly crushing *Endurance*. Supplies, equipment and the party's dogs were offloaded on to a temporary camp on the ice and Crean, among the most experienced of the party, was placed in charge of the sledges.

Endurance sank in November 1915, leaving twenty-eight men camped on the ice. Shackleton hoped that, as the drift continued, the party could strike out for land to the west or that they could drag the small lifeboats towards open seas. But either way it was a hopeless task. The nearest land, the Antarctic Peninsula or one of the remote offshore islands, was perhaps 350 miles (560 km) away and there was no sign of a break in the relentless field of ice. Dragging the boats, which each weighed around one ton (1,000 kg), was horrendously hard work. Yoked in harness, eighteen men at a time could manage only 200 or 300 yards (180 m – 270 m) before collapsing exhausted.

Last Supporting Party. The last men to see Scott alive near the Pole and reunited in 1913 on the journey home: (l–r) Bill Lashly, Lt Evans and Tom Crean.

For gallantry. The Albert Medal awarded to Tom Crean for his life-saving march of 35 miles (56 km) to save the stricken Lt Evans.
CREAN FAMILY

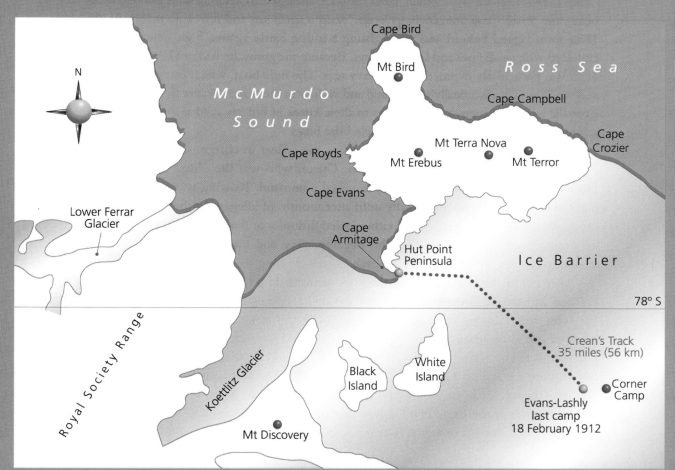

Tom Crean's incredible eighteen-hour solo trek to save the lives of Evans and Lashly in February 1912.

The boat-hauling ordeal, though futile, was Shackleton's way of keeping the men occupied and he leant heavily on the support of Crean and Frank Wild to keep order and maintain morale. Amid signs of growing unease among the restless and distressed sailors, the only men Shackleton could fully trust were Crean and Wild.

By late March 1916, after more than a year of entrapment, mountain tops could be seen in the distance but the party had drifted beyond the most northerly reaches of the Antarctic Peninsula. In early April, clear signs of loose and broken ice could be seen and small tongues of open waterways were visible which offered the first chance to launch the boats.

The three lifeboats, loaded with boxes of food and equipment, were launched on 9 April about 250 miles (400 km) above the Antarctic Circle. Initially, the boats towed Crean's sledges behind but it was soon realised that the extra weight impeded movement and they were quickly cut adrift.

Crean was assigned to the smallest and most vulnerable craft, a 20 foot 8 inch (6.3 m) cutter called *Stancomb Wills* which, from the start, struggled to keep up with the two other boats, the *James Caird* and *Dudley Docker*. With a small sail and fewer men to row, the *Wills* soon lagged behind and was fighting a losing battle against high winds and seas cluttered with small floes and large icebergs. Because the gunwales had not been raised, the *Wills* was particularly exposed to the heavy seas. The little boat, which carried eight men and supplies, was chronically overloaded and sat low in the water. Waves frequently broke over the sides and men were often up to their knees in bitterly cold water. All around, schools of intimidating killer whales circled the boats.

A fresh crisis arose when Hubert Hudson, the officer in charge, suddenly collapsed from a combination of fatigue and illness. Crean, who was the oldest man on *Wills*, immediately took control and quietly assumed command. Rowing was intensely hard, particularly for men who were badly unfit after months of idleness on the ice. While one group took turns at the oars, others either bailed furiously or fended off dangerous chunks of ice. All hands were soaked by the freezing spray and most were seasick. In spare moments, the men picked the ice off each other's clothing.

After a tiring first day's rowing, the boats were tied up to a large floe and tents were erected. But the ice floe split apart during the night, tipping two men into the water and the tents were quickly dismantled. It was a long and miserable night and Shackleton resolved not to camp on an ice floe again. The ordeal by water was resumed at dawn and the men were cheered when the flotilla finally left the clutches of the ice, the first time they had met open seas since *Endurance* entered the Weddell Sea. But away from the occasional shelter of the ice, the boats were even more at the mercy of the heavy seas in the dangerous eastern reaches of the Bransfield Strait between the Drake Passage and the Weddell Sea. Strong currents flow in one direction and winds, frequently reaching gale force, blow in the other.

Despite Crean's stewardship, the *Wills* laboured badly and more than once came close to capsizing as heavy waves engulfed the craft. Frank Hurley, the Australian photographer, watched one moment of drama from another boat and reported: 'Disaster was only averted by greatest exertion of her crew and Crean's skilful piloting.'

Many of the men were also struggling to cope. Seasickness was a constant problem for the cold, wet sailors and some were inflicted with debilitating bouts of diarrhoea. At times the only sustenance was dog food eaten cold, and at night the only man allowed on to an ice floe was the cook, Charles Green, who brewed up precious mugs of steaming hot milk. Men shivered uncontrollably in the freezing temperatures and sleep was fitful as the boats rocked back and forth in the swell. By morning the men were sheathed in a white coating of frost. Before long another member of Crean's crew collapsed and another reported severe frostbite in his feet.

With *Wills* limping along in the rear of the flotilla, Shackleton worried that Crean's vessel would be lost in the rough seas. His worst fears were nearly confirmed when a huge wave swamped the craft; but the next wave tipped the boat over the other way and the water poured out. Anxious to avoid losing Crean's party, Shackleton fixed a line between the *Wills* and his vessel, the *James Caird*, but it was only a temporary reprieve.

The seventh day at sea broke with the encouraging sight of the mountain tops of Clarence and Elephant Islands about 30 miles (48 km) in the distance. Progress was very slow in the heavy, lumpy seas and the deteriorating condition of the men, particularly those under Crean's command in the *Wills*, was causing great concern. Few had enough strength to row and at least four of the eight men had virtually collapsed, while others were weakening.

Crean remained an indomitable figure. Those in the other boats frequently lost sight of the *Wills* in the semi-darkness and mountainous seas and Shackleton could be heard calling out to Crean above the din of the sea, always fearing the worst. Hurley recalled: 'Then against a white spume a dark shape would appear and though the tumult would come, faint but cheering, Tom Crean's reassuring hail, "All well, Sir".'[10]

Limping along like a lame duck, the *Wills* inevitably slowed the progress of the *Caird* and *Docker* who were reluctantly forced to wait for Crean to catch up. Thomas Orde Lees, who was in the *Docker*, wrote: 'We could but sympathise with her occupants as, having a wholly inadequate spread of canvas, she was heavily handicapped and her crew had the harder work on the oars, besides which her low gunwale rendered her much the wettest boat of the three.'[11] Dawn broke on the morning of 15 April with the cliffs of Elephant Island almost within touching distance and the *Caird* and *Wills* gathered near the eastern extremities of the island. A small sheltered bay was spotted as the craft ventured along the bleak shores of the island and it was decided to take the *Wills*, the lightest and most manoeuvrable, ashore first.

Crean the animal lover. The pups were born a few days before *Endurance* became irretrievably trapped in the ice and Crean later trained the animals to pull sledges.

Tom Crean on *Endurance* in 1915.

The *Stancomb Wills*, which only survived the terrible seven-day journey from the ice to Elephant Island because of Crean's skilled seamanship. The boat, only 20 ft 8 ins (6.3 m) in length, is seen here taking men to the *James Caird* for the voyage to South Georgia.

Shackleton joined Crean on board *Wills* and a route was found through the dangerous rocks guarding the entrance to the beach. When *Wills* came to a shuddering halt on the rocky beach it was 497 days since they had last stood on solid ground.

Crean had once again demonstrated his incredible endurance and indestructibility. Where others had buckled, Crean had stood firm and was one of only two of the eight men from the *Wills* still capable of standing after the punishing seven-day voyage from the ice. Those in the *Wills* had suffered far more than the men on the larger, more seaworthy vessels, *Caird* and *Docker*. Orde Lees reported: 'The *Stancomb Wills* had had a very bad time of it, taking in water, if anything, in greater quantities than we had.' The men were a pitiful sight. Shackleton reckoned that 10 of the entire 28-man party were 'off their heads'.

The first landing place was named Cape Valentine, but the beach was exposed to high tides and Shackleton asked his loyal lieutenants, Crean and Wild, to go in search of a safer haven. Taking *Wills*, the men returned late into the night with word that a more suitable spot had been located about 7 miles (11 km) along the coast. It took five hours to sail the few miles in a freshening gale and on arrival the dishevelled group was greeted by a heavy

Crean, Shackleton and Worsley after the incredible march across the interior of South Georgia. The irrepressible Crean is still smiling after the ordeal. (L–r): Tom Crean, Ernest Shackleton, Ingvar Thom (Norwegian whaler) and navigator Frank Worsley.

Relief finally came on 30 August when the Chilean steamer, *Yelcho*, finally penetrated the ice at the fourth attempt and moored off Elephant Island, four and a half months after the *James Caird* had sailed. Crean and Shackleton rowed ashore to discover that all twenty-two men had survived and Crean, the consummate sailor, knew what the men missed most. Standing up at the front of the rowing boat, he tossed packs of cigarettes to the men who leapt upon the tobacco like 'hungry tigers'.

Shackleton, a peerless leader, was enormously grateful for Crean's contribution to the extraordinary survival of the *Endurance* party. According to Shackleton, Crean had been 'splendid throughout' and, on another occasion, he simply said: 'I cannot speak too highly of Crean . . .'.

Crean had no time to recover from the two-year ordeal of *Endurance*. Less than three months after assisting with the rescue on Elephant Island, he was back in naval uniform and plunged into the war. He was restored to duty at Chatham Barracks in early November 1916 and transferred to *Colleen*, the shore establishment at Queenstown, in March 1917. A little later he was stationed at the large Berehaven naval base at Castletownbere in west Cork.

Crean broke off from war duties briefly to return home in September 1917 to marry Eileen Herlihy, the daughter of a local publican in Anascaul, known as Nell. Tom and Nell's first child, Mary, was born in December 1918, a month after the First World War came to an end. Crean's long naval career was also drawing to a close and the departure was hastened in 1919 when he suffered head injuries and a damaged eye in a fall while serving on the cruiser, *Fox*. He finally retired from the navy on 24 March 1920 after serving for twenty-seven years. According to his commanding officer's final report, Crean was a man of 'great ability and reliability'.

The 42-year-old Crean returned to Kerry in 1920 to find dangers of a different sort in his homeland as Ireland's long struggle for independence was moving to a climax. Like many Irishmen who had served with the British forces during the war, Crean was vulnerable to charges of disloyalty. His distinguished service in the Antarctic counted for little in the environment of rebellion, and the grim reality of the time was brought to his front door almost immediately after arriving home.

His return to Kerry coincided with a renewed IRA offensive against the British which was aimed particularly at members of the Royal Irish Constabulary. The IRA operation had lethal consequences for Crean's brother, 48-year-old Sergeant Cornelius Crean, who was shot dead alongside Constable Patrick McGoldrick in an ambush near Ballinspittle, County Cork, on 25 April 1920.

In the volatile climate Crean, the perennial survivor, wisely decided to keep his head down and vowed that he would never discuss his exploits in the Antarctic with Scott and Shackleton. While some attributed the silence to Crean's self-effacing nature, the truth is that it was safer to maintain a low profile. It was an unwavering stance he retained for the rest of his life.

Crean also had other responsibilities. Two more girls were born to Nell in the early 1920s – Kathleen and Eileen – and the additional responsibilities persuaded Crean to retire from the ice. Shackleton tested Crean's resolve in 1920 when he invited him to join his new *Quest* expedition. Crean, by now forty-three and perhaps influenced by Nell's firm hand, turned down his old boss. In response to Shackleton's invitation, Crean quipped: 'I have a long haired pal now.'[14]

Crean settled down in the quiet refuge of Anascaul, although the family was hit by tragedy in 1924 when daughter Katherine died at the age of four. On a happier note, Crean finally achieved his ambition of opening a pub in Anascaul. The pub, which he proudly called the South Pole Inn, was first opened in 1927 and is open to this day.

Tom Crean's quiet life came to a premature end in 1938 when he suffered an attack of appendicitis. He was rushed to the nearest hospital in Tralee for the straightforward operation. But there were no surgeons available in Tralee and Crean was transferred to the Bon Secours Hospital in Cork city, a slow journey of about 75 miles (120 km) along the poorly made roads of Kerry and Cork. The delay was fatal and on 27 July 1938 – a week

Left: Family man. Tom Crean, pictured in the late 1920s with his wife, Nell, and two children, Mary (left) and Eileen (centre). CREAN FAMILY

Bottom left: The South Pole Inn, Anascaul, home of Tom Crean and a site of pilgrimage for people around to the world to pay tribute to a true hero. BRIAN LUCEY

Below: Recognition. The statue of Tom Crean opposite his home in Anascaul, which was unveiled in 2003. MICHAEL SMITH

Facing page: The last picture taken of Tom Crean, sitting outside the South Pole Inn.

after his sixty-first birthday – the man who had survived unimaginable hardships and dangers in the Antarctic died from what is today a commonplace ailment.

Crean's body was carried through Anascaul on the shoulders of friends and old naval comrades and was buried in a tomb at Ballynacourty, a short distance up the hill from the South Pole Inn. Lt Evans, who was only alive because of Crean's great courage, sent a special wreath with the message: 'In affectionate remembrance from an Antarctic comrade.' Those who served with Crean on three voyages to the ice always remembered the cheerful, dependable Irishman with great fondness. Frank Debenham, a geologist on Scott's expedition, said Crean was a 'unique' character. A more colourful tribute came from Tryggve Gran who recalled that '[Crean was] a man who wouldn't have cared if he'd got to the Pole and God Almighty was standing there, or the Devil. He called himself the 'Wild Man of Borneo' and he was.'

Unfortunately, the years were unkind to the memory of Tom Crean. Despite his outstanding feats, Crean faded from the spotlight soon after his death and before long he was the forgotten man of Antarctic exploration. Even in Ireland he was an obscure figure and it was not until 2000 that the first biography of Tom Crean – *An Unsung Hero* – brought his incredible exploits to a wider audience. Recognition followed quickly as Ireland discovered a hero most never knew existed. A fine statue was erected opposite the South Pole Inn in Anascaul and Irish schools began teaching children about the extraordinary adventures of the farmer's son from Kerry.

It is also fitting that Tom Crean is remembered in the Antarctic with two notable landmarks. The Crean Glacier lies across the centre of South Georgia and Mount Crean, an 8,366 ft (2,550 m) peak in Victoria Land, stands as a permanent and majestic monument to the continent's unsung hero.

PATRICK KEOHANE

1879–1950

Keohane with the Manchurian pony Jimmy Pigg.
PLYMOUTH MUSEUM

PATRICK KEOHANE was a man of the sea. He grew up in sight of the sea, served most of his life at sea and Keohane's final days were spent overlooking the waters of one of the great naval ports in the world. Yet Keohane's fame was earned on land, many miles from the water, in the most remote place on earth, as a notable member of Captain Scott's expedition to the South Pole in 1911–12.

Keohane's early days in Ireland were a rehearsal for his later life at sea, though his upbringing could not have been further removed from the wastes of Antarctica. He came from an isolated spot at Barry's Point, the most easterly reach of the Seven Heads Peninsula in west Cork, which lies opposite the remote settlement of Coolbawn and little more than 2 miles (5 km) from the port of Courtmacsherry. Opposite Barry's Point, about 5 miles (8 km) across Courtmacsherry Bay, is the Old Head of Kinsale. It is an area steeped in seafaring traditions.

The sheltered anchorage at Courtmacsherry (*Cúirt Mhic Seafraidh*) was attractive to the early Norman invaders, who made landfall in the area sometime during the twelfth century and planted roots which are still evident today. Among the earliest arrivals were the De Barrys who gave their name to Barry's Point and nearby Barryroe, while a branch of the Hodnett family, originally from Normandy, settled around Lislee, changed their name to *MacSeafraidh* (son of Geoffrey) and soon discovered it was anglicised to MacSherry.

The name Keohane was associated with the area for many centuries. By the mid-nineteenth century there were at least fifty Keohane households scattered throughout the rolling hills of the Seven Heads Peninsula and around the townships of Clonakilty, Timoleague and Courtmacsherry. According to some etymologists, the name Keohane is peculiar to west Cork while some believe it is a variant of Keenan or Kinnane and others say it derives from the ancient Gaelic word *cano*, meaning wolf cub.

The Keohanes of Barry's Point were typical members of the local community in the late nineteenth century, eking a living off the land and supplementing their existence by fishing in local waters. It was a no-frills, close-knit community and two of the local families were brought together in 1877 when Timothy Keohane and Julia Moloney, both from Barry's Point, were married at Courtmacsherry. Over the next twenty-one years, Timothy and Julia produced twelve children, though one died in infancy.

The eldest son of Timothy and Julia Keohane was Patrick Keohane, although there is some confusion about the actual date of birth. The baptismal record gives a date of 20 March 1879 and the local register shows 2 June 1879. In later life Keohane always listed his birth date as 25 March 1880. His father, Timothy, was a busy man who farmed a parcel of land and ran a small fishing boat to help sustain his large family. Aside from family duties, Timothy Keohane was also a long-serving voluntary member of the Courtmacsherry lifeboat service.

The coastguard station, one of Ireland's oldest and a focal point for the local community, was then based at Barry's Point and a short walk from the Keohane family home.

Above: The old boathouse at Barry's Point, which was close to the Keohane family home at the most easterly tip of the Seven Heads Peninsula in Cork. Timothy Keohane, Patrick's father, was coxswain of the Courtmacsherry lifeboat which was stationed at Barry's Point.

MICHÉAL HURLEY/TOM MULCAHY

Left: Timothy Keohane, father of Patrick Keohane. The Courtmacsherry lifeboat, with Timothy Keohane as coxswain, was among the first vessels to reach the torpedoed liner *Lusitania* in 1915. Tim Keohane served as coxswain for twenty-three years.

Founded in 1825, the Courtmacsherry coastguard earned a place in history in 1915 when the passenger liner *Lusitania* was sunk by a German submarine some 8 miles (13 km) off the Old Head of Kinsale. Timothy Keohane, aged sixty-one, was coxswain of *Kezia Gwilt*, the 37 ft (11 m) long Courtmacsherry lifeboat, which was rowed from Barry's Point for three hours and was among the first rescue vessels to arrive at the scene of the slaughter, where 1,198 people were killed.

Very little is known about Keohane's early years around Barry's Point, except that he was raised in the family's Catholic tradition, managed to pick up a basic education at a school in nearby Butlerstown and grew up speaking both Irish and English. Like five of his brothers and sisters, Patrick left home at the earliest opportunity. His choice for a life away from Barry's Point was the obvious one of joining the Royal Navy. Keohane enlisted on 6 June 1895, following the well-trodden path of many young Irish boys flocking to the services in search of regular work, passable wages and a degree of security.

On enlistment at Queenstown, he gave his date of birth as 25 March 1880. He was among the enthusiastic band of 4,000 youngsters a year from all walks of life who tried to enlist in the Royal Navy, the world's most powerful fighting fleet whose nickname was the 'senior service'. While many fell by the wayside, Keohane, the young man of the sea, thrived during his naval apprenticeship on the old wooden training ship, *Impregnable*, at Devonport, Plymouth.

Patrick Keohane was small for his age, standing only 5 foot 1 inch (1.55 m) in 1895 when he signed on as Boy 3rd Class. He added a few inches in height during his first years and reached the rank of Able Seaman in 1897. Keohane, who was evidently happy with his chosen career, immediately signed on for twelve years of continuous service.

Later spells of training took him to the Devonport gunnery ship, *Cambridge*, and the torpedo school aboard *Defiance* before he was posted to the cruiser *Amphion* in September 1900 for a tour of duty in Pacific waters, a spell which lasted almost four years. Keohane was back in more familiar territory from November 1904 when he served on *Emerald*, the harbour training vessel at Queenstown. Towards the end of 1906, Keohane began a 2½ year stint on *Sapphire II*, a depot supply ship for the Channel Fleet based at the Portland naval base.

In keeping with his modest, unfussy manner, Keohane passed quietly and efficiently through the ranks and in 1907, at the age of twenty-seven and with twelve years of service under his belt, he was promoted to Petty Officer, 1st Class. His navy record shows that each of Keohane's commanding officers reported his conduct and ability as 'very good'. To friends, Petty Officer Keohane was always known as Patsy.

By March 1910, Keohane was serving on board *Repulse*, a 14,000-ton Royal Sovereign-class battleship, which was once rated among the fleet's most potent weapons. But advances in warship design quickly overtook *Repulse*. The emergence of the formidable new Dreadnought class of warships in 1906 – the 'all big gun' armaments of the

Dreadnoughts replaced the mixed calibre armoury – left *Repulse* virtually obsolete overnight and within a year of Keohane's appointment the vessel was consigned to the scrap yard.

It was during his spell on *Repulse* in 1910 that Keohane decided to abandon his familiar naval routine and apply to join Captain Scott's expedition to the South Pole. Although the precise circumstances are unclear, it is likely that Petty Officer Robert Forde, another Corkman, was the link which took Keohane from the relatively comfortable berth on *Repulse* to the dangerous and largely unknown Antarctic continent.

Forde knew Keohane from several earlier naval postings and they had much in common. Both had left Cork to join the navy as raw teenagers and the men served together on *Amphion* and *Emerald*. Forde had also served on the cruiser, *Talbot*, where he got to know Lieutenant Teddy Evans, later to be Scott's deputy on the British Antarctic Expedition. As Scott's No. 2, Evans was given responsibility for recruiting men and fitting out the expedition's ship, *Terra Nova*. By 1910 he was sifting through a deluge of 8,000 applications from eager volunteers but Evans rejected the bulk of the appeals and turned to the men he knew best. He selected three men from *Talbot* – Forde and two English seamen, Frank Browning and Harry Dickason – and is thought to have recruited Keohane on the personal recommendation of Forde.

Keohane, a sturdy and dependable character with fifteen years' distinguished service behind him, signed up for the expedition on 7 May, just three weeks after Forde. Three days later he arrived at West India Docks in London to join *Terra Nova*. Keohane was quickly installed alongside the experienced naval Petty Officers who formed the backbone of the 31-man shore party who were to set up a winter station and carry out much of the expedition's hardest work, particularly the back-breaking task of man-hauling sledges across hundreds of miles of ice and snow. At 5 foot 7 inches, Keohane was a shade smaller than most of his comrades but there was no doubt about his physical capabilities and mental toughness, while few had more experience of the oceans than the man brought up overlooking Courtmacsherry Bay.

Scott was also impressed with the thirty-year-old Keohane. When the pair first met for an interview in London, Scott emphasised that the expedition did not offer any extra wages and he wondered why Keohane had volunteered for a potentially dangerous mission into the unknown. Keohane, in typically laconic style, replied that he 'always wanted to see what's on the other side of the hill' and was recruited on the spot. *Terra Nova* sailed from London on 1 June 1910. The ship, a poor sailer and desperately overladen, lumbered across the oceans to Melbourne where Scott received the shock news that Roald Amundsen, the most adept Polar explorer of the age, was also driving south and poised to race the British to the Pole.

Undeterred by the threat, the expedition reached McMurdo Sound in the Antarctic in early January 1911 after surviving the full force of a Southern Ocean hurricane. A suitable landing place was found at Cape Evans, Ross Island, and work began immediately

to erect a base camp hut and unload tons of supplies, teams of dogs and the Manchurian and Siberian ponies which Scott intended to deploy to drag sledges on the first leg of the journey to the Pole. The versatile Keohane was quickly into action, helping Forde and Davies, the ship's carpenter, to assemble the prefabricated hut which was to be the expedition's home for two years. It was completed in twelve days and Frank Debenham, the geologist, reported that Keohane was a 'wizard with the paint brush'.

Although slightly cramped, the hut provided a reasonably comfortable shelter for the twenty-five men scheduled to spend the winter at Cape Evans, plus stables for the ponies and kennels for the dogs. Another six men under Lt Victor Campbell, including Dickason and Browning, were dropped off by *Terra Nova* to explore an area to the north of McMurdo Sound.

In keeping with naval tradition, a wall of packing cases kept the living quarters of Keohane and the other 'men' at Cape Evans separate from the officers' bunks. The two groups maintained a respectable distance from each other by eating at separate tables and rarely mixing during the leisure time. Latrines, which were built close to the main hut, were discreetly partitioned for officers and men. The four naval Petty Officers – Tom Crean, Edgar 'Taff' Evans, Robert Forde and Keohane – were allocated their own private corner of the hut and Keohane's bunk was flanked by those of his two Irish colleagues, Crean and Forde.

The 25-man party spent the long Antarctic winter preparing for the spring assault on the Pole, knowing that 400 miles (640 km) along the coast Amundsen's group, with their well-trained and expertly driven dog teams, were doing the same. Keohane and the other seamen were constantly busy on a myriad of tasks in preparation for the journey. Like all the Petty Officers, Keohane was a multitasker capable of handling a range of different jobs, and the scientists, in particular, frequently sought their help to repair or modify clothes and equipment. Griffith Taylor, the geologist, admitted: 'All the scientists learnt something of many handicrafts through contacts with stalwarts of the navy.'

The valuable work of Keohane and Forde in erecting the hut at Cape Evans was recognised by an unusual drawing in the *South Polar Times*, a newspaper produced by expedition members during the 1911 Antarctic winter. Keohane is depicted top left, being held aloft by Forde, while painting the hut.

Facing page: Patrick Keohane lending a hand with the permanent task of shifting snow from around the hut at Cape Evans, 1911. PLYMOUTH MUSEUM

The atmosphere and camaraderie at Cape Evans was mostly very good and the men generally rubbed along together without too much stress, despite the close confines and the inevitable difficulties of coping with the 24-hour-a-day darkness of the Antarctic winter. But there was one potentially explosive dispute involving Keohane, normally a mild-mannered character. The trigger for the dispute was the emotive subject of Irish nationalism. The argument broke out on 22 June 1911 when, unusually, both officers and the men from the ranks joined together to celebrate Midwinter's Day, the point in the Antarctic calendar when the sun begins its slow journey towards reappearance in late August. A lavish dinner was prepared and most of the party got noisily drunk as the drinks flowed freely. It was an uncommonly boisterous occasion and some of the traditionally reserved naval officers even shed their inhibitions to dance with each other.

At one point during the revelry the subject of Ireland came up and Keohane waded in. The sensitive topic went down like a lead balloon among the hut's largely unsympathetic ranks of officers and scientists, who were mostly drawn from the conservative well-mannered English middle classes and reared on an unquestioning diet of upholding the Empire.

Scott recorded the disagreement by writing in his diary: 'Pat Keohane had grown intensely Irish and desirous of political argument.'[1] Herbert Ponting, the expedition's photographer, went further and wrote: '. . . the mind of the Irishman, Keohane, ran to his native politics and he sought vainly for either an opponent or a sympathiser with whom to exchange views.' Keohane, said Ponting, became 'over vehement' in stating his case but did not elaborate.[2]

The heat was taken out of the row by the unlikely intervention of Oates. Although his aristocratic background and privileged education at Eton made him the quintessentially English army officer, Oates had spent over three years in Ireland – he had been stationed at the Curragh, Dublin's Marlborough Barracks and Ballincollig – and had developed a certain fondness for the country. Oates was far more familiar with the theme of Irish nationalism than any of the other Englishmen at Cape Evans and quietly and diplomatically stepped in to defuse the situation.

According to Ponting's account, Oates 'tactfully led [Keohane] to more timely subjects' and the argument was quickly forgotten. The irony of the minor fracas was that, when independence came a decade later, Keohane was forced to flee Ireland because of his service with the British Royal Navy. Keohane's account of the expedition, which he wrote in two personal diaries and an extended log, did not mention the midwinter dinner argument.

All disputes were set aside in the Antarctic spring when the attack on the South Pole began. The procession of sixteen men, ponies, teams of dogs and two motor tractors hauling tons of supplies started to filter away from Cape Evans in late October 1911. First away were the two stuttering tractors under the stewardship of Lt Evans, though these broke down within a week and the men resorted to man-hauling the sledge.

Keohane in August 1911 putting the finishing touches to his model of *Terra Nova*. Keohane continued with his hobby of building models in later life and the *Terra Nova* was eventually donated to Plymouth Museum.

Keohane was in the vanguard of the foot sloggers, leading the shaky pony Jimmy Pigg out of Cape Evans on 31 October with another struggler in the care of Dr Edward Atkinson, the naval surgeon. The main group followed a day later and within a week the party was strung out across the Ice Barrier on the first leg of the 1,800-mile (2,880-km) round trip to the Pole.

Jimmy Pigg began the trek hauling a load of 589 lb (267 kg) and soon began to lag behind. 'Surface could hardly be worse,' Keohane wrote in his diary on 13 November. 'Ponies and men going down a foot at times.' Three days later he reported that all the ponies were very fit – 'except the crocks'. Even when the loads began to ease, Jimmy Pigg and two others continued to labour badly, often sinking up to their bellies in the soft clinging snow. The weaker animals needed a five-minute rest at the end of each mile and few expected them to survive very far into the march.

Scott's aim was to coax as many ponies as possible up to 400 miles (640 km) across the flat Barrier stage to the foot of the Beardmore Glacier, which cuts through the

Keohane and Jimmy Pigg ready to set foot on the Ice Barrier at the start of the march to the Pole in 1911.
PLYMOUTH MUSEUM

Transantarctic mountain range and leads up to the Polar Plateau. The first pony was shot on 24 November, though Jimmy Pigg continued to defy all expectations and somehow managed to plod along in the thoughtful care of Keohane. After around 300 miles (480 km), the sight of the mountains on the horizon brought a welcome change of scenery, but with feed stocks dwindling, the ponies were coming to the end of their journey.

It was Keohane's selfless care and a moment of inspiration which kept Jimmy Pigg on the march for so long. By regularly shooting ponies along the march, the men discovered it was difficult to find an animal who was content to lead the procession. But Jimmy Pigg, despite his frailty, appeared happy leading the convoy and Keohane, sensing that he might keep the animal alive for a little longer, volunteered to march out in front. 'I made Pigg lead and so I prolonged his life,' Keohane wrote in his log of the expedition.

The party, by now down to fourteen men and five ponies, came to an abrupt halt in early December when a blizzard struck as they neared the bottom of the Beardmore

Keohane before embarking on his round trip of nearly 1,200 miles (1,800 km) towards the South Pole.

Glacier. Warmer temperatures made everything wet and strong winds made it impossible to stray very far from the tent. Scott reported: 'The tempest rages with unabated violence'. In the freakishly warm temperatures, equipment, stores and clothing became saturated and pools of water were left on the floor cloth every time anyone entered. Keohane, according to Scott's diary, composed an apt rhyme:

'The snow is all melting and everything's afloat,
If this goes on much longer we shall have to turn the tent upside down and use it as a boat.'[3]

The violent storm raged for almost four days, trapping the men in their tents. More seriously, the delay meant they were already eating into rations set aside for the draining climb up the Beardmore Glacier. The trek over the soft, drifted snow was horribly slow when the march finally resumed. All hands floundered and the ponies could manage only a few paces at a time before grinding to a halt. On 9 December, the last of the ponies were shot. Jimmy Pigg, the poor beast that no one thought would survive the depot-laying journey a year earlier, was among the last to die.

The site of the slaughter was called Shambles Camp. For some it was a 'black day' but Keohane was pleased that slices of pony flesh livened up the 'hoosh', the dull pemmican mix that was their staple diet. 'Ponies meat is so good in the hoosh,' he reported. Most of the party were relieved to be rid of the decrepit animals and some positively enthused at the prospect of the rigorous labour of man-hauling the sledges. 'Thank god the horses are now all done with and we begin the heavier work ourselves,' one man wrote.

For much of the Barrier stage, Keohane shared a tent with Lt Evans, Atkinson and Charles Wright, the young Canadian scientist. But on 27 November he swapped places with seaman Bill Lashly and joined Scott's tent alongside Apsley Cherry-Garrard and Edward 'Bill' Wilson, who was Scott's best friend and only confidant. Another rearrangement in early December took Keohane in with Scott, Oates and Wilson. The dog teams, though fit, were ordered back to Cape Evans, leaving twelve men at the foot of the Beardmore to man-haul their own sledges in three teams of four. Two of the four-man support parties were scheduled to be sent back over the next month, leaving the final four men with a journey of more than 1,200 miles (1,900 km) to the Pole and back. At this stage, however, the choice of the four men had not been made.

Three man-hauling teams began the horrendous 125-mile (200-km) slog up the Beardmore on 10 December. The soft snow was a punishing ordeal, the men advancing as little as 4 miles (6 km) a day in terrible conditions. Keohane recorded a 'very bad surface' and Scott admitted the pulling was 'extraordinarily fatiguing'. A substantial depot of food and supplies was laid at the bottom of the climb and the teams again rearranged, with Keohane pulling alongside Cherry-Garrard and Crean in a team under the leadership of marine lieutenant Henry 'Birdie' Bowers.

The daunting Beardmore Glacier, the pathway to the South Pole, which Keohane climbed with Scott in 1911. The glacier is among the world's largest and slices through the Transantarctic Mountains for 125 miles (200 km), rising 10,000 ft (3,000 m) to the Polar Plateau.

The daunting struggle up the Beardmore Glacier, December 1911. The men dragged the sledge, which weighed around 800 lb (360 kg), uphill for nearly two weeks and were drained by the ordeal. (L–r): Cherry-Garrard, Bowers, Keohane and Crean. Figure at the rear is unknown.

Soon after starting the climb Keohane and several others were struck by a severe attack of snow blindness. Bowers reported that Keohane was as 'blind as a bat' and sticking plaster was placed over his goggles, leaving only a small spy hole to give him limited vision as the team dragged the sledge weighing around 800 lb (360 kg) or 200 lb (90 kg) per man. The strain of the daily toil began to tell on Keohane. In his diary, Scott wrote that Keohane was 'the only weak spot' in Bowers' team, though he admitted that the snow blindness was causing difficulties.

The unrelenting grind continued through a mixture of hard blue ice or soft deep snow, with Lt Evans' team – Atkinson, Lashly, Wright and Evans – emerging quite clearly as the weakest unit. All four had man-hauled more miles than anyone else and the Beardmore was draining their remaining strength. The pulling was so hard that the teams were forced to rest every few hundred yards and breathing became more laboured as the men climbed higher towards the Polar Plateau, which rises to nearly 10,000 ft (3,000 m) above sea level. In desperation, the teams of Bowers and Lt Evans resorted to relaying their sledges, which meant going back and forth with partial loads and effectively marching 3 miles (5 km) to advance every single mile.

A week after starting the climb, they ran into a perilous area of half-hidden crevasses which threatened to swallow a man and sledge at any moment. Keohane said: 'Can't go 5 yards from the tent in safety.' Climbing the Beardmore gave Scott the chance to weigh up the options of who to send back with the First Supporting Party and who would continue the drive south. He kept a particularly close watch on Keohane and Cherry-Garrard who were evidently feeling the effects of the hard work. On 14 December Scott swapped sledges with the group of Bowers, Cherry, Crean and Keohane to see whether defective sledge runners were causing the faltering progress. The result of the change, he declared, was that '[we] pulled theirs easily, whilst they made quite heavy work with ours. I am afraid Cherry-Garrard and Keohane are the weakness of that team, though both put their utmost into the traces.'[4]

On the same day, a few hundred miles to the south, Amundsen's five Norwegians were celebrating their arrival at the South Pole. Unaware of the triumph, Scott's three parties continued to weave their way through a maze of crevasses and slog up the Beardmore. On 20 December, after reaching the Plateau and climbing to a height of around 7,000 ft (2,100 m), the twelve men camped near the latitude 85° S. After almost two months of exhausting effort, they had travelled about 550 miles (880 km) towards the Pole and Scott announced the names of the four men who were going back to Cape Evans.

With the Pole still approximately 350 miles (560 km) away to the south, Keohane, Atkinson, Wright and Cherry-Garrard, the First Supporting Party, were selected to return. Scott wrote: 'All are disappointed – poor Wright rather bitterly. I dreaded this necessity of choosing – nothing could be more heart-rending.' The decision infuriated Wright who believed Lt Evans was shirking and should be sent back instead. In a terse diary entry, Wright scrawled: 'Scott a fool. Too wild to write more tonight.'[5] Keohane, in his own matter-of-fact manner, did not record his personal feelings. He merely wrote: 'Tonight Captain Scott told the first party off which is Mr Wright, Dr Atkinson, Mr Garrard and myself. Now about 85°.'[6]

From the hints given in his diary during the ascent, it was no surprise that Scott sent Keohane back, but there was another important indicator which pointed to Keohane's return. Keohane was the odd man out of the four seamen – Keohane, Crean, Lashly and 'Taff' Evans – who began the climb up the Beardmore with Scott. What tied Crean, Lashly and Evans together was that all three had served with Scott on the *Discovery* expedition a decade earlier. Only Keohane had not been on *Discovery*.

Next day the First Supporting Party went on a little further south to 85° 15' S, reorganised the sledges and prepared to turn back. Keohane's only comment was: 'Sorry to part with old Crean.' Cherry-Garrard said there was a 'very mournful air' about the camp as the two groups prepared to separate and Wilson admitted it was 'wretched parting' from the group. Scott, surveying his prospects, wrote an optimistic footnote in his notebook: 'We ought to get through.' He added: '[we] said an affecting farewell to the returning party who have taken things very well, dear good fellows as they are. [We] have weeded out the weak spots and made the proper choice for the returning party.'[7]

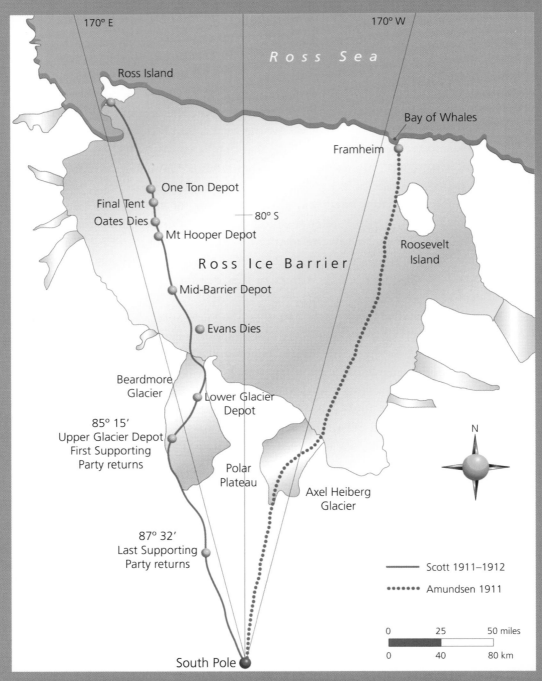

Scott's tragic march to the Pole, 1911–12. Patrick Keohane turned back with the First Supporting Party at the top of the Beardmore Glacier and Crean returned with the Last Supporting Party, some 150 miles from the Pole.

The First Supporting Party, under the calm, unspectacular leadership of Atkinson, turned north on 22 December, taking 3½ days' food to reach the next depot. Going down the Beardmore Glacier, the party covered a remarkable 23 miles (37 km) on the first day and 19 miles (30 km) the next. Even the weather was fairly kind, the temperature hovering around 0 °F (– 18 °C) and unexpectedly bright sunshine replacing the blustery snow falls. But Keohane was soon a victim of the treacherous crevasses which had caused so much trouble on the uphill climb. In one heart-stopping spell of twenty-five minutes he plunged into crevasses to the full length of his harness on eight separate occasions. 'Little wonder he looked a bit dazed,' Cherry-Garrard remembered. It was, he added, a 'much to be avoided record' of mishaps.

Locating the supply depots was critical, particularly as Scott's plans left precious little margin for emergencies in the run between each depot. Food began to run out as the party neared the cache halfway down the Glacier and Wright reported that dinner one night was a slice of plum pudding and seven caramels. 'Feel happy but by no means full,' he said. 'Hope to heaven the fine weather continues or we will have to go short.' Once re-provisioned, the group trekked over 40 miles (65 km) to the next depot at the foot of the Beardmore with only 3½ days' full rations. The men reached the bottom on 28 December and Keohane said: 'Start Barrier journey tomorrow and glad to be rid of that glacier.'

Once revived by a full stomach, the men had rations for seven days to cover 45 miles (72 km) to the next cache, which was a decent margin provided the weather held. However, the ample meals played havoc with Keohane's digestion, much to the annoyance of Wright.

Wright, a 24-year-old Canadian-born physicist, was an uncompromising character who occasionally lacked patience with his companions and showed little sympathy for Keohane's obvious discomfort. An indifferent Wright scribbled in his diary: 'Patsy has got belly ache' and he added: 'He must have a small tummy.' Next day he wrote: 'Keohane makes an awful fuss about his indigestion.'[8] Keohane's problems continued and two days later he was struck down by a debilitating bout of dysentery. Atkinson administered a dose of brandy and ordered Keohane into his sleeping bag early. Wright's only comment was: 'Hope he bucks up tomorrow.'

The daily distances were commendably good, despite the niggling ailments and poor visibility which hampered navigation. On 3 January they made 14 miles (22 km) and nearly 17 miles (27 km) the next. But all four were growing increasingly hungry, a clear sign that the diet of 'hoosh' sprinkled with a few cuts of pony meat was inadequate. On 6 January, about 47 miles (75 km) from Mount Hooper Depot, Keohane's brief diary entry read: 'Getting awful hungry lately.' A further worry nagging away was that the line of depots had not been suitably replenished by the men left at Cape Evans. Atkinson, fearing the worst, decided to keep a small amount of rations in reserve, regardless of the growing hunger.

By 13 January, the poor conditions and terrible visibility had slowed the march to a trickle. Keohane reported: 'A bad day.' It was 26 miles (42 km) – at least a good two days of marching – to the substantial One Ton Depot and a much-needed feed. Images of great feasts and a full stomach filled the imagination as the men plodded slowly north. One night, Keohane wrote in his diary: 'As I lay in my bag here I think of all the food I have ever left behind and that I would not eat. I wish I had it now.'[9]

Mercifully the well-stocked One Ton Depot was reached on 15 January where the men indulged in an ample dinner, rounded off with hot cocoa and sticks of chocolate. 'We could hardly move when we finished,' a replete Keohane told his diary. 'We are as happy as sand boys.' As an afterthought, he wrote: 'Hope the southern party are close to the Pole now.' That night, a few hundred miles to the south, Scott was camped 27 miles (43 km) from the Pole, just two days away from discovering that Amundsen had won the race.

A visibly restored Keohane, Atkinson, Wright and Cherry-Garrard resumed the march to Corner Camp, about 120 miles (190 km) away, with fourteen days' rations and the backing of surprisingly good weather. The good fortune did not last. Atkinson was suddenly crippled by diarrhoea and vomiting which Wright put down to the orgy of overeating at One Ton Depot. On 18 January Atkinson's condition forced them to make camp after covering only 2½ miles (4 km), though morale improved a few days later as the familiar landscape around Hut Point and Cape Evans came into view. Atkinson 'bucked up' a little and the party managed almost 19 miles (30 km) on 23 January, with Corner Camp passed a day later.

The First Supporting Party reached the *Discovery* hut at Hut Point late on 26 January 1912. A day earlier Amundsen had returned to his base camp after the successful 1,800-mile (2,880-km) journey to the South Pole. While Scott's teams were generally hungry on the march, Amundsen discovered that he had put on weight. Keohane, Atkinson, Wright and Cherry-Garrard had been out for close to three months and covered 1,164 miles (1,860 km), averaging a very creditable 16 miles (24 km) a day on the return from the top of the Beardmore Glacier. The four had man-hauled for at least two-thirds of the entire trek, one of the longest Antarctic sledging journeys ever undertaken. 'Arrived in Hut Point after a heavy pull at 7.20pm,' Keohane's straightforward diary entry reported. 'Had a good feed and a lot of brandy before bag.'

After a short rest, the four men finally walked into Cape Evans on 28 January, carrying the encouraging news that Scott's party was last seen on the Polar Plateau going strongly towards the Pole. Based on the First Supporting Party's experience, particularly the comparative ease of the return march, it seemed a mere formality that Scott would reach the Pole and get back safely.

A few days later, *Terra Nova* reappeared after wintering in New Zealand and Cape Evans was in celebratory mood. *Terra Nova* carried sacks of mail from home, fresh supplies

Facing page: Patrick Keohane. The classic portrait was taken on 29 January 1912 shortly after Keohane returned from his Polar trek.

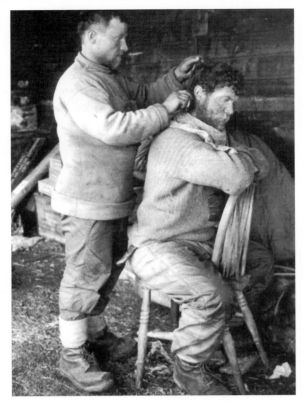

Keohane getting a much-needed haircut after eighty-seven days on the march. The stylist is Russian groom Anton Omelchenko.

and a few replacements for the men heading home after one season in the Antarctic. The ship also carried a team of mules from the Indian Army which Oates had arranged to be sent down for the second season's sledging programme.

But the relaxed, confident atmosphere of Cape Evans was punctured on 19 February when Crean staggered alone into Hut Point with the alarming news that Lt Evans was close to death out on the Barrier. Crean had courageously walked the last 35 miles (56 km) alone, leaving Lashly to nurse the critically ill Evans, who was stricken with scurvy. The shocking state of Crean, Lashly and Lt Evans was a wake-up call which for the first time raised concern about the safety of Scott's team. Atkinson, the most senior officer at Hut Point, first rushed out with dog teams to save Lt Evans and Lashly and prepared to send another party on to the Barrier to help steer Scott's men home. Although there was no real sense of alarm, the problem was whom to send.

Atkinson, the only doctor, was needed to treat the gravely ill Evans. Wright was the best-equipped to make the journey but had been ordered to take responsibility for weather readings at Cape Evans and Atkinson, a naval officer accustomed to obeying orders without question, blindly followed Scott's instructions. By a process of elimination, Atkinson was left with Cherry-Garrard and the Russian dog driver, Dimitri Gerov, to make the 170-mile (270-km) dash to One Ton Depot and guide Scott back. It was a near-impossible task for Cherry-Garrard, a university graduate in his early twenties and the wrong man for the important job. He had no experience of driving dogs and could not navigate, while the glasses he wore to combat chronic short-sightedness fogged up in the cold. In more than one sense, Cherry-Garrard was travelling blind.

Leaving Hut Point on 25 February, Cherry-Garrard and Dimitri hurried south as fast as possible and reached One Ton Depot on 3 March. They stayed for six days, wondering whether to continue driving south but fearing they might miss Scott in the hazy conditions.

To compound Cherry-Garrard's problems, a mix-up in orders had left One Ton short of dog food and Scott had left emphatic orders that on no account should the dogs be risked. Cherry-Garrard, a man who had never been in charge before, was reluctant to take the initiative by driving south, killing the weaker dogs as he went to feed the stronger animals. Nor did he believe that Scott was in any serious danger. Temperatures plummeted to –37 °F (–38 °C), Dimitri suffered badly from the chilling cold and dog food was running low. Cherry-Garrard, with just enough rations to make the return trip to Cape Evans, reluctantly left One Ton on 10 March unsure whether he was right or wrong.

To the south, perhaps three days' travelling by well-managed dog teams, the life was ebbing away from Scott's party. 'Taff' Evans was already dead, Oates was on the brink of committing suicide and Scott, Wilson and Bowers were facing the inevitable end. On the day Cherry left One Ton Depot, Scott wrote in his diary: 'Things steadily downhill. With great care, we might have a dog's chance, but no more.' Two days later he said: 'God help us!'

Cherry-Garrard arrived back to Hut Point on 16 March, the day before Oates crawled from the tent to die with the immortal last words: 'I am just going outside and may be some time.' In Cherry's own words, 'We were not unduly alarmed about the Polar party at present, but began to make arrangements for further sledging if necessary.'

Based on the experience of the two supporting parties, it was calculated that Scott would arrive at Hut Point on 26 March. Hopes rose one night when they were awakened by five or six knocks on the window, and Atkinson yelled out: 'They're in.' Keohane leapt up, calling 'Who's cook?' and lit a candle. The men rushed outside to discover the tapping was made by a dog wagging its tail against the window.[10] But the reality began to sink in as the days passed and Atkinson, sensing the danger, decided to go in search of Scott, even though his options were limited. Cherry-Garrard and the dogs were incapable of another journey after the run to One Ton Depot and the newly landed ponies were still at Cape Evans.

A further concern was that Lt Campbell's six-man party, which had failed to rendezvous in the north with *Terra Nova*, was long overdue at Cape Evans. Caught between a rock and a hard place, Atkinson proposed taking Keohane on a quick trip on to the Barrier in the faint hope of locating Scott, trusting that Campbell's party would make its own way in.

The omens were not good. A blizzard raged shortly before departure, with the strong winds making visibility very poor and the chances of finding Scott even more remote. Twice in the hours before leaving they thought they saw men approaching from a distance, but both proved false alarms. Keohane's diary recorded the keen sense of disappointment. 'I thought I could see the party off the point this afternoon. We all went out to the sea ice to meet the party who turned out to be seals. Last night one of the dogs knocked the window. We all jumped out of our bags and went out but could see nobody.'[11]

Atkinson was fortunate to have the strong, reliable Keohane as a travelling companion in the very difficult circumstances. '[Keohane] was cheerful and willing and proved of the very greatest service during a very trying time,' he later recalled. On 27 March, Keohane

Left: The field diary which Patrick Keohane kept during the desperate attempt to locate Scott's doomed party in March–April 1912. Keohane and Dr Atkinson endured appalling conditions and were driven back by very low temperatures. They were unable to find Scott.
MIKE O'SHEA, IRISH EXPLORERS TRUST

Below: Search party. The men assembled for a team photograph in October 1912 before setting out to discover the bodies of Scott, Wilson and Bowers. Keohane sits in the middle of the front row.

and Atkinson packed up eighteen days' food for themselves and one week's rations for the Polar party and stepped back on to the Barrier. It was bitterly cold, though accurate readings were impossible because the thermometer broke early into the journey and Keohane was left to estimate the temperatures. On the first day he guessed at -10 °F (-23 °C). Travelling was very difficult and the pair managed only 9 miles (14 km) on the first day out. More than 40 ° frost that night made it hard to get a decent night's sleep. A four-man tent, they quickly discovered, was a very cold place for two people on the edge of the Barrier in low temperatures. Keohane reckoned that temperatures next day plunged even lower to -15 °F (-26 °C) and the surface was appalling, restricting their advance south to another 9 miles (14 km).

On 29 March the pair managed a marginally better 11 miles (17 km) in thick, drifting snow. 'Wind spraying up surface. V bad' Keohane scribbled in his field diary. On the same day, about 120 miles (190 km) to the south, Scott was still pinned down in his tent by a blizzard just 11 miles (17 km) from One Ton Depot and made the final entry into his diary: 'It seems a pity, but I do not think I can write more. For God's sake look after our people.'[12]

The next day, 30 March, arrived with Atkinson in a hopeless position. The men struggled southwards across the Barrier for a while in swirling snow and temperatures in the region of -15 °F (-26 °C) and came to halt some 8 miles (12 km) south of Corner Camp. He was by now 'morally certain' that Scott's party had already perished and yet his basic humanity compelled him to continue the search, even if his chances of locating survivors were impossibly small. In whiteout conditions and without a definite rendezvous point, it was like looking for a needle in a haystack.

Keohane and Atkinson had struggled close to 60 miles (100 km) from Cape Evans in dreadful weather with almost no hope of finding the lost men and Atkinson remembered: 'Our condition was bad, and owing to low temperatures we had got no sleep.' Keohane was more succinct and simply wrote: 'Awful travelling.' A depot of one week's rations was left for Scott, and the two men, utterly worn out and emotionally drained by the forlorn search, gratefully turned for home. A strong following wind helped drive them along and despite the fatigue, Keohane and Atkinson walked into Hut Point late on 1 April. Their faces and hands were frozen and Atkinson declared: 'We reached Hut Point after dark. We were both glad to be in and to get some sleep.'

The men, shaken by the ferocity of the low autumn temperatures and difficult travelling conditions, were physically drained by the short trip. Cherry-Garrard observed: 'Their bags were bad, their clothes very bad . . . they must have had minus forties constantly. They are much in want of sleep, poor devils. Keohane did well and is very fit.'[13] It was the last attempt to find Scott alive. Cherry-Garrard reasoned that going out again would serve no purpose and be a 'useless risk' for the two men. He added: 'They did right to come back.' Three days later the temperature sank to -33 °F (-36 °C).

The pressure on Atkinson was unrelenting as he and Keohane made their way back to Cape Evans. Campbell's party was still long overdue and despite his own fatigue, he felt obliged to go in search of the missing men, last seen miles up the coast to the north of Cape Evans. A small party, including Keohane, was assembled to go in search. In poor light and worsening weather it was a highly risky venture.

According to Gran, it was 'a hopeless enterprise.' In a biting, driving wind, the six men left Cape Evans for the 15-mile (24-km) trek to Hut Point on 13 April and arrived exhausted a day later where Cherry-Garrard was still recovering from his journey to One Ton Depot a month earlier. Only Keohane looked fit and the other men needed two days to recuperate before embarking on the next leg of the trip towards Butter Point. Keohane revived spirits by making pancakes which, said Gran, were 'of a size and quantity that left us gasping'.

The four-man search party – Atkinson, Keohane, Williamson and Wright – set off on 17 April in fading light and very low temperatures. Moving cautiously along the shore, the quartet managed to travel 13 miles (20 km), although on one occasion, Keohane had to go back and pick up some gear which fell off the sledge, which increased his mileage. At night temperatures plummeted to -43 °F (-42 °C) and Wright reported: 'No sleep.' The plan was to travel north along the coast, hoping that the sea ice had frozen solid enough to take the weight of a man and a sledge. But the sea ice was breaking up and the sight of penguins milling around increased fears that open water was nearby.

The men were stunned when temperatures dropped further to -45 °F (-43 °C) and they became increasingly anxious about the wisdom of the trip. Wright, who was opposed to the journey, said Atkinson should never have 'chanced his arm' looking for Campbell. On 20 April the party camped at Butter Point, where *Terra Nova* had dumped supplies for Campbell's party. But all hopes of travelling along the coast were dashed by the sight of ice breaking up and drifting out to sea. For the second time in three weeks, Atkinson was forced to turn for home without finding his lost companions.

Keohane reported the sea ice 'rather dangerous' as the four men slowly made their way back in half-light, completing a laudable distance of 10 miles (16 km) on the first day. Travelling as fast as possible, the party hurried along the treacherous coastline but was soon hit by worsening weather. The morning of 23 April opened with a blizzard and temperatures down to -22 °F (-30 °C), which forced Atkinson to change his plans and make a run for the safety of Hut Point before conditions deteriorated any further. The party pushed along, covering the last 15 miles (24 km) to Hut Point at a relative gallop. A relieved Keohane reported: 'Arrived Hut Point after completing 15 miles and "B" glad to.'[14]

The hurried trip across precarious sea ice in fearsomely low temperatures and poor light had taken a heavy toll on the men, particularly Atkinson and Wright. Atkinson admitted: 'I have never known a journey have such an effect upon a party in such a short time.' Cherry-Garrard welcomed his colleagues back to Hut Point and observed: 'They have had a difficult and dangerous trip and it is a good thing they are in.' Atkinson was also full of praise for the steadfast work of Keohane, who was a tower of strength during these difficult weeks of searching for Scott and Campbell. He wrote: 'Petty Officer Keohane behaved splendidly on the Barrier in the latter end of March and beginning of April and again on this journey.'[15]

The thirteen-strong wintering party settled down at the main base camp at Cape Evans and turned their minds to the spring season's sledging. Keohane and Williamson, another naval Petty Officer, were in charge of daily life at the hut and in preparing equipment for the spring trips. 'This winter is passing a lot better than I thought it would under the circumstances,' Keohane wrote. But one question dominated all their thoughts: should they go in search of Campbell's lost party to the north or head south to find the bodies of Scott's men? A free vote was held and by a margin of twelve from thirteen – one man abstained – the group elected to ignore the living and search for the dead.

The eleven-man search party for Scott left Cape Evans on 29 October, rested briefly at Hut Point and set off across the Barrier where they met temperatures down to -30 °F (-34 °C). The men, leading the seven Indian Army mules, aimed to make One Ton Depot, a journey of about 150 miles (240 km), in twelve days and if necessary push on to the Beardmore in search of the bodies. Keohane, leading a mule called Begum, found the animals pulled the loads of 670 lb (300 kg) better than the sorry ponies who had struggled a year earlier.

On 12 November, Wright, leading the group, spotted a dark object poking out of the snow about 11 miles (17 km) south of One Ton Depot and realised it was a tent. Inside they found the bodies of Scott, Wilson and Bowers and the notes and dairies which revealed how the party had reached the Pole and discovered that Amundsen had beaten them by a month. They also learned that seaman 'Taff' Evans had died at the foot of the Beardmore and how Oates, crippled by frostbite, had crawled from the tent in temperatures of -40 °F (-40 °C) when the suffering became too much to bear.

Like all the men, Keohane particularly admired the bravery of Oates, whose body has never been found. After hearing the circumstances of his death, Keohane was overheard to say: 'Captain Oates did just what we all expected of him, sir; he was a fine man that, sir; not much talk about him, but chock full of grit.'[16] In sombre mood, Atkinson read the burial service, the tent was collapsed over the bodies and a 12 ft (4 m) cairn built on top. It was midnight when they finished.

The return to Hut Point was a slow, unhappy affair, particularly as the conditions of the mules had deteriorated. But on arrival they discovered that Campbell's party had returned safe and sound at Cape Evans. The expedition, now restored to nineteen men, awaited the arrival of *Terra Nova*. To their surprise, Lt Evans, now recovered from his near-death experience on the Barrier, was on board when the ship sailed into McMurdo Sound on 18 January 1913 to learn of Scott's fate.

Homeward bound. The search party gather for a last picture together as the expedition makes its way home in 1913.
Back row (l–r): Keohane, Williamson and Hooper; centre (l–r): Gran, Lashly and Crean; front row (l–r): Cherry-Garrard, Atkinson and Nelson.

Keohane's last role in the British Antarctic Expedition was to help erect a 12 ft (4 m) wooden cross on top of the 700 ft (230 m) Observation Hill, which has commanding views of Hut Point Peninsula and the Barrier, in memory of Scott, Wilson, Bowers, Oates and 'Taff' Evans. The steep climb up the hill took eight hours and at the recommendation of Cherry-Garrard, the final words of Tennyson's *Ulysses* were carved on the cross: 'To strive, to seek, to find and not to yield.'

Terra Nova left the Antarctic on 26 January, arriving in New Zealand on 9 February with the first official news of the disaster. By June, the ship was back in Britain and on 26 July 1913 Keohane joined survivors at Buckingham Palace to receive Polar medals from King George V. Soon after, he was promoted to Chief Petty Officer, the highest naval rank he would achieve.

A silver fob watch given to Keohane by Dr Edward Atkinson, who assumed command of the expedition after Scott's death in 1912. The inscription on the back reads: 'P Keohane In remembrance of 3 years in the Antarctic'.
MIKE O'SHEA, IRISH EXPLORERS TRUST

Keohane was back in west Cork a year later where he married Bridget Mary 'Ivy' O'Driscoll, the twenty-year-old daughter of Michael O'Driscoll, commanding officer of the Courtmacsherry coastguard station. The marriage took place at Barryroe Church, Courtmacsherry on 21 April 1914, with Keohane in full naval uniform and proudly wearing his Antarctic medal. Coastguards formed a ceremonial arch with bayonets and Keohane's sledging flag from *Terra Nova* flew on the bridal carriage. The only child of Patrick and Ivy Keohane was born at Courtmacsherry on 12 March 1915. Her name, Sheila Nova, was taken from Scott's ship.

At the outbreak of war in 1914 Keohane went back to the familiar surroundings of *Impregnable*, the naval training ship at Devonport where his career had begun two decades earlier. He was stationed on *Impregnable* from January 1914 until July 1917, where he used his skills and long experience of the sea to turn out the next generation of seamen. Keohane did not see active service until August 1917 when he was posted to *Cornwall*, a 10,000-ton cruiser escorting convoys across the Atlantic.

A card commemorating the wedding of Patrick Keohane and Bridget Mary 'Ivy' O'Driscoll at Courtmacsherry on 21 April 1914. TOM MAGUIRE

The sledging flag Patsy Keohane took on the trek towards the South Pole. The swallow-tailed flag shows the cross of St George and the Irish harp embroidered with the slogan *Erin Go Braugh* (Ireland Forever). The tradition of attaching flags to sledges is thought have been introduced in the 1850s by Leopold McClintock from Dundalk, County Louth. PLYMOUTH MUSEUM

Impregnable, the navy training ship at Devonport where Keohane was stationed during the First World War. Keohane served his apprenticeship on *Impregnable* in the mid-1890s and he returned to the ship from 1914 until 1917 to help train the next generation of sailors.

It was a particularly dangerous moment in the war as both sides grappled for supremacy of the seas. Unable to mount a direct offensive against the stronger British fleet, Germany stepped up the U-boat campaign against merchant shipping in early 1917, hoping to cut off the precious lifeline of food and materials to starve Britain into surrender before America entered the war.

Keohane spent five months on convoy protection duties in the Atlantic with *Cornwall* and in June 1918, with the war entering its final stages, he served on the battleship *Valkyrie*, which formed part of the navy's powerful 13th Destroyer Flotilla in the Grand Fleet. He was still serving on *Valkyrie* when the war ended on 11 November 1918. Keohane left *Valkyrie* in March 1919 and spent the next year at a variety of shore stations, finally ending up assigned to *Vivid* in the Devonport dockyard. *Vivid* was the last appointment of Petty Officer Patrick Keohane, whose official naval career came to an end on 30 May 1920 in the same port where his service had begun twenty-five years earlier.

But Keohane, now forty years of age, was not ready to put his feet up and in June 1920 followed in his father's footsteps by joining the coastguard service. He was first stationed at Omeath on the County Louth shore of Carlingford Lough and after a brief stay moved a few miles down the coast to Clogher Head. At Clogher Head, he was confronted with the realities of Ireland's mounting rebellion against British rule.

Keohane, like many of the 200,000 Irishmen who served in the First World War, returned to Ireland to find the political landscape had changed forever. Any association with the British left them vulnerable and Keohane was especially exposed because the coastguard, which was a branch of the Royal Navy, represented a potent symbol of the British military presence in Ireland. In addition, Ivy Keohane's family – the O'Driscolls – were also coastguards and the coastguard stations had become regular targets.

Stations as far apart as Donegal and Kerry were hit in a fresh wave of anti-British attacks and the Howes Strand base, across the bay from the Seven Heads Peninsula, was attacked twice in a month during the summer of 1920. Courtmacsherry also came under attack and, shortly after, Keohane moved the family out of the area for the last time. He never went back to live on the Seven Heads Peninsula.

The attacks continued and the old Clogher Head coastguard station was burnt down. In July 1921 Keohane was transferred to Dundalk, which itself had to be evacuated a few months later. After a brief stay at Dun Laoghaire (then Kingstown), he was posted to the station at Cushendall, County Antrim. The appointment, which took effect in April 1922, coincided with the end of British rule in the twenty-six counties of Ireland and was Keohane's last posting in his native country.

Deeming Ireland to be unsafe, Keohane left Cushendall in March 1923 and moved to the UK, where he took up a number of coastguard appointments. He was appointed Station Officer at Portsoy on the northeast coast of Scotland in September 1928 and later went to Coverack, a picturesque fishing village on the Lizard Peninsula in Cornwall.

Coverack, with its long seafaring traditions, was strongly reminiscent of the area around Courtmacsherry Bay and Keohane, the new Station Officer, was comfortable in the surroundings. The family lived in the coastguard office cottage in the charmingly named Sunny Corner Lane and each Sunday, the Keohanes hired a taxi for the 10-mile (16-km) trip to the nearest Catholic church in the village of Mullion.

The family were popular in the village, particularly when Keohane entertained locals with enthralling stories from the Antarctic. It was something he could never have done in post-independence west Cork. Keohane was a regular speaker at the packed Village Hall and he spiced up his stories by showing his skis and sleeping bag from the expedition. 'Small boys in Coverack were fascinated with his Polar gear,' a local historian remembered.[17]

The busy seaways and rugged Cornish coastline ensured that Keohane was kept busy co-ordinating rescues. He was called into action twice in thirty minutes one night in March 1932 when two ships ran into trouble during storms battering Coverack Bay. After being woken in the early hours, Keohane feared that one ship, a Belgian trawler, was in danger of running aground. He rushed outside in the darkness and lit a bundle of rags to warn the vessel and was astonished when the warning was totally ignored. Keohane fired maroons to summon the lifeboat whose crew soon discovered that the trawlermen had abandoned ship and the vessel was drifting helplessly.

Almost immediately, Keohane was called into action again when distress rockets were fired to signal that another vessel, the *Ocklinge*, had run aground elsewhere along the coast. Onlookers witnessed the drama from the shore and one Coverack resident, a retired master mariner, applauded Keohane's efficient work as being of a 'most praiseworthy character.' He told Keohane: 'To fire two rockets over two ships in the short space of time that occupied was, I think, the smartest bit of rocket work I have ever known.'

Keohane stayed at Coverack for three years before moving along the Cornish coast to Looe, another old fishing port, in late 1932. He moved to the Isle of Man in 1934, where he was appointed District Officer of the Ramsey Coastguard and was later promoted to the rank of Divisional Inspector. He remained as Divisional Officer on the Isle of Man when war broke out in September 1939 and only retired from the post in 1941. Although now sixty-two years old, Keohane was anxious to serve again and signed up to be an instructor at *Valkyrie*, the radar and telegraphy training school at Douglas on the island.

Valkyrie was the top-secret shore establishment based in the Douglas Head Hotel and in a few seafront boarding houses, which trained more than 30,000 men and women to operate wireless telegraphy and radar. Among those at *Valkyrie* at the same time was Jon Pertwee, a naval intelligence officer who became famous as television's *Doctor Who* in the 1970s.

The Isle of Man, which was situated away from the major areas of military value, was a relatively peaceful haven during the war and a great deal safer than the heavily bombed

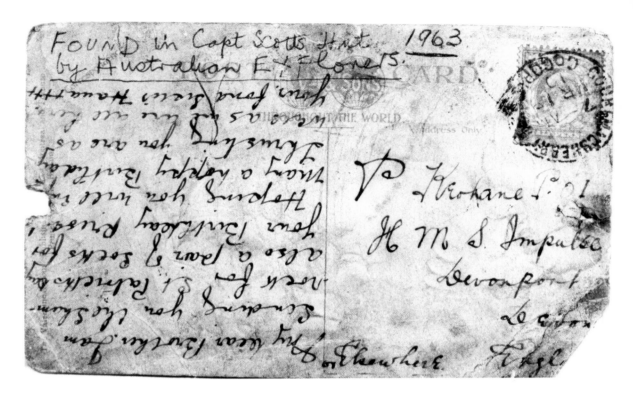

naval port of Plymouth where Keohane's daughter, Nova Keohane, lived with her husband, Patrick Madigan from Limerick. Keohane was evidently concerned about his daughter's safety as the bombing raids intensified, eventually resulting in the loss of more than 1,000 civilians in 59 separate bombing missions to hit the city. In response, Nova Keohane joined her parents on the Isle of Man and two of her children – Patrick and Vincent – were born there.

Keohane and his enlarged family remained on the Isle of Man until the war came to an end in 1945, when he finally retired. He was sixty-six years old and had been associated with the sea, wearing one uniform or another, for precisely fifty years.

The Keohanes moved back to Plymouth in 1945, the spot where Keohane's naval career had begun half a century earlier. He was comfortable in the city, one of the great ports of the world with a rich seafaring past. Apart from being the seat of British naval power, Plymouth had also for centuries been a centre of exploration and discovery. Francis Drake, the first Englishman to circumnavigate the globe, sailed from Plymouth in 1577, the Pilgrim Fathers took the *Mayflower* to colonise America in 1620 from the same quay and the epic voyages of James Cook in the eighteenth century and Charles Darwin in the nineteenth both began on the dockside at Plymouth.

Keohane had his own links with history after moving to Plymouth in 1945. Captain Scott was born at Outlands, a country house at Stoke Damerel, then a suburb of Plymouth and close to the Devonport Dockyards. Although the original building was destroyed in the war, Scott's birthplace was less than a mile from Keohane's new home in Birchfield Avenue, Plymouth.

The Harp that once in Tara's Halls
The Soul of Music Shed,
Now hangs as mute on Tara's Walls
As if that Soul were Fled.

Above and facing page: A postcard with a tale to tell. The postcard was written in March 1910 by Hannah Keohane, the younger sister of Patsy Keohane. The card, depicting shamrock and an Irish harp, was sent to celebrate St Patrick's Day.

It was posted in Courtmacsherry and addressed to Petty Officer Keohane at Devonport Docks in England where he was serving on HMS *Repulse* prior to joining Captain Scott's expedition to the Antarctic. Hannah appears to have misunderstood the ship's name and sent the card to HMS *Impulse*. She was also unsure of Keohane's exact where-abouts and scribbled an afterthought to the address: 'Or Elsewhere' (bottom centre).

Keohane left *Repulse* in May 1910 to join Scott's *Terra Nova* and navy bureaucrats forwarded the postcard to the expedition's base at Cape Evans in the Antarctic. But the card arrived only after Keohane's departure from Cape Evans in 1913. Some kind soul thoughtfully pinned the card to the wall of the hut where it remained untouched for fifty years. The postcard was rediscovered in 1963 by a team of Australian scientists who 'redirected' it back to the sender, Hannah Keohane in Courtmacsherry (top left). Sadly, Keohane had died in 1950, years before the card was returned, and Hannah had died in 1947. The wording of the postcard reads: 'My dear Brother. I am sending you the shamrock for St Patrick's Day, also a pair of socks for your birthday present. Hoping you will enjoy many a happy birthday. Trusting you are as well as we are all here. Yours, fond sister Hannah'. CLONAKILTY MUSEUM

Keohane made a nostalgic return to the family home on the Seven Heads Peninsula in 1948, though it was apparent that the wounds of Ireland's War of Independence had not fully healed in west Cork. Keohane's long association with the navy and coastguard authorities was still unpopular in some quarters and he discovered that it was not possible to celebrate the local man who had marched to 85° S with Scott. Some still regarded Keohane as 'very blue', a pointed reference to his links with the British.[18]

At around the same time, Keohane's first-hand account of the expedition was sought by the makers of a new film, *Scott of the Antarctic*. Keohane was among the few remaining survivors of those who had climbed the Beardmore Glacier and stood on the Polar Plateau with Scott. Among those also consulted by the film-makers were Lt Evans, Cherry-Garrard and Wright. Keohane was among five survivors of the *Terra Nova* who went to Ealing Studios to watch the film being made and he met Larry Burns, the Belfast-born actor playing Keohane on the big screen. In December 1948 he travelled to London for the premiere of the film, which has since become a classic.

Recognition of a different type emerged almost half a century later in 1997 when a mountain in the Antarctic was named after him. Mount Keohane (77° 36' S 162° 59' E) rises to 4,100 ft (1,250 m) on the north side of the Taylor Valley in Victoria Land which runs into McMurdo Sound. It stands about 50 miles (80 km) from the old hut which Keohane helped to build at Cape Evans.

Although affected by illness in later life, Keohane lived peacefully at his home in Birchfield Avenue and outlasted many of his old comrades from the Antarctic. Keohane never lost his love of the sea and was occasionally seen sailing a small boat in the nearby waters. Patrick Keohane died on 31 August 1950, aged seventy-one, and was buried in Ford Park cemetery in Plymouth, about a mile from the sea. Cherry-Garrard, his sledging comrade from 85° S, wrote a suitably warm tribute to Keohane, saying he was 'a dependable Irishman who took things as they came without worrying overmuch'. He was, said Cherry, a 'useful and cheerful man in difficult times'. His easy-going nature and versatile qualities were 'doubly welcomed' in the testing final year of the expedition.

Cherry-Garrard summed up Patrick Keohane with the charming, down-to-earth judgement which recalled his comment to Scott in 1910 on wondering why he wanted to join the Antarctic expedition. 'He was a man who wanted to see what was on the other side of the hill – and he saw!'

ROBERT FORDE

1875–1959

Forde at the start of the Western Party expedition, November 1911.

ROBERT FORDE emerged from a remote settlement near Kilmurry in the ancient parish of Moviddy which lies amidst the grassy slopes of County Cork, about 15 miles (24 km) to the west of Cork city. Bandon is a dozen or so miles (20 km) to the south of Forde's birthplace and Béal na mBláth, the small village close to where Michael Collins was assassinated in 1922, is a brisk walk across the hills from the area where Forde was brought up.

Moviddy parish has long been fertile farming ground and George Forde, Robert's father, was a steward for local landlords. It was enough of a foothold to provide a decent living for the family and over the years George Forde and his wife, Charity Payne, produced three sons and two daughters. The three boys were William, Robert and Samuel and the two daughters, Sarah and Charity. Robert Forde, the fourth child, was born on 29 August 1875.

The Fordes were among the concentration of Protestant families in the area whose predecessors probably came over from England and Wales during the Munster Plantation, Ireland's first mass plantation. The process began around 1580 as punishment for the Desmond Rebellions and accelerated into the 1600s with settlers pouring into places such as Youghal, Kinsale and the city of Cork. Bandon, founded in 1604, was at times inhabited solely by Protestants. It is likely that Forde's ancestors came to Ireland by way of the 'Undertakers', wealthy colonists – including Sir Walter Raleigh, who held 40,000 acres of estates around Youghal – on condition that they brought across tenants from England and Wales to work the lands.

The early arrivals brought their own slice of history. With or without the 'e', Forde is one of the oldest topographical surnames still in existence. It is an ancient Anglo-Saxon name originating in the early Middle Ages and was usually given to a person living near a shallow river crossing or ford. In Ireland it may have been adapted from Fourhan or Foran (*Fuarthán* or *Fuarathán* which is sometimes translated as 'cold little ford').

The exact location of Robert Forde's birthplace is not known. His birth records list only the parish of Moviddy as the place of birth and it must be assumed that the family's home or hamlet has disappeared over the years. But it is probable that Robert Forde's family, though they did not know it, had illustrious relatives.

Among the Fordes' near neighbours in the Anglican community of Cork in the nineteenth century was the immediate family of the legendary American car maker, Henry Ford. It is probable that the two families, who shared the same name and faith and lived only a few miles apart, were related. Henry Ford's grandfather leased a farm at Lisselan near Ballinascarthy, about 15 miles (24 km) from the Forde family home and William Ford, Henry's father, went to school at nearby Kilmalooda. The family emigrated to America in 1847 to escape the Famine and Henry Ford, creator of the popular mass-produced motor car, was born near Detroit, Michigan, in 1863. Although the precise relationship may never be properly established, photographs of Robert Forde and Henry Ford in later life show a remarkable likeness between the two men, even though they were born twelve years and many thousands of miles apart.

Little is known about Robert Forde's early life in west Cork, except that he did not follow his father on to the land. In late 1891, only a few months after his sixteenth birthday, Forde made the short trip to Queenstown and joined the Royal Navy. Forde, who was usually known as Bob, formally entered the navy on 7 November 1891 as Boy 2nd Class and was to serve for almost twenty-nine years.

Forde, a thick-set youngster of 5 foot 8 inches with a mop of dark brown hair, was sent to *Impregnable*, the naval training ship at Devonport in Plymouth, then the greatest naval seaport in the world. Forde was the first of the three sturdy, resourceful men from Munster who were schooled in the art of seamanship on *Impregnable* and who subsequently made their reputations on expeditions to the Antarctic. Apart from Forde, the two other Antarctic stalwarts who learned the ropes on *Impregnable* were Tom Crean from Kerry and Patrick Keohane, also from west Cork.

Entering the world's biggest and most powerful navy clearly held no fears for Forde, who adapted better than most boys to the tough training regime which ensured that only the strongest and best-equipped survived the two years of intense instruction. The navy of the late Victorian era could pick and choose its recruits from the thousands of young lads who applied to join and only one in ten managed to complete the rigorous training course. A weak chest or swollen joints were as likely to mean rejection as much as failing to add up a row of figures or read a few lines from a training manual. Forde, in every sense, passed muster.

About 4,000 teenage boys a year were put through their paces in the training programme on board *Impregnable* and other ships. Apart from demonstrating physical capabilities, youngsters took lessons in basic subjects like reading, writing and arithmetic and were taught a range of other vital skills ranging from navigation and signalling to swimming and firing a rifle. Boys were able to make occasional visits home and their few personal possessions were kept in a small wooden 'ditty' box.

About 1,000 youngsters a year passed through the hands of hard-boiled instructors on *Impregnable*, which was moored in the busy estuary of the Tamar and Plym rivers that separates the counties of Devon and Cornwall. *Impregnable*, a three-masted wooden craft in an era of motorised vessels, was the last of the great Victorian sailing ships and a throwback to an earlier age. Built in 1860 under the original name *Howe*, *Impregnable* was effectively obsolete even before being launched and made only one journey before being adopted as a training ship. The ship looked strangely out of place alongside the steel grey warships jostling for space in the narrow waterways around Devonport Dockyard but for many decades was responsible for instructing countless thousands of young sailors.

Forde moved easily through the training, first transferring across the Tamar to the sister ship, *Lion*, and later to *Vivid*, the shore barracks at Devonport where he celebrated his

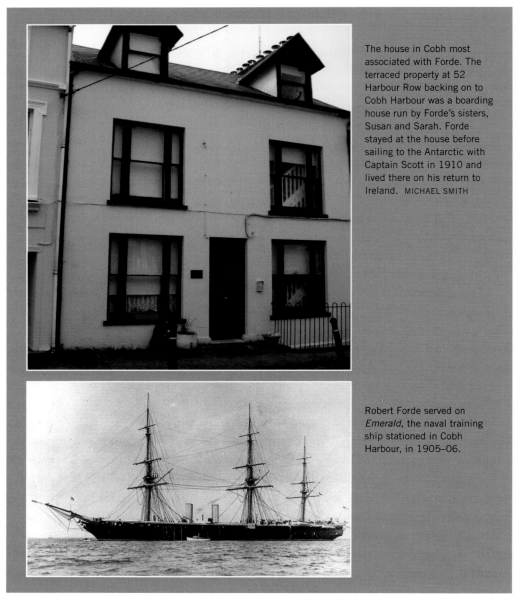

The house in Cobh most associated with Forde. The terraced property at 52 Harbour Row backing on to Cobh Harbour was a boarding house run by Forde's sisters, Susan and Sarah. Forde stayed at the house before sailing to the Antarctic with Captain Scott in 1910 and lived there on his return to Ireland. MICHAEL SMITH

Robert Forde served on *Emerald*, the naval training ship stationed in Cobh Harbour, in 1905–06.

eighteenth birthday by earning the rating of Ordinary Seaman. By 1894 Forde was promoted to Able-bodied Seaman and for the next few years served on a variety of ships and training vessels, including time at the *Cambridge* gunnery school where he learned how to load and fire torpedoes. In February 1902 he was appointed Petty Officer Second Class and in November 1904, at the age of twenty-nine and a strongly built 5 foot 9 inches tall, Forde was promoted to Petty Officer First Class. Other appointments followed, including nearly four years with the cruiser *Amphion* in the Pacific station. It was while serving on *Amphion* that Forde first served alongside Patrick Keohane, another Corkman from the Seven Heads Peninsula who was destined to join him on Scott's South Pole expedition in 1910.

Forde was also stationed with Keohane on *Emerald*, an ageing warship which had seen better times and was seeing out her final days as a harbour training vessel at Queenstown. Originally named *Black Prince*, the cruiser was built in 1861 and for a brief period was ranked among the world's most powerful warships. However, advances in naval technology soon left *Black Prince* out of date and by the time of Forde's appointment, the vessel was living on borrowed time as *Emerald*, permanently moored in Monkstown Bay and with her own pier to the shore at Ringaskiddy. A little later, Forde served on the cruiser *Talbot*, part of the Channel Fleet, where he rubbed shoulders with three men – Frank Browning, Harry Dickason and Lieutenant Teddy Evans – alongside whom he would also serve in the Antarctic.

It is not known how Forde came to volunteer for Scott's expedition, though it is probable the connection was Lt Evans from *Talbot*. Evans was a key figure in the expedition who had once nurtured his own ambitions to reach the South Pole. Evans, a determined go-getter who saw exploration of the Antarctic as a means of advancing his naval career, had developed the taste for adventure on two earlier journeys to the south. In 1903 and 1904 he served on *Morning* which had been sent to relieve *Discovery*, Scott's ship that was trapped in the ice of McMurdo Sound. Scott, too, had been planning to go back to the Antarctic and reach the South Pole ever since returning from the *Discovery* expedition in 1904. Scott was even more determined after Shackleton, his great rival, marched to within 97 geographic miles (111½ statute miles or 179 km) of the Pole in 1909.

Evans, a boisterous 29-year-old character who might have been plucked from the pages of *Boy's Own* comic, initially tried to drum up support for his own expedition. But he reckoned without the influence and status of Scott, whose *Discovery* expedition provided the popular and political support Evans could never match. Evans finally agreed to sail as second-in-command on Scott's British Antarctic Expedition.

Much of the work in selecting men and fitting out the ship fell to the eager Evans, who turned to the dependable and experienced seamen he knew from earlier postings. Among the men he selected was Forde, the burly, reliable 34-year-old Petty Officer from west Cork, who was then serving on *Ramillies*, a 14,000-ton battleship in the Channel Fleet patrolling UK territorial waters. He was, said Evans, a 'fine fellow'.

Forde officially enlisted on the British Antarctic Expedition on 16 April 1910 and travelled to London soon after to catch his first sight of *Terra Nova*, the whaling vessel which was to carry the party to Antarctica. The ship, a grubby remnant of the Arctic whaling fleet, gave off a foul smell, appeared worryingly small and was considered by some to be dangerously overcrowded for the long and hazardous voyage through the Antarctic pack ice. *Terra Nova* left London docks on 1 June 1910, heavily overladen with stores and equipment. Lt Evans would later paint over the ship's Plimsoll line (the marker showing

Left: Forde (back row, centre) with some of *Terra Nova*'s crew en route to the Antarctic. He stands alongside Petty Officer Edgar 'Taff' Evans (with pipe), who died with Scott on the return march from the South Pole in 1912.

Facing page (top): Officers and crew of *Terra Nova* in Lyttelton, New Zealand, October 1910, shortly before departing for the Antarctic. Petty Officer Robert Forde stands in the front row (far right). Others in the picture include Scott (front row, centre) and Lt Teddy Evans who recruited Forde to the expedition (seventh from left, partly obscured by pole).

Facing page (bottom): Forde's versatility with his hands was important in the Antarctic. After *Terra Nova*'s arrival at Cape Evans, Forde (left) was a key figure in building the expedition's base camp hut, which stands to this day.

the legal limit for the loading of a ship), to avoid the inquisitive gaze of the harbour authorities who might condemn the vessel as unseaworthy. After brief stops at Madeira and the South African port of Simonstown, the ship reached Melbourne on 12 October 1910, where a surprise was waiting for Scott. On arrival he found a telegram from the Norwegian, Roald Amundsen, announcing that he was preparing to race Scott to the South Pole.

Terra Nova pulled into the New Zealand port of Lyttelton a little later to pick up the nineteen Manchurian and Siberian ponies and thirty-four dogs that were central to Scott's transport plans and to collect any last-minute supplies before embarking on the tricky 2,500-mile (4,000-km) journey through the ice to the Antarctic mainland. Nothing was more important than the prefabricated wooden hut which Scott was taking south to provide shelter for the men during the planned two-year stay in the south and Forde's versatility and adaptability was quickly apparent.

Forde was an obliging and capable man who could turn his hands to a multitude of tasks. On enlistment to the navy, he described himself as a painter and on the quayside of Lyttelton Harbour he soon demonstrated his skills as a carpenter. Under the watchful supervision of Frank Davies, the ship's carpenter, the part-assembled hut was laid out on the quay. Forde, joined by Keohane and Petty Officer George Abbott, marked the beams and joists and cut the tongue and groove boards to measure in readiness for a quick assembly on reaching Antarctica.

Terra Nova crossed the Antarctic Circle and on 4 January 1911 reached McMurdo Sound, the inlet in Ross Island, where the expedition's base was established about 15 miles (24 km) from where Scott had moored *Discovery* in 1902. The site, beneath the slopes of the smouldering volcano, Mount Erebus, is a headland originally called The Skuary in deference to the skua birds found the area and subsequently renamed Cape Evans after Lt Evans.

Forde was called to carpentry work immediately on landing and worked flat out with Davies, Keohane and Abbott assembling the hut, while everyone else unloaded the supplies and animals from the ship. The hut-building team worked longer hours than anyone, starting at six o'clock in the morning and finishing around midnight before collapsing exhausted into their tent. In a flurry of non-stop work, Forde and his companions finished the hut in just twelve days.

The hut, which measures 50 ft (15 m) in length and stands 25 ft (7.5 m) high, accommodated a shore party of twenty-five men and adjoining stables for the ponies. Insulation against the brutal Antarctic climate was provided by thick layers of dried, shredded seaweed sewn into jute quilting and strips of Ruberoid, the waterproof covering. Windows were double-glazed and the floor consisted of wooden boards, a further quilt of seaweed, rolls of felt and olive-green linoleum.

The hastily erected building has survived a century of battering by the world's most hostile climate and still stands to this day as the most enduring and recognisable symbol of the Heroic Age of Antarctic Exploration. Lt Evans said that the results were 'little short of marvellous' and one of the expedition's scientists noted: 'We thought we should be warm and we were.' Scott declared that it was misleading to call the new building a hut and added: 'Our residence is really a house of considerable size, in every respect the finest that has been erected in the polar regions.'

The next priority was to lay down a line of food and equipment depots on the Ice Barrier for the first stage of the journey to the Pole, which was scheduled to begin the following spring. With the approach of autumn and 24-hour-a-day darkness, a thirteen-man team was hurriedly pulled together for the 350-mile (560 km) round trip on to the Barrier before the weather closed in. Forde, who had already proved a strong and versatile figure, was an automatic choice for the trip. It should have been a routine affair but in the event the depot-laying journey was a sorry episode which was partly responsible for the expedition's tragic end.

The journey was broken into two parts, the first stage to establish two depots fairly close to Cape Evans – at Safety Camp on the edge of the Barrier and Corner Camp about 50 miles (80 km) from Cape Evans – and the second stage to build a substantial cache of supplies some 160 miles (250 km) further south. However, the journey began with the men already tired after the heavy work of unloading the ship and establishing base camp and it was quickly apparent that the ponies, which were crucial to Scott's plans, were painfully inadequate.

Taking fourteen weeks' food and fuel, eight ponies and twenty-six dogs, the depot-laying party marched south in late January 1911, with Forde leading an animal called Blücher who had barely survived the sea journey south. However, the party's inexperience of travelling over the ice was soon apparent and Dr Edward Atkinson, one of only two doctors on the expedition, had to be left behind after developing a severely blistered heel.

The ponies, too, were suffering in the low temperatures and often sank up to their bellies in the soft snow. One animal went lame soon after starting and many looked pitifully weak and thin even before the real labour of the journey had started. The bitter cold sapped their strength, the heavy work of pulling sledges made them sweat profusely and the beasts laboured badly, slowing the march to a snail's pace. One member of the party wrote that 'all the care in the world could do little for the poor ponies'.

No one was more sceptical about the ponies than Captain Lawrence 'Titus' Oates, the Inniskilling Cavalry Officer whose expertise with horses had earned him a place on the expedition. Inexplicably, Scott did not send Oates to the Far East to buy the ponies, even though the animals were crucial to the expedition's chances of reaching the Pole. Oates was appalled when he first set eyes on the animals in the days before *Terra Nova* sailed south. He dismissed them as 'a load of old crocks' and a bunch of 'wretched old cripples', but it was too late to buy replacements.

After establishing Safety Camp and Corner Camp, the party turned south on to the Barrier, the vast flat sheet of ice which stretches for hundreds of miles to the south and leads to the Transantarctic Mountains and the Polar Plateau. Temperatures dropped sharply and the winds picked up as they penetrated the Barrier. The ponies, each dragging 600 lb (270 kg) loads, struggled badly. 'It is pathetic to see the ponies floundering,' Scott wrote. To ease their woes, Scott decided to travel at night when temperatures were even lower and the ground harder, but the faltering pace of the march was dictated by the worsening condition of the poor animals. A two-day blizzard inflicted more distress on the ponies, particularly Blücher.

The unfortunate Blücher was an emaciated wreck after only a short time on the march and soon unable to pull a full load. Some wag nicknamed the beast 'Misery' and Forde cut the sledge load to 400 lb (180 kg) in the hope it would help. But even that was beyond the pathetic animal and the weight was soon cut to only 200 lb (90 kg). Finally, Forde had to put on the harness and help Blücher drag the sledge. He found it impossible to keep up with the rest of the party and drifted off the pace to the rear of the caravan. He was soon joined by Keohane with Jimmy Pigg and Lt Evans with Blossom, who were also struggling to cope. By 12 February, only two weeks after leaving Cape Evans, Blücher had virtually given up and the other two were on the brink as the party camped at Bluff Depot, about 100 miles (160 km) from Cape Evans.

Evans said that Forde and Keohane showed 'extraordinary aptitude' in coaxing the wretched beasts forward but it was a fruitless exercise. 'It would have been cruel to continue with them, they were so wasted, and even their eyes were dull and lustreless,' Evans recalled.

Scott, who was particularly anxious to protect the ponies for the Polar march, faced a tough decision as the party camped at Bluff Depot. Oates, the acknowledged expert, urged him to push the weaker animals as hard as possible to the south before shooting them and storing the meat to feed the overland parties. But Scott rejected the idea and instead ordered Evans, Keohane and Forde to escort the three weakest ponies back to the safety of Cape Evans. A contemptuous Oates had a side bet with Tryggve Gran that Blücher would be dead within a week and that Jimmy Pigg would not last much longer.

Forde, Keohane and Evans began the return journey on 13 February and were beset by another bout of foul weather only a few miles after leaving Scott. It was the last straw for Blücher who simply lay down in the snow and refused to budge. Forde tried to coax the weakened animal back on to his feet, but his legs could not support even his own weight.

Even a hard nut like Forde was upset by Blücher's inevitable fate and found it hard to end the animal's misery. Instead Keohane volunteered to deliver the *coup de grâce*, taking his knife and slitting the animal's throat. Evans said it was 'a rotten day' and noted that there was 'hardly any blood' afterwards. The loss of Blücher did nothing to improve their position, with approximately 90 miles (145 km) of the journey still ahead and both Jimmy Pigg and Blossom unlikely to survive the trek. Forde assumed responsibility for Blossom, bodily lifting and pulling the animal in the faint hopes of avoiding another slaughter. 'I felt I ought to kill this animal but I knew how angry and disappointed Scott would be at the loss,' Evans wrote. Blossom, assisted by the careful attention of Forde, somehow staggered along in distress for another 30 miles (48 km). To Evans he looked like a 'spectre against the white background of snow'. Shortly after, Blossom collapsed and died. A cairn of snow was built over the corpse and Forde, Keohane and Evans resumed the march north with the last remaining pony, the run-down Jimmy Pigg.

The party rested at Safety Camp for a couple of days and were soon joined by a few other stragglers from the unhappy depot-laying party, where the news was equally grim. Scott learned that Amundsen had established his base a few hundred miles along the coast in the Bay of Whales and had assembled more than 100 trained and expertly driven dogs to speed the Norwegian assault on the Pole. What Scott did not know was that Amundsen's faster-moving dog teams had also deposited tons of supplies further south on the Barrier and the Norwegian's base camp was also a little closer to the Pole.

Jimmy Pigg, who at one stage appeared to be living on borrowed time, somehow survived and miraculously regained a little vigour with the aid of a few good feeds on the return march. By 22 February, Forde, Keohane and Evans were reunited with Scott and learned that another pony had died elsewhere on the march. Three more animals perished soon after, leaving Scott to assess the full scale of the shambolic depot-laying journey. Six of the eight ponies had died, the key supply depot had been laid 30 miles (48 km) further north than planned and it was evident that the start of the Polar journey would have to be delayed because of the fragility of the ponies. As a greeting, Jimmy Pigg bit the other surviving animal on the neck.

The entire depot-laying party was soon reassembled at Hut Point, the site of the old *Discovery* expedition hut, while they waited for the autumnal sea ice to freeze over before making the final journey of 15 miles (24 km) along the coast to Cape Evans with the two surviving ponies. But Scott was impatient and decided to head back to Cape Evans and leave six men, including Forde and Keohane, at Hut Point to wait for the sea ice to harden enough to take the weight of the animals.

The men left behind were forced to remain in the cramped quarters of Hut Point, which offered few home comforts, for a month. The only relief was a few short trips to drop more supplies on to the Barrier. On the last supply trip in mid-March, Forde was given a pointed reminder about the dangers of travelling late in the season when a blizzard hit the sledging party and temperatures suddenly plunged to -32 °F (-35 °C). It was their first experience of deep cold and one man wrote that it was cold enough to 'teach you how to look after your footgear, handle metal and not to waste time'. Next day the thermometer dropped further to -42.5 °F (-42 °C) and in late April, with the men still camped at Hut Point, the sun dipped below the horizon, not to be seen again for four months.

Forde, Keohane and their companions waited longer than anticipated at Hut Point, which was barely half the size of the main hut at Cape Evans and was rather spartan. Days turned to weeks and Scott was growing concerned at the delay. 'I cannot understand why the Hut Party doesn't return,' he wrote on 9 May. 'I wish it would return and shall not be free from anxiety until it does.' Four days later, the Hut Point party finally made it back across the ice with the two surviving ponies in darkness and nearly 50 °F of frost. It was 13 May, the sun had disappeared for winter, the thermometer had dipped below -20 °F (-29 °C) and the men had been gone for nearly four months. Hut Point's billowing blubber stove left the men with blackened faces, but Gran said all were in 'good shape', while Scott reported: 'Men and animals in good form'.

Despite the hazards, Forde adapted well to the challenge and showed that he was a good all-rounder, capable of dealing with all manner of tasks around the hut or on the march. He was strong in the sledging harness, able to turn his hands to most maintenance jobs and soon recognised as a very good cook in the most difficult circumstances. No job seemed beyond him and Forde's genial nature made him a popular figure with most of his companions.

Charles Wright, the physicist, also noticed that Forde kept a paternalistic eye on Lt Evans. In his diary, Wright observed: '[Forde] looks after Evans like a child.' However, Forde was feeling the cold and it is possible that he was more susceptible to the very low autumnal temperatures than some of his companions. In a telling entry to his diary, Wright reported that Forde was 'given to complaining about cold feet and hands'.

Winter passed slowly in preparation for the great march south in the spring. During the day the party worked on myriad tasks for the push south, with seamen like Forde embroiled in making sledges, sewing sleeping bags and weighing foodstuffs. 'No one is idle,' Scott wrote in his diary.

However, the defining moment of Forde's expedition to the Antarctic came in early September 1911, a couple of weeks after the sun fully returned and almost two months before the major southern journey to the Pole began. In September, with barely a few hours of daylight available, small sledging parties began to venture on to the ice, partly to get accustomed to travelling and partly to check on the state of the nearest supply depots after the winter onslaught. Temperatures hovered around the -30 °F mark (-34 °C) as the first parties ventured outside. One proposed excursion was to take a small group on a near 50-mile (80-km) trip to the depot at Corner Camp. The idea was to carry some fresh supplies and to 're-mark' the site for the men treading south in the coming weeks.

The ever-eager Lt Evans offered to lead the trip, assisted by Forde and Tryggve Gran, the Norwegian ski expert. Scott was unsure about the value of the trek and concerned that the dangerously low early spring temperatures posed a serious risk to the men.

When pressed for permission, he snapped: 'If you people want to suffer, for Heaven's sake, go!'[1] But he refused to allow Evans to risk any of the dogs or ponies.

Gran, a 22-year-old who had been skiing since childhood, also had concerns. He was worried about Forde's lack of experience with skis and knew the hazards of travelling in the early spring conditions. Forde, who had just celebrated his thirty-sixth birthday, had found little spare time to practise skiing during the dark months at Cape Evans and Gran sensed danger ahead. He warned: 'He may have a difficult time. These September journeys are reckoned to be the worst that polar explorers have to go through. We shall see.'[2]

Evans, Gran and Forde left the comparative cosiness of Cape Evans early on Saturday, 9 September 1911, dragging a sledge carrying almost 600 lb (270 kg) of food and equipment with each man pulling the equivalent of more than his own body weight. (Gran, for example, was among the largest of the twenty-five men at Cape Evans and weighed 186 lb or 84 kg.) Despite Scott's misgivings, the men were warmly toasted by their comrades at dinner the night before leaving.

The three men were immediately taken aback at the penetrating cold and heavy pulling needed to drag their sledge forward in the hazy twilight. Temperatures on the edge of the Barrier were at least 20 °F lower than at Cape Evans and the months of inactivity in the hut left them unprepared for the sudden hard labour of hauling the weighty sledge. Forde, showing early signs of vulnerability to the low temperatures, was the first victim of the raw cold when his nose became frostbitten. Evans had to apply warmth to Forde's nose while Gran cooked a much-needed hot meal.

The group trekked from 8 a.m. until 9 p.m., stopping only briefly for a quick lunch. At the end of the hard slog, they had covered 20 miles (32 km) and found that temperatures had plunged to -43 °F (-42 °C). Gran opened his diary with the revealing comment: 'It takes all my strength to grip this pencil.' Evans recalled: 'We got little or no sleep that night. The cold seemed to grip us particularly about the feet and loins'.[3]

Despite the intense cold and heavy going, the men arrived at Safety Camp, where they dug out the depot and marked it with a fresh black flag before continuing south towards Corner Camp. By the end of another exhausting day, the trio had travelled about 12 miles (18 km) but were already feeling the effects of the toil.

After a hot meal, the men climbed into their sleeping bags and huddled together for warmth. The temperature nudged -60 °F (-51 °C) as the men shivered and fidgeted hoping to trap any little pockets of warmth inside their bags. Moisture from their bodies and breath formed ice in the sleeping bags, though they managed to snatch some welcome sleep. 'Nature nursed us somehow into a sort of mild unconsciousness,' Evans wrote.

Day three brought no let-up, with the hazy conditions making it difficult to find a course and the cold wind lashing their bodies. Gran reported 'extremely laborious' going and frostbitten fingertips. Evans somehow managed to find some comfort from a slight rise in temperatures and was positively cheered when the thermometer recovered a little to

Forde (centre) on 30 August 1911 building sledges with Tom Crean (left) and Taff Evans

show −30 °F (−34 °C). 'Warm enough after what we had experienced earlier,' he announced. It did not last. A blizzard descended on the tent soon after the men camped and any hopes of a warmer snap evaporated when the thermometer sank to a numbing −73.3 °F (−58 °C) or 105 °F of frost. No one slept that night.

The party struck south again in hazy conditions, straining their eyes in the hope of spotting the cairn marking the site of Corner Camp. Fortunately the sun broke through in mid-afternoon and the depot suddenly emerged from the gloom. On arrival, it was discovered that the marker flag had been ripped to shreds by the winter winds. In daytime temperatures well below −30 °F (−34 °C), Forde, Gran and Evans worked feverishly to dig out the old cache, repack the depot with new supplies and rebuild the cairn, which was topped off with a new marker flag. The piercing wind blew incessantly and chilled them to the bone. Gran said restocking the depot was a 'pretty hard job' in the bitter cold and Evans noted: 'It was the coldest day's work I ever remember doing'.[4]

Conditions in the open were close to intolerable and none of the party wanted to hang around for too long. Evans, eager to get back to safety, decided to make a rapid dash for Hut Point, about 35 miles (56 km) away, without camping. Marching through the night with a lighter sledge, the group steered by the stars and made only brief stops for a warming mug of tea or a quick bite to eat. 'The hot tea seemed to run through my veins,' Evans wrote. Overhead, the glittering bands of light from the aurora shimmered and wavered in a magnificent natural spectacle to herald their return. But Forde and Evans were struggling, despite the brisk pace of the return march. Forde's hands were particularly bad after several bouts of frostbite and the only slice of good fortune was the mercifully clear weather, which at least allowed Evans to plot a decent course.

The three men strode north at a steady rate and by mid-afternoon on 14 September they walked into the small wooden hut at Hut Point, shattered but grateful that the ordeal was finally over. Evans, Gran and Forde had managed to cover about 35 miles (56 km) in twenty-four hours, despite the intense cold and lacerating winds. It was the longest unbroken march yet made across the Barrier. 'It has been a considerable march in such cold without sleep for several nights,' Gran wrote in his diary. 'We must be quite content with our achievement'.[5]

All three showed signs of the strain, particularly Forde. As the strongest member of the team, it is likely that Forde did more work than anyone on the forced march back and was clearly feeling the effects. Gran reported: 'Forde, whom I must admire for his strength and energy, began to weaken, to feel the cold and show other signs of exhaustion.'[6]

A piping hot meal was prepared but Gran's sleeping bag was so iced up that he was unable to climb in to get a rest. Instead he proposed making the final 15-mile (24-km) sprint to Cape Evans. But in semi-darkness and with Forde and Evans still recovering, it would have been folly. Rest was more important. Forde rustled up another dish of hot pancakes and with the benefit of a full stomach Gran remarked that 'things began to look a lot better'. Forde and Evans slept for fourteen hours, not counting a brief interval halfway through the night when Gran woke the pair with a bowl of steaming hot porridge. Sheltered from the bitter winds and sub-zero temperatures, no one had any problem sleeping.

Forde, Gran and Evans awoke on the morning of 15 September and covered the final miles to Cape Evans in seven hours. It had taken almost seven days to make the round trip of nearly 100 miles (160 km) to Corner Camp. 'It is really quite strange to lie in a warm cubicle and to be able to drop off to sleep without waking the next instant from cold,' a relieved Gran wrote.

But Forde had paid a heavy price for the short journey on to the Barrier. The frostbite, which he mentioned on the march, was far more severe than either Gran or Evans realised. Large blisters had developed on the fingers and thumb of his right hand, making them appear like bloated sausages. The hand had turned black and the immediate concern was that he might lose two or three fingers. Gran observed that 'Forde's fingers are much more frostbitten than anyone realised'. Edward Atkinson, the expedition doctor, weighed up the risks of amputating part of Forde's hand in the restricted confines of the hut, but decided to wait to see whether the wounds responded to treatment. Atkinson, more than anyone at Cape Evans, knew about Forde's suffering.

During midwinter Atkinson had ventured outside in the dark and became lost within a few hundred yards of the hut. With winds blowing at 45 mph and temperatures down to -28 °F (-33 °C), Atkinson quickly became disorientated and wandered around aimlessly for five hours before being found by search parties. Like Forde, he suffered severe frostbite and developed sausage-like blisters on one hand. Fortunately, Atkinson escaped amputation and now hoped that Forde would too. Forde was lucky and, helped by Atkinson's careful nursing, did not lose any fingers to the surgeon's knife. But his hand never fully recovered from the effects of the severe frostbite suffered on the Barrier in September 1911 and he wore gloves for the rest of his life to hide his wounds.

Scott was furious about the injury and uncharitably blamed Forde for taking unnecessary risks, which overlooked the appalling conditions and over 100 °F of frost. But Scott was worried that Forde's injury would upset his carefully drawn plans for the sledging season. With Forde incapacitated, he faced having to make alternative arrangements. Even before the frostbite, Scott had decided not to take Forde on the South Pole journey and wanted the Irishman to travel with a party of geologists on a three-month trip to the Western Mountains. Forde, understandably, was upset at being excluded from the Polar journey but Scott believed that his muscle and resourcefulness would be important to the Western Party.

Scott's more immediate concern was delaying or postponing the geological trip because of Forde's hand. In his diary, Scott wrote: 'On [the Corner Camp] journey Forde got his hand badly frostbitten. I am annoyed at this, as it argues want of care; moreover, there is a good chance that the tip of one of his fingers will be lost and if this happens or if the hand is slow in recovery, Forde cannot take part in the Western Party. I have no one to replace him.'[7]

Forde, with his hand heavily bandaged, made only a limited recovery over the following weeks and Scott was left with little choice but to delay the start of the Western Party trek. But his plans were thrown into further disarray when Frank Debenham, one of the two scientists scheduled to make the journey, twisted his knee playing football on the ice and was also laid up. The only consolation, said Scott, was that Debenham's footballing injury gave Forde a little more time to recover. The omens were hardly encouraging and Griffith Taylor, the laconic geologist who was leading the party, wrote: 'We shall start west with Forde's right arm useless and Debenham's leg crocked!'.[8]

The original plan was for the four-man Western Party – Taylor, Debenham, Gran and Forde – to leave Cape Evans on 21 October, about ten days before the bulk of the party started south on the main journey to the Pole. But the injuries to Forde and Debenham delayed departure until 14 November, two weeks after Scott's team had embarked on the first stage of the march to the Pole. Forde's incapacity was a problem in a small party. With his hands still heavily bandaged more than two months after the frostbite attack, he was limited in the tasks he could carry out and his effectiveness, particularly around the camp, was restricted. As they prepared to leave Cape Evans, Gran pointed out that Forde 'still has two useless fingers'.

Another handicap was that Debenham had a very low opinion of Forde. Debenham, a scholarly 27-year-old geologist from Australia, was a man with strong opinions, who wielded a waspish pen. Forde was among his targets, though not his only victim. He found Gran a 'great disappointment' and a 'dangerous companion for sledging', dismissed the biologist Nelson as 'weird' and once admitted: 'I don't like being alone' with Lt Evans.

Debenham had reservations about Forde from the very start of the expedition. On first catching sight of Forde in New Zealand, Debenham said he was one of the 'most besotted-looking ruffians I had ever seen.' He went further after learning that Scott had selected Forde for the Western Party. In one gratuitous entry to his diary, Debenham wrote: 'Forde is the least gifted of the remarkable seamen we have with us here and tho' very big is perhaps the least strong.' However, Debenham did condescend to admit that Forde was very anxious to please and added: 'I have no doubt we shall get on quite well together.'[9]

The Western Party expedition, which left Cape Evans in mid-November, was scheduled to study the geology of the coast around Victoria Land as far north as Granite Harbour, a journey of about 130 miles (210 km) along the coast. It was a potentially dangerous trek and Scott urged great caution in his formal instructions to Taylor. He warned: 'You must remember that violent storms occasionally sweep up the coast and that changes of weather are quite sudden, even in summer.'

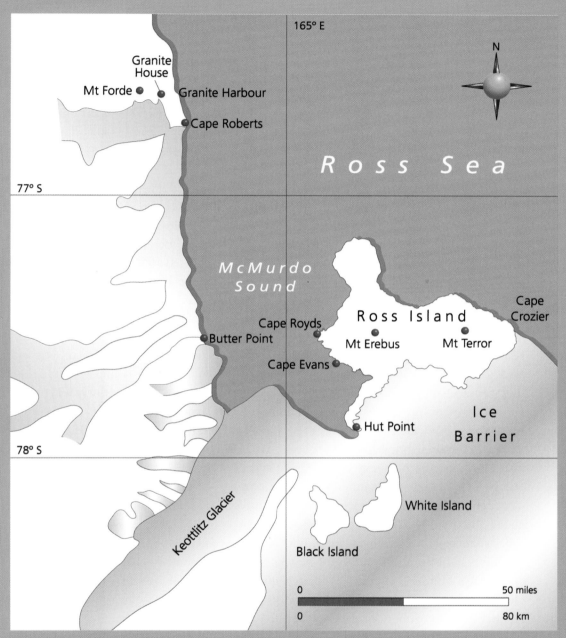

The area around McMurdo Sound and Granite Harbour where Forde explored in 1911.

Progress was very slow from the start and the men were forced to relay the cumbersome sledges, moving one ahead and going back for the second. Effectively this meant walking 3 miles (5 km) for every mile gained and at times the group counted themselves lucky to advance a mile in two hours of hard toil. The combined weight of close to 1,350 lb (600 kg) was back-breaking, particularly as Debenham, still suffering from his knee injury, was effectively a passenger limping alongside and unable to pull properly. Some days yielded only a few miles of ground, despite hours of exhausting pulling over loose snow and icy ridges. 'I've never had a heavier grind than this,' a disenchanted Gran reported. 'All are more or less exhausted.'

Gran painted a negative picture of the little group struggling over the ice. 'Our team makes an extraordinary procession, something like a family on a Sunday's promenade,' he wrote in diary. 'Deb limping along at the sledge side, Taylor lean and gaunt and Forde old and grave.' The men switched to travelling at night to make use of the harder ground and the speed picked up a little when the imaginative Forde helped arrange makeshift 'sails' on the sledges to take advantage of favourable winds. 'Forde was Bo'sun and made a good job of it,' Taylor said.

Progress was slow and each mile gained took an enormous struggle, although the site of Granite Harbour approaching did raise morale a little. By 30 November the party had reached its goal and Gran reported an ideal camping site and ample supplies of seals and birds to eat. A campsite was chosen and named Cape Geology, while the resourceful Forde immediately went to work on constructing a field kitchen from a cave in the granite rocks. He laid a sledge and seal skins across the top to form a roof and placed the blubber stove inside the hollow. Helped by Gran, a flue was added and moss was stuffed in the cracks to keep out the draught. While the stove smoked badly, it provided welcome snatches of heat for the group. A mucky blend of soot and oil soon built up, seeping on to the floor and Forde spread gravel around their feet to mop up the mess.

Gran paid tribute to Forde as 'master mason' of the modest little shelter, which stood about 3 ft (1 m) high before the roof was attached. The rough, makeshift sanctuary was called Granite House from a story in Jules Verne's popular book, *Mysterious Island*. Forde proudly told his companions that the new kitchen was 'as good as many an Irish shebeen.'[10]

Forde's humble creation has for a century withstood the ravages of the Antarctic climate and is now protected as a site of historic interest by the internationally recognised Antarctic Treaty. American geologists visited Granite House in November 1959, about eight months after the death of Forde. They found a sledge and ice axe belonging to the Western Party and several books, which were in perfect condition and subsequently returned to the owners and survivors of the expedition, Taylor and Debenham. A New Zealand party inspected the site in 1990 and reported that the sledge had disintegrated and some of the walls had partially collapsed. Inside were scraps of discarded food tins, a sealskin and assorted lengths of cord. But the moss which Forde had painstakingly stuffed

Granite House, the makeshift field kitchen which Forde built at Granite Harbour during the Western Party expedition in 1911. The structure is still standing after almost 100 years and is protected by the Antarctic Treaty as a site of historical interest.

into the cracks eighty years earlier was still visible and doing its job of keeping out the cold draughts.

Forde turned his hand to creature comforts, rigging up a regular source of drinking water by channelling melting snow into a small reservoir, which came close to providing the men with the luxury of running water. He also demonstrated the art of hunting and butchering seals and showed that he was, without doubt, the best cook among the four. Forde, Taylor announced, was our 'most expert' chef.

The most bizarre incident of the journey occurred on 15 December when Gran woke to report an astonishing dream about Amundsen. In his dream, Gran was reading a telegram which revealed: 'Amundsen reached Pole, 15–20 December'. Amundsen and four companions, in fact, reached the South Pole on 14 December 1911, a month before Scott's party arrived.

Christmas was celebrated in style, with a sumptuous meal of seal steak and fried bird's eggs, followed by plum pudding and caramel. The four men from different countries – Forde from Ireland, Australian Debenham, the Norwegian Gran and Taylor from England – rigged up sledging flags celebrating their own national identities. Forde, who did not have his own sledging pennant, showed another bit of inventiveness in order to run up an Irish flag from a scrap of cloth. He cut out a white harp from a linen specimen bag and sewed it on to a fragment of green burberry cloth, which Taylor admitted was both 'patriotic and striking'.

Christmas Day 1911 on Western Party journey to Granite Harbour. The flags depict the international flavour of the party, with Norwegian Tryggve Gran (back, right), the Australian geologist Frank Debenham (front, left) and Griffith Taylor, the expedition leader, who lived in Australia. Forde (back, left) stands in front of his flag, which bears the Irish harp. It was made from a linen specimen bag and sewn onto a piece of green burberry. Forde's hand shows the effects of the severe frostbite which forced him to return home early from the Antarctic.

The party was due to be relieved in the middle of January by the return of *Terra Nova*, which had overwintered in New Zealand. The first glimpse of the ship was seen on the morning of 11 January 1912, but the build-up of ice near the shore prevented *Terra Nova* getting close enough to lift the men off the headland. By 1 February *Terra Nova* had disappeared from sight and Taylor faced a difficult choice. The party could try to make its way along the coast towards Cape Evans but the risk was that the sea ice would not be solid enough to cross until at least the end of March, another nine weeks. Travel overland was also very difficult and the other grim possibility, which Scott had suggested if *Terra Nova* failed to reach the men, was to build a stone shelter and sit out the winter waiting for relief at least a year later.

A few days later Taylor decided to make a run for it, first along the coast and then across a succession of glaciers which drain into the sea in that region. Stashing most of

All-rounder Forde. Apart from building the stone shelter, modifying their equipment and adding his great strength in the sledging harness, Forde was the party's best cook.

their surplus equipment and geological specimens, the group set off on 5 February for the testing journey of around 100 miles (160 km) to Cape Evans. Although the sledge was light, the men were stiff and out of training after two months of gentle geological work around Granite Harbour and in Gran's words, they found it 'enormously heavy going' clambering over the glaciers.

The dangers were ever present and although Forde crashed down a crevasse, the hazards of travelling over the unstable sea ice were far worse. After careful consideration, Taylor preferred to risk the glaciers and crevasses.

By 15 February the men had come to the Blue Glacier, an area riddled with crevasses, about two-thirds of the way to Cape Evans. Fortunately, most were narrow and shallow fissures which meant they were only waist-deep. Halfway across the glacier, Gran suddenly spotted the ship. 'For a moment, we just stood and stared,' said Taylor. Fearing that the ship might not spot them, the men hurried down the glacier as fast as possible. At the bottom they found a 30 ft (10 m) drop and a pool of icily cold water. While making the descent, the sledge began to slip and Forde was pulled over by his harness and crashed on top of Gran. The sledge followed, falling on top of both men. 'It nearly broke in the middle,' Taylor reported. The rushed descent worked and within half an hour the four men, though slightly bruised and battered, were on board *Terra Nova*. They had been away for exactly three months.

Autumn was closing in and *Terra Nova*'s captain, Harry Pennell, knew the ship risked getting trapped by the ice in McMurdo Sound. Speed was vital, first to offload fresh supplies for those staying at Cape Evans for another year and then to pick up the nine men going home after just one season in the Antarctic. Among the nine members of the shore party going home were Taylor and the gravely ill Lt Evans, who had barely survived a 1,500-mile (2,400-km) trek on the main Polar journey.

Forde, too, was forced to go home. Atkinson, who had just returned from a 1,000-mile (1,600-km) round trip supporting Scott's Polar party, examined Forde's injured hand and made the decision that another year in the south would be too dangerous. Forde's right hand was still in bandages from the frostbite of September and Atkinson was left with little choice.

Terra Nova, with Forde on board, steamed out of McMurdo Sound on 7 March 1912, still unaware of the tragedy of Scott's party slowly unfolding a few hundred miles away on the Barrier. The ship reached the New Zealand port of Akaroa on 1 April before proceeding to Lyttelton a few days later where the crew discovered for the first time that Amundsen had beaten Scott to the South Pole. Another ten months passed before news reached the outside world that Scott's party of five had died on the return from the Pole. The party perished just 11 miles (17km) from One Ton Depot, the supply cache which Scott had originally planned to build 30 miles (48 km) further south on the ill-fated depot-laying journey year earlier.

Forde, it appears, reported back for duty with the navy in 1912 but was given a long time off to recuperate from his Antarctic wounds. In June 1913 he was given the honorary position of 'shipkeeper' to *Terra Nova* when the expedition made a poignant return to the Welsh port of Cardiff, where he was photographed on deck with old Antarctic comrades, Crean, Keohane and Lt Evans. Forde remained with *Terra Nova* for two months while the expedition was formally wound up and the old ship was made ready to resume more traditional duties in the seal hunting grounds around Newfoundland.

Forde did not return to full naval duties until October 1913, two years after the spring journey with Lt Evans and Gran which forced him to leave the Antarctic. He was posted to the shore station at Devonport Dockyards where, for the next few months, he was able to observe the relentless countdown to the First World War. Forde served on *Indus*, the Devonport guardship, from February to August and on 2 August 1914, just two days before Britain formally declared war on Germany, he was posted to the cruiser *Endymion*, serving in the northern patrol.

The Western Party on board *Terra Nova* in February 1912 at the end of the three-month expedition to Granite Harbour (l–r): Taylor, Debenham, Gran and Forde.

Forde had a busy war, serving on six different ships or shore stations. The longest posting was to *Hilary*, one of the many merchant vessels requisitioned and armed by the navy in 1914 to supplement the mainstream fleet of warships. Forde was appointed to *Hilary*'s maiden voyage as an armed merchant ship in December 1914 and served until April 1916 in the 10th Cruiser Squadron, which mounted the blockade of the North Sea waters and patrolled the approaches to Europe from the north. A year after Forde's tour of duty ended, *Hilary* was sunk by a German U-boat off the Shetland Islands.

The blockade, like the cordon imposed during the Napoleonic Wars a century before, was a highly effective weapon and helped sway the war at sea in favour of the British navy. The sheer size and overwhelming firepower of the powerful British Grand Fleet prevented the outgunned Germans from launching many large-scale attacks by sea and apart from isolated incidents, most of the German fleet remained in port for much of the conflict. As a result, only one major naval engagement took place during the entire war, the Battle of Jutland in May 1916. Among those killed at the Jutland, the largest sea battle in naval history, was Harry Pennell, captain of *Terra Nova* on the voyage to Antarctica.

In December 1916, Forde joined the newly built *Resolution*, a 29,000-ton battleship on her first voyage of active service. Forde would spend almost all his remaining years with the navy on board *Resolution*, a 'Revenge' class destroyer which also formed part of the Grand Fleet.

Forde survived the war and, after almost twenty-nine years of service, retired from the navy on 17 June 1920. He returned to Queenstown – renamed Cobh in 1922 – and lived quietly, buttressed by his naval pension and a small additional sum for the disability suffered while on duty in the Antarctic. Forde, who was a matter of weeks from his forty-fifth birthday when he left the navy, never worked again. He spent the remaining thirty-nine years of his life at 52 Harbour Row, Cobh, a neat terraced house a stone's throw from the bustling Cobh Harbour where his older sisters, Charity (known as Susan) and Sarah, ran a modest boarding house for seafarers and travellers. Forde, the man who could turn his hand to most tasks, was always available to help his sisters with odd jobs around the house, despite the restriction of his injured hand. Even in later life Forde was rarely seen in public without gloves. He never married.

The return to Cobh was, however, fraught with risk for Forde. Like most Irishmen who had served in the war, he was vulnerable to charges of being pro-British at a time when opinions were polarised by the rush to independence. Forde's Anglican background gave even further reason to keep his head down, particularly with the increased attacks against the Protestant community which resulted in thousands of Protestants fleeing Cork around this time. The 1926 census shows that in Cobh alone, 55 per cent of Protestants left the town in the fifteen years between 1911 and 1926, although Forde elected to remain behind.

He chose to keep a discreet silence and rarely spoke about his twenty-nine years' service with the Royal Navy. Even his exploits in the Antarctic were highly sensitive because the expedition was a navy-led enterprise and it was not until many years after returning home that Forde felt comfortable enough to talk openly. Nevertheless, Bob Forde became a familiar figure in the quayside pubs around Cobh Harbour. He took to drinking heavily in later years and when his sisters died in the 1940s, Forde lived alone in the small house in Harbour Row. He went to Cork in 1948 to watch *Scott of the Antarctic*, Charles Frend's feature film on the expedition. Sitting alongside Forde in the cinema was Nell Crean, the widow of Tom Crean, his old companion from *Terra Nova* who had died ten years earlier.

Robert Forde photographed in Cobh in 1950 at the age of seventy-five.

Henry Ford, the legendary American car-maker, who was probably related to Robert Forde. Both families came from the same area of County Cork and photographs show a remarkable likeness between the two men.

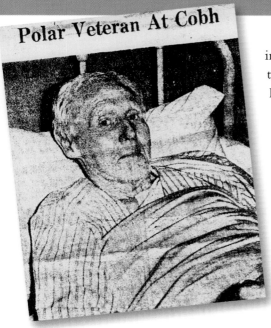

Polar Veteran At Cobh

Illness dogged Forde's later years and he spent periods in and out of hospital. He lived long enough to witness the first crossing of the Antarctic continent by Dr Vivian Fuchs in the mid-1950s, though the old warrior sniffed contemptuously at the expedition's use of modern motor tractors to cross the frozen wastes. 'We had to do it on foot,' the unimpressed 82-year-old said from his hospital bed. He died on 13 March 1959 at the age of eighty-three. He was the last survivor of the three outstanding characters from Munster – Crean, Keohane and Forde – who bunked together and made history in the Antarctic half a century before.

The last known photograph of Robert Forde, aged eighty-two, during a spell in hospital.

ERECTED BY
ROBERT FORDE
(WITH CAPT. SCOTT B.A. Ex. 1910/13)
SUSAN E. FORDE
DIED 19 TH JAN. 1942
SARAH FORDE
DIED 9 TH MARCH 1948
THE ABOVE
ROBERT FORDE
DIED 13 TH MARCH 1959.

Robert Forde's grave at the Old Church Cemetery, Cobh.
The wording on the headstone was composed by Forde himself.
MICHAEL SMITH

Forde is buried in the Old Clonmel (Old Church) Cemetery in Cobh, the last resting place of many seafarers from the area. He lies alongside his two sisters, Sarah and Susan. The wording on the headstone, which he chose for himself, proudly records Forde's service with Scott's British Antarctic Expedition, something he might never have been able to disclose in earlier decades. Jack Doyle, the celebrated boxer and showman from Cobh, lies close by and Old Clonmel Cemetery is also the last resting place for many of the unfortunate victims of the *Lusitania*, sunk by a German U-boat in 1915 while trying to reach Cobh.

Forde's role in the *Terra Nova* expedition was overlooked for many years, partly because of his reluctance to speak publicly about his year on the ice and partly because the focus of historians was largely on the leaders like Scott. It was not until after his death that Forde was formally recognised by the naming of Mount Forde (76° 53' S, 162° 05' E), a mountain overlooking Granite Harbour in Victoria Land.

Recognition of Forde's life took a little longer to appear in Ireland. But in 2009, on the fiftieth anniversary of his death, a fine stone monument to Robert Forde was unveiled on the Promenade in Cobh. Funds for the memorial were raised by local subscription, and among those present at the unveiling ceremony to pay tribute to Forde were modern-day Irish adventurers Pat Falvey and Frank Nugent. Appropriately, the memorial overlooks the sea.

The memorial to Robert Forde overlooking Cobh Harbour. The memorial was erected in 2009, thanks to the generous support of local people. MICHAEL SMITH

The inscription on the Forde memorial reads: 'In memory of Robert Forde RN 1875–1959 Who served on *Terra Nova* with Captain Scott and took part in the 1910–1913 British Antarctic Expedition. Interred in the Old Church Cemetery, Cobh'. MICHAEL SMITH

MORTIMER McCARTHY
1882–1967

and

TIMOTHY McCARTHY
1888–1917

Above: Timothy McCarthy. Few images of Tim, thought to be the youngest of the McCarthy brothers, have survived.

Left: Decorated. Mortimer McCarthy wearing the Polar Medal for the *Terra Nova* expedition, which he received from King George V in 1913.

THE HISTORIC TOWN OF KINSALE provided a fitting backdrop for the lives of Mortimer and Timothy McCarthy, one of only two sets of brothers who served with Scott and Shackleton during the Heroic Age of Exploration to the Antarctic in the early years of the twentieth century. Though the brothers never served together in the Antarctic, they featured strongly in the two most dramatic episodes of the era – Scott's last expedition and the epic survival story of Shackleton's *Endurance*.

Mortimer and Timothy McCarthy hailed from the little community of Preghane in the Lower Cove area of Kinsale, overlooking the Bandon River estuary and close to the star-shaped, seventeenth-century Charles Fort, which once stood guard over the narrow entrance into Kinsale Harbour. It is a place steeped in the traditions of the sea and with a reputation of turning out generations of skilled seamen, particularly those adept at handling small boats.

Although it is impossible to positively establish a clear line back to the Gaelic aristocracy of Cork and Kerry, the early McCarthy family of Lower Cove were probably drawn from the old clan, once among the most powerful in the area and a lineage which can trace its origins back to Oilioll Olum, King of Munster, in the third century. Oilioll's descendants included Cárthach, whose family later took the name *Mac Cárthach* (Sons of Cárthach).

Very little is known about the far more modest background of the McCarthys of Preghane except that in May 1881 John McCarthy of Lower Cove married Mary Forde from Garrylucas, the small sandy bay at the neck of the Old Head of Kinsale. The couple, who were married at Ballinspittle, farmed a scrap of land and fished in local waters while producing a family of six children. The four boys were named Mortimer, Timothy, James and John and the two daughters, Anne and Mary.

There is some confusion about the precise date of Mortimer's birth because, in the care-free manner of sailors down the age, he lied about his age to get a berth on his first ship and went through life giving a series of different birthdays which in time became more and more distant from the truth. However, the most reliable information is that Mortimer, who was named after his grandfather, was born on 15 April 1882. Official naval records, which relied on Mortimer's version of events, gave his date of birth as 15 April 1878, although in later life he regularly shaved years off his age to keep his job. Timothy McCarthy – often called Tadhg – was a more straightforward case whose date of birth was 15 July 1888.

Families in the Preghane (*Préachán*) area of Lower Cove survived for generations working the land and fishing in coastal waters with small craft known as drievers. With *Préachán* in Irish meaning 'crow', locals reputedly called the little cluster of families of Lower Cove the 'crow people' after the populous black choughs seen in the area.

The McCarthy children picked up a simple education at a school near the British garrison at Charles Fort, and away from the classroom, the boys helped their father around the farm or on the fishing boat. Slowly but surely the McCarthy boys learned the traditional skills of the small-boat man. Almost inevitably, the McCarthy boys went to sea when the time came to seek a better life.

Mortimer McCarthy's colourful and long life at sea began in 1894 when he was only twelve years old, though the actual circumstances surrounding his enlistment have been lost. Somehow the lad persuaded the ship's Master that he was sixteen and he was taken on, possibly because he was already a practised seafarer. It was the beginning of an extraordinary and prolonged career at sea which spanned close to seventy years. Over the next sixteen years Mortimer worked his way upwards on a variety of merchant ships, serving as an Able Seaman on cargo vessels plying the trade routes of the world. By 1900 Mortimer was employed on ships taking thousands of troops and supplies to South Africa for the Boer War. Among the seamen in the same waters at the time was a young Irish-born merchant naval officer, Ernest Shackleton.

Mortimer, who was then known to his shipmates as Murty or Mac, was a chirpy, self-confident character who stood 5 foot 7 inches tall and was known for his agreeable humour and fine all-round skills as a sailor. Mortimer was every inch the archetypal seaman, a lively, impish wanderer with an endless fund of thrilling and heavily embroidered yarns, a flowing handlebar moustache and fondness for hard liquor.

During the early years of the century he was based in the Welsh port of Barry and in 1907, while serving on the 7,500-ton *Oswestry Grange*, he made his first recorded visit to New Zealand. He evidently liked what he found and in the following years gravitated increasingly towards the country where he would eventually put down his roots.

New Zealand became his adopted home and he once 'jumped ship' there. Telling the ship's Mate he had a letter to post before sailing, Mortimer strode off down the quay and never looked back. By chance, he later bumped into the same Mate in another port and was asked pointedly if he had yet managed to post his letter. 'Yes, sir, thank you,' McCarthy firmly replied and strode off once again.

By 1910, Mortimer was serving as bosun on the cargo vessel *Arapawa*, which operated from the main New Zealand ports of Wellington and Lyttelton. By chance, Lyttelton was also the port of choice for *Terra Nova*, the exploration ship under the command of Captain Robert Scott which was being made ready for sailing to the Antarctic. *Terra Nova* arrived in Lyttelton on 28 October for a month of refitting and loading supplies before embarking on Scott's attempt to reach the South Pole. After two weeks in dry dock getting a niggling leak fixed, *Terra Nova* was back at sea by 12 November and the final preparations for sailing south were being made.

One of the last-minute items was the addition to the crew of the much-travelled seaman, Mortimer McCarthy. The events leading to his appointment are unclear, though he joined on the eve of *Terra Nova* sailing. It must be assumed that either Lieutenant Harry Pennell, the ship's captain for the voyages to and from Antarctica, or Lieutenant Teddy Evans, Scott's deputy who was in charge of selecting the men, needed another experienced hand to take the ship to the expedition's base camp.

Mortimer's posting on *Arapawa* came to an end on 24 November and a day later he was appointed as Able Seaman on *Terra Nova*, the day the expedition headed south from Lyttelton. When asked what wage he expected, Mortimer said: 'Just what the others are paid.' The 28-year-old Mortimer gave his age as 32. After a brief stopover to pick up last stocks of coal at Port Chalmers, *Terra Nova* finally headed to the Antarctic on 29 November 1910 amid a fanfare of flag waving, marching bands and cheering crowds. An excitable flotilla of little craft accompanied the ship down the narrow channels of Port Chalmers and out to sea at the start of the long and hazardous voyage across the Southern Ocean.

The plan was a simple enough one of taking *Terra Nova* to McMurdo Sound, where the 31-man shore party and supplies for at least two years would be dropped off. The ship would only be able to remain for a few weeks before the autumnal Antarctic ice blocked off their retreat. *Terra Nova* was a veteran of the Arctic whaling fleet, a 744-ton sealer of just 187 ft (57 m) in length. Built in Scotland in 1884, *Terra Nova* was also dangerously overloaded for a round trip of nearly 5,000 miles (8,000 km) through the roughest seas on earth to the Antarctic continent and back. More than sixty men, nineteen ponies, over thirty dogs and countless boxes of food and equipment were jammed into every corner and crevice of the ship and the Plimsoll line was conveniently painted out to avoid any embarrassing questions from the port authorities.

Terra Nova's dangerous overloading left precious little spare room or comfort for those on board. The crew had to share hammocks and each time a sailor reported for duty he was instantly replaced by another jumping in for a rest. It was also discovered that the stinking pony stalls were directly above their heads and the animals' urine seeped slowly on to the sailors as they slept.

The seaworthiness of *Terra Nova* was a major concern as the vessel entered the notoriously rough waters of the Southern Ocean. 'We must hope for a fine passage,' Lieutenant Victor Campbell wrote in his diary. Storms were inevitable on the run south and Tryggve Gran, a member of the shore party, shared the general anxiety. 'The ship is overloaded, so let's hope we don't run into bad weather,' he wrote.

Within twenty-four hours *Terra Nova* was struck by a full-scale hurricane and came close to sinking. Coal sacks and supply boxes were scattered around the decks in the tumult, two ponies died in the storm and a dog was hurled overboard by one crashing wave and instantly thrown back on board by the next. Some waves measured up to 35 ft (10 m) and winds increased to force 11, or over 70 mph.

At the height of the storm the bilge pumps became blocked by coal dust and other debris and all hands were sent below with buckets to bail for their lives. Some stood up to their necks in cold filthy water trying to get the pumps working properly. 'The water was gaining fast and things looked serious,' Campbell said. Improbably enough, the reassuring sound of sailors singing sea shanties could be heard above the roar of the storm.

McCarthy, who was helmsman, took the full brunt of the storm and struggled to keep his feet in the turbulent seas. It is unlikely that McCarthy had ever met such ferocity in all his years at sea. Herbert Ponting, the photographer, recorded the ordeal and wrote: 'Often the waves swept over the stern, almost carrying the helmsman off his feet and he was frequently knee-high and sometimes waist deep in water.'[1]

Few on board had any sleep for forty-eight hours and the relief was immense when the storm finally blew itself out. 'It was a corker and nearly the end of the Expedition,' one scientist wrote. Another said that at the peak of the storm the chances of foundering were 100 to 1, while Scott prayed that the ship would not meet another violent bout of weather before reaching the Antarctic coast. His pleas were answered and the next challenge for Pennell, *Terra Nova*'s captain, was to navigate a path through the Antarctic pack ice. The ship spent three weeks zigzagging through the choking band of ice which surrounds the continent ice and *Terra Nova*'s boilers guzzled over 60 tons of coal before the ship finally reached McMurdo Sound in early January 1911.

Initially all hands were kept busy for up to eighteen hours a day unloading supplies, helping to erect the expedition's hut and building shelters for the dogs and ponies at Cape Evans on Ross Island. There was also time for a near catastrophe when *Terra Nova* ran aground, threatening to leave the entire ship's crew and landing party marooned on the continent. Strong currents drove the vessel towards shore and Pennell had to take decisive action. Tons of supplies were shifted in the holds and, on Pennell's command, the crew ran back and forth together across the decks – a process called sallying – to roll the ship off the rocks.

Scott, watching horrified from the shore, faced the miserable ordeal of handling more than sixty men forced to overwinter in the Antarctic unless *Terra Nova* could be refloated. 'A terribly depressing prospect,' he said. However, Pennell's quick thinking saved the ship and lusty cheers from the crew signalled to Scott that *Terra Nova* had managed to get off the rocks. Scott said: 'The relief was enormous'.

After three weeks of frantic activity, *Terra Nova* sailed from McMurdo Sound on 27 January, leaving Scott's main party of twenty-five to prepare for the assault on the Pole in the following spring. *Terra Nova*'s remaining task was to carry a splinter group of six men under Lt Campbell to explore King Edward VII Land a few hundred miles to the east. *Terra Nova* sailed alongside the cliffs of the Ice Barrier for about 400 miles (640 km), an area first seen by Crozier and Ross and last visited by Shackleton three years earlier. To their amazement another ship came into sight as they entered the Bay of Whales, an indent in the Barrier first discovered by Shackleton. The ship was *Fram*, carrying a team of Norwegians under the command of Roald Amundsen to a camp on the Barrier. Although Amundsen had telegraphed Scott to warn him he was racing the British to the Pole, no one expected to find *Fram* in the Bay of Whales, because camping on the shifting, unstable Barrier was regarded as impossible.

A postcard showing *Terra Nova* in New Zealand on the eve of her departure to the Antarctic. The card is postmarked 29 November 1910, the day
the expedition sailed from Port Chalmers. TOM MAGUIRE

7199 B

THE SOUTH POLAR EXPEDITION: CAPTAIN

T AND HIS EXPLORATION SHIP, "TERRA NOVA."

Mortimer McCarthy with the crew of *Terra Nova* after returning to the Antarctic in November 1910. McCarthy stands in the back row (far right) with his arms folded, wearing a hat. Also pictured is Robert Forde from Cork (front row with dog). Bill McDonald (standing, second from left) and Bill Burton (standing, fourth from left) returned to the Antarctic with McCarthy in 1963.

Campbell went aboard *Fram* for breakfast, hoping to discover a little of Amundsen's plans and a short while later he returned the compliment by entertaining Amundsen to lunch on *Terra Nova*. One perceptive scientist said the Norwegians looked like 'dangerous rivals'. However, the presence of Amundsen prompted Campbell to abandon plans for the King Edward VII Land expedition and instead *Terra Nova* went back to McMurdo Sound with news of their discovery.

The detour left *Terra Nova* with a tight schedule to drop off Campbell and sail north before the thickening ice of autumn trapped the ship for the winter. Pennell was also worried about a shortage of coal for the long return journey, particularly if the pack proved difficult to penetrate on the way back. He hurriedly took *Terra Nova* out of McMurdo Sound on 9 February and on 17 February dropped Campbell's party to the north at Cape Adare. After unloading a hut for the six men, Pennell beat a hasty retreat northwards on 20 February 1911 and promised to return to pick up the men in eleven months.

Scott had asked Pennell to explore the seas around Cape Adare, a headland discovered by Crozier and Ross in 1841. Two days after dropping off Campbell, *Terra Nova* picked out a chunk of uncharted land in the distance which was named Oates Land after Captain Lawrence Oates, the Inniskilling Dragoon officer and the expedition's expert on horses. It was the only major geographical discovery of the three-year *Terra Nova* expedition and it would be nearly half a century before anyone ventured on to Oates Land.

However, the ice in the area was particularly dangerous and *Terra Nova* came perilously close to becoming trapped as the ship skirted along the coast. A quick count found forty-seven icebergs in the immediate vicinity and Pennell, wisely abandoning any hopes of getting closer to land, turned the ship northwards. *Terra Nova*, battered by a hurricane on the way down to the Antarctic, endured another heavy storm on the return journey to New Zealand. Once again the wretched bilge pumps were blocked, but the ship managed to battle through unscathed. Four months after leaving to a fanfare, *Terra Nova* slipped quietly and almost unnoticed into Lyttelton in the early hours of 1 April 1911.

The ship, with McCarthy again at the helm, left Lyttelton for the second time on 15 December 1911 carrying holds stocked with fresh supplies, seven new pack mules recruited from the Indian Army and a handful of replacements for the men due to leave the Antarctic after just a single season. Following a fairly peaceful trip south, *Terra Nova* sailed alongside Cape Adare in early January, picked up Campbell's party and dropped the men further down the coast in Terra Nova Bay. It was planned that Campbell would spend about five weeks exploring the area and only a small stock of six weeks' food and two weeks' sledging rations, plus a few minor items of gear, was dumped on shore.

Terra Nova re-entered McMurdo Sound on 4 February 1912 expecting to hear heartening news of Scott's advance to the Pole. At this stage, eight of the sixteen men who struck out for the Pole nearly three months earlier were still out on the ice and their condition was unknown. The most recent arrivals at base camp were the four men of the

First Supporting Party – Atkinson, Cherry-Garrard, Keohane and Wright – who returned on 26 January with encouraging reports that their eight companions were last seen in good spirits on the Polar Plateau, over 300 miles (480 km) from the Pole. But the mood of cautious optimism was shattered two weeks later when Tom Crean from the Last Supporting Party staggered in after a miraculous hike of 35 miles (56 km) on his own to report that Lt Teddy Evans and Bill Lashly were camped on the Ice Barrier, with Evans on the brink of death. Crean had left Scott about 150 miles (240 km) from the Pole, but the shocking state of the Last Supporting Party raised the first serious doubts that Scott's men would get back alive.

Pennell, a capable 29-year-old navigator, now faced a major dilemma. Although Scott's fate was still in the balance, autumn was closing in and *Terra Nova*, once again, was at serious risk of becoming trapped. At the same time, *Terra Nova* was due to pick up Campbell's party, which had been left at Terra Nova Bay with only a small quantity of provisions and shelter for the coming winter.

Pennell's priority was Campbell. He had left Campbell with the clear message to expect *Terra Nova* in the days between 18 February and 1 March, but no one reckoned on the appalling conditions. Visibility was poor and the pack ice unexpectedly thick in the region, which cast doubts on getting the ship close enough to shore. At one stage, Campbell's men were virtually confined to their sleeping bags for thirteen days by high winds and blizzard conditions, making it impossible for *Terra Nova* even to see the beleaguered men.

After being thwarted in the first attempt to reach Campbell, the ship was driven back to Cape Evans to collect the desperately ill Lt Evans. Soon after, *Terra Nova* steamed out of McMurdo Sound and drove north in a fresh attempt to reach Campbell. But the pack ice, which had blocked the first attempt, remained stubbornly in place. The ship briefly came within 35 miles (56 km) of the shore but was repulsed and on 6 March, Campbell's diary recorded: 'Although I shall not give up until 15 March, I begin to think something must have happened. Either the ship is ashore or there is too much pack for her to get in, or she is damaged in these gales and blown north.'

Next day, the struggle was abandoned and *Terra Nova* turned north towards New Zealand, unaware of the fate of either Scott or Campbell. Hundreds of miles to the south, Scott's party was falling to pieces on the final leg of the return from the South Pole. Edgar 'Taff' Evans was already dead, Oates was in final throes of his agony and Scott appeared to have accepted that he, Wilson and Bowers were doomed. The day after *Terra Nova* sailed Scott wrote in his diary: '. . . God help us . . .We are in a very bad way . . .'. In Terra Nova Bay, Campbell's party dug out a cave from the ice, slaughtered as many seals as they could find and prepared to spend eight to ten months in isolation. It was named Inexpressible Island.

Terra Nova ran north and immediately hit another brutal storm, the worst they had ever experienced. The ship's log recorded a storm force 9 to 11, which Pennell called a 'severe storm'. (The maximum storm rating is force 12.) In the semi-darkness, with icebergs all around, Pennell fought a desperate rearguard action to keep the vessel afloat. It was impossible for the crew to sit down for a hot meal – the only food was what the hard-pressed men could hold in the hands. Ponting said it was 'magnificent to watch her fighting the mountainous seas' threatening the ship. 'One minute she would be in an ocean valley, with waves ahead and astern higher than her maintop, the next she would be on the summit of one of these watery peaks.'

McCarthy, as helmsman, stood like a rock throughout the storm. Griffith Taylor, the geologist, reported one occasion when huge waves swamped McCarthy. 'It broke down the canvas screen protecting, but didn't dismay the jaunty McCarthy,' he added, continuing: 'He had back luck later, also. For climbing the ratlines to free some tackle his helmet was knocked off. It nearly came inboard on an incoming wave over the lee bulwarks, but not quite. However, all that cheery McCarthy said was, 'Maybe 'twill make the gales lessen a bit !'[2]

McCarthy's experience and quick thinking also saved *Terra Nova* from a collision when he spotted an iceberg looming out of the heavy seas. Only the white spume spreading from the bows was visible in the gloomy grey seas and scudding clouds. Taylor

remembered: 'Very early on the 17th every one was on deck busy furling sail when McCarthy suddenly spotted an iceberg dead ahead. Luckily we just had time to steer clear.'[3] *Terra Nova* survived the beating and sailed into Lyttelton on 3 April 1912, still unaware of what had happened to Scott or Campbell. But they did discover that Amundsen had beaten Scott to the Pole.

Mortimer was discharged from *Terra Nova* on 4 April while the ship underwent another major refit, which lasted four months. While the ship was being made ready for another voyage south, Mortimer went back to sea to earn a living by serving on two local merchant ships, *Mararoa* and *Mokora*.

On 1 December, four days after completing his last voyage on the *Mokora*, Mortimer McCarthy was back on board *Terra Nova* in Lyttelton Harbour as the ship prepared to sail

Mortimer McCarthy, a studio photograph probably taken after his return from the Antarctic in 1913.
CLONAKILTY MUSEUM

Facing page: Mortimer McCarthy at the wheel of *Terra Nova* during the precarious journey from New Zealand to McMurdo Sound in the Antarctic. The ship almost sank during a hurricane but Mortimer eventually completed three round trips of 5,000 miles (8,000 km) each to the continent.

Stoker McCarthy's Polar Medal. MCCARTHY FAMILY

h to the Antarctic for the third time. Flags and bunting were stored in readiness
celebrations to mark the achievement of Scott reaching the Pole. Lt Evans, hav
vered from his perilous escapade, was also on board when the ship sailed on
ember and re-entered McMurdo Sound on 18 January 1913 – precisely one year

Antarctic. The one piece of good news was that Campbell's party, which many feared had also been lost at Terra Nova Bay, had survived against the odds and managed to work their way back to Cape Evans.

Terra Nova left Antarctica for the last time on 26 January 1913, just eight days after her arrival. Most of the shore party was horribly seasick on another tempestuous journey through Southern Ocean gales and a maze of icebergs. 'Just after midnight, the hurricane was so strong you couldn't stand on deck,' Gran once wrote. 'The sea got up awfully and ship was tossed about like a cork. Things worked loose and below decks it was chaotic.'

The New Zealand port of Oamaru was reached on 10 February and news of the tragedy cabled back to London. Two days later *Terra Nova* crept into Lyttelton with her flags at half mast and a small crowd standing silently on the quayside.

Terra Nova, with Mortimer steadfastly at the helm, had travelled around 15,000 miles (24,000 km) on three hazardous voyages back and forth to the Antarctic and never went south again. The ship returned to her old haunts in the Arctic sealing trade and sank off Greenland in September 1943 after colliding with ice. The engine room pumps, which had caused so much trouble during three voyages to the Antarctic, were again blocked and nothing could stop the seas flooding in.

Mortimer McCarthy returned to the UK on board *Terra Nova* in June 1913 and joined the expedition's survivors a month later for a visit to Buckingham Palace where he received a Silver Polar Medal from King George V. Mortimer also had his own personal souvenir from his Antarctic voyages: frostbite had claimed two fingers from one hand.

Just as one member of the McCarthy family left the ice on *Terra Nova*, another was poised to take his place in the Antarctic. While Mortimer was collecting his Antarctic medal, younger brother, Timothy, was on the verge of joining *Endurance* for Shackleton's newest venture, the Imperial Trans-Antarctic Expedition.

Tim McCarthy, another experienced seaman from the McCarthy family, was an ideal man for Shackleton's purposes. He is thought to have signed up for service in the merchant fleet at the age of sixteen and a year later in 1905 joined the Royal Navy Reserve, the volunteer force for professional seafarers where he was assigned to *Aeolus*, the cruiser deployed as guard ship at the Queenstown naval base. He was an ebullient, popular and good-tempered character who was widely recognised as a first class sailor. Tim stood 5 foot 8 inches in his socks and was distinguished by an impressive set of tattoos on his right arm bearing images of a heart, an anchor and a cross.

Tim McCarthy's entry into the story of Antarctic exploration began on 1 August 1914, just two weeks after his twenty-sixth birthday, when *Endurance* sailed from London on the first leg of the long journey south. Tim, like most of the crew, was recruited only to take

Endurance down through the Weddell Sea to the Antarctic coast, deposit Shackleton's shore party at Vahsel Bay and escape north before the ice trapped the ship. Shackleton's grand plan to make the first-ever coast-to-coast crossing of the continent was of little consequence to a seaman like Tim.

A far greater concern was the looming war with Germany and whether the ship might get caught up in the hostilities. It is not known how Tim McCarthy came to be recruited to *Endurance*, though his experience and willingness must have been important factors. It seems likely that he was picked by Frank Worsley, the New Zealand-born captain of *Endurance* who was another highly experienced man of the sea who knew a good sailor when he saw one.

Endurance, with twenty-eight men on board, evaded German warships on the run south and reached the treacherous waters of the Weddell Sea at the end of 1914. By 19 January 1915 the ship was captured by the ice, never to be released. The Weddell Sea, among the most dangerous seas on earth, is surrounded on three sides by land and relentless currents drive the choking ice in a slow circular movement like a cement mixer, crushing anything in its clutches. Stuck fast in the ice, the ship drifted past the planned landing site of Vahsel Bay and normal ship's routine was abandoned as winter descended.

Throughout the long dark winter, the monumental force of the ice slowly but inexorably strangled the life from *Endurance*. By the time the ship sank in November 1915, the twenty-eight men and about fifty dogs were camped on the slowly moving ice, waiting for the drift to carry their ice floe northwards to warmer waters where they could launch their three small lifeboats into open seas.

Tim McCarthy was universally popular and a man whose buoyant sense of humour and unhurried, easy-going manner provided a little light relief, particularly to the men feeling the strain of isolation on the drifting ice floe. Little affected his demeanour and everyone had a good word for the cheerful sailor from Kinsale. Worsley said he was the 'most irrepressible optimist I've ever met' and Thomas Orde Lees, the expedition's storekeeper, wrote: 'McCarthy is a witty Irishman with a splendid gift of repartee.'

His irrepressible humour was evident when Tim almost drowned soon after *Endurance* became trapped. While attempting to dig out a path in the ice, Tim slipped and fell into the bitterly cold water. Shipmates quickly dragged him out and, according to Orde Lees, the cheery Irishman shrugged off the narrow escape with a dismissive comment: 'He said it was warm enough until the water overflowed down his neck.'

Tim's expertise with small boats came to the fore in April 1916 when, after more than fifteen months trapped in the ice, the drift carried the floe towards patches of open water. Shackleton ordered the twenty-eight men into the three lifeboats in an attempt to reach dry land and wisely picked Tim to serve alongside him in the *James Caird*, the largest of the boats. The three craft – *James Caird*, *Dudley Docker* and *Stancomb Wills* – pushed away from the ice floe on 9 April, with the initial target of reaching the northern tip of the

Antarctic Peninsula or the nearby Deception Island where a passing whaling ship might be found.

But all three vessels struggled badly in the heavy, icy seas and the boats were eventually turned towards the uninhabited but more easily accessible Elephant Island. The seven-day journey to Elephant Island was a dreadful ordeal. Rolling seas and threatening icebergs were a constant danger, the men were soaked by crashing waves, and food was often dog rations eaten cold. The only relief came from the occasional mug of hot milk and at night the men huddled together for warmth in the small boats, which gathered together for shelter in the lee of a convenient iceberg. They woke in the morning either soaked to the skin or to find frost covering their bodies and most men were violently sick once the boats took to sea again. Rowing was a terrible strain for the cold, severely drained men. A final indignity was frequent bouts of diarrhoea.

At least a third of the men were on the brink of collapse as the ominous, brooding peaks of Elephant Island came into view on 15 April. The three vessels were beached on the rocky shore, the first time they had been on firm land in nearly seventeen months. Although heavily punished by the nightmare journey, Tim McCarthy was among those still capable as the battered crews made their way ashore.

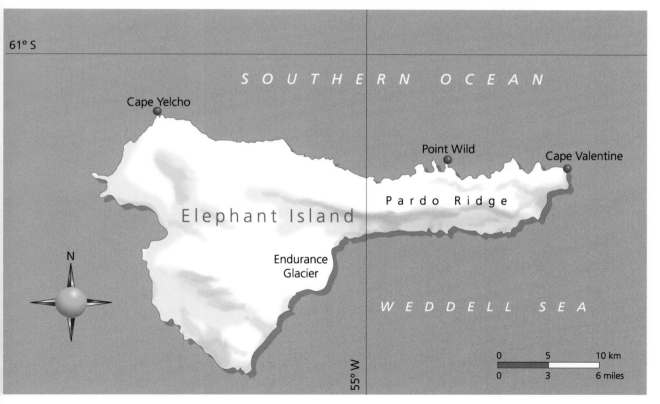

Elephant Island, the tiny refuge in the Southern Ocean reached by the crew of *Endurance* in 1916. Leaving twenty-two men behind on the beach, Shackleton, Crean and McCarthy sailed to South Georgia in the *James Caird* to fetch rescue.

Tim McCarthy with the *Endurance* party, stuck in the ice of the Weddell Sea in September 1915. McCarthy stands in the back row (seventh from right). Also pictured against the backdrop of the stricken *Endurance* are Shackleton (front row, third from left) and Crean (front row, fourth from left). *Endurance* sank two months after this photograph was taken.

The bleak, forbidding Elephant Island where the *Endurance* party landed in April 1916. CON COLLINS

It was soon obvious that the beach was likely to be flooded at high tide and Shackleton rounded up the fittest men to search for a more suitable place to make camp. Tim, who had excelled in the *James Caird*, joined Frank Wild and Tom Crean to take the *Stancomb Wills* along the coast to scout for an alternative landing site. The group returned at nightfall to report the discovery of a small spit which offered reasonable shelter, adequate fresh water from nearby glaciers and ample wildlife to stock the larder. It was named Cape Wild (now called Point Wild).

Elephant Island is a remote and isolated spot, just 23 miles (37 km) long and far from any known shipping routes. No one knew the men had landed on the island and Shackleton realised that the only prospect of survival was to sail for help to the whaling stations on South Georgia, about 800 miles (1,200 km) across the Southern Ocean. His choices were strictly limited, with at least ten of the men incapable of making another long boat trip and neither the *Dudley Docker* nor *Stancomb Wills* likely to survive the dangerous open seas. He decided to take six men in *James Caird* and leave twenty-two behind at Cape Wild.

Tim McCarthy, tough, cheerful and a small-boat man to his finger tips, was an obvious choice to sail in the *James Caird*. He was among the most accomplished sailors on *Endurance* and in many respects was more equipped for the journey than even Shackleton, whose years at sea were spent in large cargo or passenger ships. Shackleton knew his limitations

Tim McCarthy.
He was twenty-
seven years old
at the time of
this photograph.

and recognised the value of Tim McCarthy. In one revealing exchange shortly before the departure of *James Caird*, he confessed to Worsley: 'Do you know, I know nothing about boat sailing?' Worsley laughed at the improbable remark before Shackleton insisted: 'I'm telling you that I don't.'

But Shackleton, like Worsley, recognised a good sailor in Tim McCarthy. In *South*, his book on the expedition, Shackleton wrote: 'McCarthy, the best and most efficient of the sailors, always cheerful under the most trying circumstances and who for these reasons I chose to accompany me on the boat journey to South Georgia.'[4] The other five members of the crew of the *James Caird* were Shackleton as leader, Worsley the navigator with almost thirty years of seafaring behind him, the hardened Antarctic veteran Crean, trawlerman Vincent, and McNish, the ship's carpenter whose skilled hands had made the *Caird* seaworthy.

At just 22 ft (7m), the modest-looking *Caird* seemed the most unlikely vessel to tackle the treachery of the Southern Ocean. Rocks were taken from the beach to provide ballast, a mast was plundered from one of the other craft to strengthen the hull and McNish, working with bare hands in freezing conditions, raised the sides with scraps of wood and fashioned a canvas decking to provide a little protection against the inevitable deluge they would meet on the high seas. Worsley called the journey an 'ordeal by water' and Shackleton said the waters south of Cape Horn in May, when the *Caird* would be crossing the ocean, were the 'most tempestuous, storm-swept area of water in the world'.

The voyage of the *James Caird* began on 24 April 1916 and hit snags from the start. McNish and Vincent were thrown into the sea while loading provisions from the beach and the vessel was half-filled with water when the plug was dislodged. McCarthy and Worsley quickly baled her dry and replaced the plug before the journey finally got under way. A four-week supply of food was taken and Worsley's only charts were a few pages torn from books salvaged from the *Endurance*'s library. Shackleton also carried a shotgun and cartridges, while McNish took a few of his carpentry tools.

Taking the boat due north to avoid the surrounding ice, the *Caird* immediately ran into a northerly gale, which threatened to drive them back into the clutches of the ice. Everyone was seasick, except the old hands Worsley and Tim McCarthy. It was, said Shackleton, a tale of 'supreme strife amid heaving waters.' Gales seemed ever present, though Shackleton ensured that the men were well fed and hot drinks were dished out at regular intervals.

McCarthy shared his four-hour watch with Worsley and Vincent and any rest was a few hours snatched by laying out a sleeping bag on the piles of stones lining the bottom of the boat. Claustrophobia often nagged at the senses as they squeezed into the cramped rest area with their noses pressed against the canvas decking. No one managed a proper rest. Worsley had nightmares of being buried alive and remembered one particular incident with some clarity: 'Once I heard muffled groans and found that McCarthy in the next sleeping bag was bumping about against me. I leaned over and freed his head from the bag and he gasped his thanks to me for "saving his life".'5

Tim McCarthy's expertise and effervescent nature were highly important to Shackleton and Worsley during the journey which was always fraught with danger and almost permanently on the brink of disaster. Worsley wrote: 'We were especially fond of McCarthy, whose optimism and cheerfulness during the boat journey were an unfailing help to all of us.'6 McCarthy seemed capable of handling anything the Southern Ocean could hurl at them. In one revealing entry on McCarthy, Worsley recorded in his log: 'When I relieve him at the helm, boat iced & seas pourg down yr neck, he informs me with a happy grin, "It's a grand day, sir."'

However, McCarthy's optimism could not conceal the worsening condition of the men, whose only comfort in the heavy seas and lashing winds was a regular and decent supply of hot food. They were constantly soaked and in spite of the cold, it was necessary to work the pumps with bare hands, a task no man could endure for more than five minutes at a time.

Sea spray, which froze on impact with the craft, built up and added a dangerous layer of extra weight which at one stage threatened to capsize the *Caird*. In desperation, the men took turns crawling along the slippery deck in the rolling seas to chip away at the ice which had grown over a foot thick. Three times it was necessary for the men to crawl outside to chop away the ice and ensure that they did not tear the flimsy canvas decking, their only protection against the bitter cold and wet of the Southern Ocean. One night a huge wave almost engulfed the *Caird*. To add to their woes, it was discovered that seawater had seeped into a water barrel and the men were inflicted with a savage thirst.

McNish and Vincent, broken by the ordeal, were struggling badly and less capable of work. Shackleton knew that making landfall was becoming increasingly urgent and turned to Worsley for his navigational brilliance to get *Caird* to South Georgia. Worsley managed to take sightings and log the craft's position only four times during the long voyage and yet managed to steer the *Caird* unerringly towards South Georgia. Had he miscalculated, the boat would have sailed into the vast expanses of the South Atlantic and the winds and currents would have made it impossible to turn back.

The first encouraging sign emerged after two weeks at sea when a piece of kelp was spotted, a clear sign of land nearby. Around noon on the fifteenth day at sea two cormorants were seen hovering overhead and the men strained their eyes hoping to see land breaking through the dark clouds blocking their view ahead. Shortly after noon the clouds parted for a brief second and McCarthy's keen eyes spotted the black cliffs of South Georgia. 'Land!' he yelled.

Night was closing in as the *Caird* came close to the shoreline at King Haakon Bay, but landing in semi-darkness and heavy rolling seas was too risky. Shackleton reluctantly ordered the *Caird* back out to sea and to wait for morning when a clear path could be found through the dangerous rocks lining the entrance to the bay. The *Antarctic* was desperate not to let them go easily. Shortly before dawn a full-scale hurricane swept down on the *Caird*, whipping the seas into a frenzy and driving the vessel towards destruction on the shore. 'None of us had ever seen anything like it before,' Worsley recalled. Somehow, the craft managed to scramble away from the rocky shoreline. But winds and high seas pounded the *Caird* throughout the day and, for the second night, the party was unable to land. All the clean drinking water had long gone and scraps of food were gulped down cold as the *James Caird* fought to stay afloat. 'I think most of us had a feeling that the end was very near,' Shackleton said.

Luckily the winds had eased by the morning of 10 May and all eyes searched anxiously for a landing place before a new storm erupted. Several attempts were made to pick a path through the reefs and dusk was falling as the *Caird* made a final bid to get ashore before darkness consigned them to another, potentially fatal, night at sea. Approaching King Haakon Bay, the *Caird* picked a path through a line of jagged rocks and came to a halt on a rocky beach. After seventeen days, one of the greatest boat journeys ever made was finally over. 'It was a splendid moment,' Shackleton wrote.

A stream of water from a nearby glacier provided the exhausted, dehydrated men with the first drink in days. Dinner was freshly killed albatross, courtesy of the eager hunters, McCarthy and Crean. However, the landfall had taken the men to the south side of the island and the *Caird*'s rudder had been lost during the difficult landing. The only means of reaching the whaling stations on the north side was to cross the mountains on foot. A new camp was made at the head of the U-shaped King Haakon Bay and the *Caird* was tipped over to form a makeshift shelter. Shackleton called it Peggoty Camp after the character in Dickens' novel *David Copperfield* who lived under a boat.

McNish and Vincent were in very poor condition after the journey and incapable of walking across the island to the whaling stations. In the face of the new emergency, Shackleton asked the dependable McCarthy to stay behind at Peggoty Camp to care for the incapacitated men while he took Crean and Worsley across the island's mountains and glaciers. McCarthy had little choice, but the weakness of McNish and Vincent left him badly exposed, particularly if Shackleton, Crean and Worsley were lost trying to cross the mountains or if the condition of his companions worsened. Shackleton recognised the dangers and said: 'These two men [McNish and Vincent] could not manage for themselves and I had to leave McCarthy to look after them. Should we fail to reach the whaling station McCarthy might have a difficult task.'[7]

Shackleton, Worsley and Crean left Peggoty Camp in the early hours of 19 May and reached the Norwegian whaling station at Stromness late the next day after an astonishing forced march which lasted thirty-six hours without proper rest. After a hot bath and a change of clothes, Worsley climbed aboard the Norwegian whaler *Samson* and went back to King Haakon Bay to pick up McCarthy, Vincent and McNish.

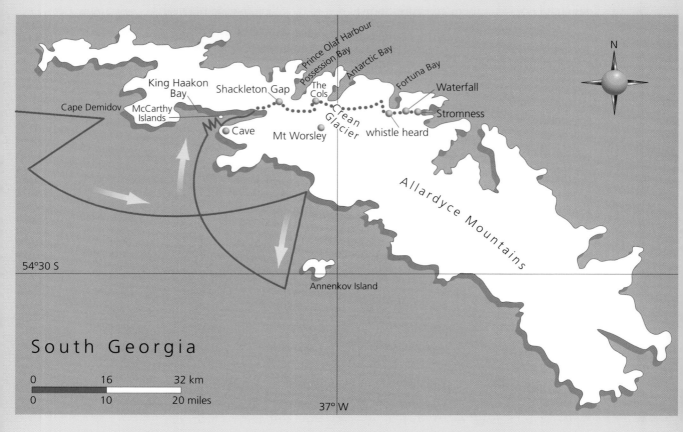

Prince Olaf Harbour
Possession Bay
Antarctic Bay
Fortuna Bay
King Haakon Bay
Shackleton Gap
The Cols
Waterfall
Cape Demidov
McCarthy Islands
Crean Glacier
Stromness
Cave
Mt Worsley
whistle heard
Allardyce Mountains
54°30 S
Annenkov Island

South Georgia

| 0 | 16 | 32 km |
| 0 | 10 | 20 miles |

37° W

The *James Caird*, with Shackleton, Crean and McCarthy on board, reached South Georgia in May 1916. Shackleton, Crean and Worsley crossed the interior, leaving McCarthy in King Haakon Bay to tend his sick companions.

An artist recreated the landing on South Georgia, 10 May 1916. The dependable Tim McCarthy was left behind on the beach to care for McNish and Vincent while Shackleton, Crean and Worsley crossed the island on foot.

He slept for almost the entire eleven-hour trip around the island and roused his companions resting under *James Caird* with sharp bursts on the ship's whistle. But he was surprised by the reception he received. As Worsley came ashore none of the men recognised the clean-shaven, smartly-dressed figure standing before them. He remembered: 'I heard McCarthy say disappointedly: 'Well, we thought the Skipper [Worsley] would have come back, anyway'. I said: 'Well, I am here' and they stared. Clean and shaved, they had taken me for a Norwegian.'[8] He had thoughtfully stuffed his pockets with pipes, tobacco, cigarettes and matches and handed them out to the eager trio. 'They fell on the smokes like tigers and were happy,' a relieved Worsley added.

Taking McCarthy, Vincent and McNish – and *James Caird* – the *Samson* endured a typical Southern Ocean storm, which kept the vessel at sea for two extra days. After landing at Stromness on 22 May, the six men were entertained by a flood of generous Norwegian hospitality. One by one, the toughened Norwegian seamen stepped forward to shake the hands of the men who had defied the Southern Ocean. In contrast, all the crew of *James Caird* wanted to know was how the war was progressing. McCarthy, Vincent and McNish spent almost six weeks resting in South Georgia waiting for a ship to take them back to Britain while Shackleton was embroiled in the first of four attempts to reach the twenty-two castaways on Elephant Island. It was not until 30 August that the men were finally lifted off the beach.

Meantime, McCarthy, Vincent and McNish finally left South Georgia on 2 July in the Norwegian steamer *Orwell*, which arrived in Liverpool on 3 August 1916 carrying a consignment of whale oil. Her cargo also included the gutsy little *James Caird*. Little is known about Tim McCarthy's life after returning from South Georgia, except that he spent some time in Liverpool with his sister Mary, who had moved to the city after marrying a man called Samuel Coleman. But Tim was never far from the sea and in 1917, less than six months after returning from South Georgia, he found a new ship.

Tim McCarthy's first posting was to *Narragansett*, a 9,000-ton oil tanker with an eventful past and a tragic future. Although built at a shipyard in Glasgow, *Narragansett* was named after a small ancient tribe of Native Americans from the Rhode Island area of the US. The English translation of their name – 'people of the small point' – has an echo of Tim's home on the headland at Kinsale.

Unfortunately, Tim McCarthy could not have chosen a worse moment to go back to sea. He joined *Narragansett* in early 1917 at a time when Germany was intensifying the war by unleashing unconditional war on all shipping. It was a desperate attempt by the Germans to sever Britain's crucial supply lines and bring the conflict to an end before the Americans, with their enormous resources and vast reserves of manpower, entered the fray. While the German battle fleet could not outgun the superior Royal Navy, the high command believed that U-boats could starve Britain into submission before America's divisions arrived in late 1917 and tipped the balance of the war in favour of the Allies.

Remarkably enough, merchant ships like *Narragansett* invariably sailed independently and without the protection of navy patrols, despite the constant threat from U-boats. As a result of the merchant fleet's vulnerability, the early days of the new German campaign warfare in 1917 were a spectacular success. In February alone – two months before America declared war on Germany – U-boats sank over 400,000 tons of mostly unprotected shipping in the Atlantic. By April, the losses had doubled to over 850,000 tons and alarm bells were ringing in London as vital stocks of food and national resources began to dwindle. Wheat supplies in April were estimated to have dropped to a bare six weeks and in May the government finally acted by ordering navy warships into the Atlantic to protect the ocean-going convoys.

Sadly, the change of policy came too late for the *Narragansett*, a lightly armed tanker carrying oil across the Atlantic in the spring of 1917 and an easy target for the U-boats. The tanker had seen drama before at sea: it was at the centre of a tense mid–Atlantic rescue

A scene in South Georgia, where stranded members of the Shackleton Antarctic Expedition made their homes after floating on an ice floe for six months. (Inset) Boatswain J. Vincent, of Hull, and Able Seaman Tim McCarthy, the first to arrive back in England.—(*Daily Sketch* Exclusive Photographs.)

A contemporary newspaper salutes the return of Tim McCarthy (right) and John Vincent from South Georgia in 1916. It is the last known photograph of Tim McCarthy.

in 1913 when 485 people, mostly Jewish immigrants from Eastern Europe travelling to America, were plucked from the sea after an explosion and fire wrecked the passenger ship *Volturno*. *Narragansett* was among the eleven ships in the vicinity to rush to the rescue of the stricken vessel in stormy weather. In spite of the risk of fire, *Narragansett* pumped 50 tons of heavy lubricating oil on to the waters to calm the seas while hundreds of survivors were rescued. *Narragansett* alone picked up twenty-nine survivors and the entire crew were awarded medals for gallantry.

Narragansett also rode her luck in 1915 during the notorious U-boat attack which sank the *Lusitania* off the Old Head of Kinsale. After picking up the *Lusitania*'s distress signals, *Narragansett* steamed towards the scene when the ship encountered *U-20*, the submarine responsible for the attack. *U-20* moved in for the kill and fired a torpedo which missed *Narragansett* by only 10 ft (3 m). It was a very fortunate escape.

However, the tanker's luck finally ran out in March 1917 when the vessel was taking a precious cargo of lubricating oil from New York to London for the Anglo American Oil

Tim McCarthy's last ship. The *Narragansett*, a 9,000-ton tanker, was sunk by a German U-boat 350 miles (560 km) off the southwest coast of Ireland on 16 March 1917.

Company and ran into the path of *U-44*, about 350 miles (560 km) off the southwest coast of Ireland. Under the command of 33-year-old Paul Wagenführ, *U-44* was a prolific killer and already credited with sinking twenty-five vessels in less than two years of active service in the Atlantic.

After undergoing repairs for a series of mechanical faults, *U-44* had returned to action only a few days before sighting *Narragansett*. But in ten days of deadly raids before *Narragansett* came into view, Wagenführ sank seven British, French and Norwegian vessels in the Atlantic in the same waters off the south and west coasts of Ireland.

Narragansett came into sight of *U-44* on 16 March 1917 and was torpedoed without warning. It was *U-44*'s biggest-ever single kill. The ship sank with the loss of all forty-six crewmen on board, including Tim McCarthy. America entered the war twenty-one days after the sinking and five months later *U-44* was sunk with the loss of all hands.

Tim, who was twenty-eight years old, was the second of the four McCarthy brothers to die in the First World War. An older brother, Patrick Joseph McCarthy – known as John – had followed elder brother Mortimer and emigrated to New Zealand. He joined the New Zealand Expeditionary Force in 1916 and was immediately thrown into the Battle of the Somme, where over 1 million men from both sides were eventually killed. John

McCarthy, aged thirty-two, was wounded in the NZEF's first day of action on the Somme and died of his wounds on 16 September 1916, only a month after Tim McCarthy returned from South Georgia.

Tim and Mortimer McCarthy from Kinsale were one of only two sets of bothers who served on Polar expeditions during the Heroic Age. By an unhappy coincidence, both families lost a son to the war. The other brothers were Frank and Ernest Wild, who served on separate branches of Shackleton's Imperial Trans-Antarctic Expedition between 1914 and 1917. Frank Wild was Shackleton's deputy on *Endurance* and Ernest 'Tubby' Wild served with the expedition's sister party in the Ross Sea, which had been sent to lay depots for Shackleton's team making the planned coast-to-coast crossing. Ernest Wild was among

Above: The death of Timothy McCarthy recorded in newspapers.

Left: Memorial card for Tim McCarthy, who was four months short of his twenty-ninth birthday when his ship was torpedoed in March 1917. McCARTHY FAMILY

only seven survivors of the disastrous venture and re-entered the navy, but died of typhoid in March 1918. Because of his Antarctic duties, Wild had overlooked getting the customary anti-typhoid vaccination.

There is no marker on Tim McCarthy's grave, though it is perhaps fitting that the inveterate seafarer should have been lost at sea. He is remembered by McCarthy Island (54° 10' S, 37° 26' W), a rocky 1-mile long (1.6-km) island which lies at the entrance of King Haakon Bay on South Georgia where *James Caird* first made landfall after the epic voyage across the Southern Ocean in 1916.

Nor did Tim McCarthy live long enough to receive formal recognition for his exploits by collecting his Polar Medal for the *Endurance* expedition and in particular, his outstanding contribution to the voyage of the *James Caird*. Tim McCarthy had been dead for almost a year before Shackleton completed the necessary paperwork and it was not until 19 June 1920 that his Bronze Polar Medal was finally awarded. The irony was that Tim only qualified for a Bronze medal because, under the rules, he had managed only one journey. To merit a Silver medal, like Mortimer, it was necessary to have made more than one voyage. In the event, Tim McCarthy's Bronze Polar Medal was collected in 1920 by his brother, the silver medal holder Mortimer.

Tim McCarthy was a well-liked and much-respected man who drew the warmest of tributes from those who served along him. Appropriately, it was Frank Worsley, another much-admired seafarer, who wrote the most sincere epitaph to his fellow seaman. Writing more than twenty years after Tim's death, Worsley remembered one of the last occasions he had seen Tim McCarthy alive. He wrote: 'How sad we should have been at parting with simple honest Tim McCarthy, had we known we should only see him once again for two days. He went down in the war, fighting his gun to the last – three short weeks after landing in England. A big brave, smiling, golden-hearted Merchant Service Jack – we, his shipmates who truly learned his worth in that boat journey, are proud of his memory.

'I always felt that, no matter where we were or what exalted company we might have been in, if Timothy McCarthy passed by he must be welcomed to a place of honour and given the best of everything, as befitted a brave man and one of nature's gentlemen.'[9]

Mortimer McCarthy's appetite for adventure was not diminished by events on *Terra Nova* and in April 1914, less than a year after returning from the Antarctic, he volunteered to join a new expedition to the Arctic. It was under the leadership of Lt Campbell, another veteran from the *Terra Nova* expedition, who was working for the Northern Exploration Company. Campbell's orders were to take the *William Barents* to Spitsbergen in the Svalbard Archipelago, more than 800 miles (1,200 km) above the Arctic Circle, to investigate potential mining claims for the company.

By 1914 the area was the centre of a minor Klondike-style rush to exploit the potential of coal, marble, iron and other deposits, though few ventures ever succeeded in making money. Companies like NEC annexed promising plots of land and posted threatening notices in three languages to deter claim jumpers. But transporting men and equipment to Svalbard was slow, difficult and very costly, while it was only possible to work for short periods of the year because of the poor weather. The dreams of making a quick killing high above the Arctic Circle soon faded and Svalbard today contains many abandoned rusting items of equipment left behind by the disappointed prospectors. However, there may have been other motives for the NEC expedition in 1914. Some believe it was a smokescreen for spying on German activities in the area.

The Svalbard Archipelago had emerged as an important weather monitoring station for shipping and in 1910 Germany established a meteorological station in the area. By 1914, with Europe edging inexorably toward war, Winston Churchill, the First Lord of the Admiralty, acted to bolster British presence on the islands and monitor German operations. At Churchill's insistence, men from the NEC are thought to have compiled bits of intelligence on German activities whilst operating under the camouflage of mineral prospecting.[10]

William Barents, with a crew of eleven seamen and five geologists, sailed from the Norwegian port of Tromso on 24 May 1914, less than three months before the outbreak of war. It was not long before Mortimer and his companions ran into the German operatives. Some weeks after landing, Mortimer and two other men were cut off from the ship by a blizzard and became lost while trying to find a route over the hills. Walking along in poor visibility, the men were relieved to come across an encampment. But relief evaporated when they discovered it was a German camp. After a few difficult moments, Mortimer and his two colleagues were informed that Britain and Germany were now at war. To embellish the story, the Germans claimed that the British naval fleet had been sunk in a major battle and that Kaiser Wilhelm's armies had invaded the north of England.

Fortunately, the German squad did not detain McCarthy and his companions and they were left to find their own way back to *William Barents*. On arrival it was discovered that at least one crucial element of the German story was perfectly true – Britain had declared war on 4 August 1914 – but the invasion was a piece of fiction. Campbell made contact with Britain and was told to carry on with the assignment, another indication perhaps that the expedition was not sent north purely to search for new mining riches. But the crew were reluctant to remain on Svalbard on the outbreak of war and most quickly made their way home to enlist.[11]

McCarthy was among those who joined the war effort in its very early days, enlisting in the Royal Navy Reserve on 1 September. Based at Devonport, Plymouth, Leading Seaman Mortimer McCarthy served for five years and was among the 30,000 officers and men, mostly merchant seafarers and former Royal Navy personnel, who volunteered for war duty with the RNR. He survived four years of war at sea, but in common with so many men, rarely spoke of his exploits at the end of the fighting. When asked, he shrugged off four years in the RNR as 'nothing much'.

By 1919, Mortimer was serving on *Ayrshire*, one of the many merchant ships mobilised to bring thousands of troops back from the front. Several voyages took him to Australia and New Zealand and sometime in the early 1920s, Mortimer decided to settle in New Zealand. Appropriately, he chose to live in the port of Lyttelton, the traditional gateway to the Antarctic. At Lyttelton he was always known as Jack.

After thirty years at sea, he began to put down roots. In 1923, at the age of forty-one, Mortimer 'Jack' McCarthy married Nellie Coughlan, the 29-year-old daughter of a fish merchant from Ballymackean on the Old Head of Kinsale. The couple were married on 13 February at the magnificent Cathedral of Blessed Sacrament in Christchurch – it resembles St Paul's Cathedral in London – and remained together for the rest of their lives.

'Jack' and Nellie McCarthy lived in Canterbury Street, Lyttelton, a few minutes walk from their harbour. The first child, John, was born in 1924 and in 1927 they had another son, Brian, followed by Gerard in 1932. The three boys were raised on vivid tales of the sea and action-packed adventures in the Antarctic, sprinkled with Jack and Nellie's

Wedding photograph of Mortimer McCarthy and 27-year-old Nellie Coughlan from the Old Head of Kinsale, County Cork. The couple were married in Christchurch, New Zealand, in 1923 and later settled in the nearby port of Lyttelton. They were married for twenty-eight years and raised three children. McCARTHY FAMILY

Mortimer McCarthy's official Identity and Service Certificate in 1919, which was stamped in Kinsale, County Cork. Although Mortimer gave his year of birth as 1878, he was actually born four years later in 1882.
MCCARTHY FAMILY

nostalgic recollections of Kinsale. Jack always retained his soft Irish accent and never forgot his Irish heritage, making several return trips to Kinsale with his family. He was remembered as a courteous, gentlemanly character with sparkling eyes, a 'peaches and cream' complexion and a trademark handlebar moustache.[12] Sadly, the happy marriage was cut short in February 1951 when Nellie died suddenly. She was only fifty-seven and passed away a few days after the couple celebrated their twenty-eighth wedding anniversary.

Mortimer 'Jack' McCarthy continued to work on ships, even as he advanced into his sixties. Any talk of retirement was breezily dismissed. 'The sea is born in me,' he once told a journalist. Mortimer did not let the simple matter of his advancing years stand in the way of a resolute determination to remain at sea. He merrily lied about his age and the exaggerations became wilder the older he became. He signed on for one voyage in 1941 claiming to be fifty years old when he was fifty-nine and in 1961, when he was aged seventy-nine, Mortimer claimed that he was a mere fifty-five years old.

He served for many years with the Union Steam Ship Company, New Zealand's leading shipping line, including lengthy service on the *Rangatira* and *Wahine*, the 'Steamer Express' ships linking the cities of Lyttelton and Wellington across the Cook Strait.

Mortimer particularly enjoyed his time on the 'Express' boats which usually returned to Lyttelton at the weekends, allowing him to attend Sunday Mass at St Joseph's church.

According to friends, he would take his 'second mass' in the bar of the Royal Hotel on the quay where he was centre of attention, drinking whisky and entertaining friends and customers with a never-ending flow of tall tales from a life at sea. When asked why he had chosen the adventurous life, Mortimer would invariably break into a smile and say: 'To find new lands for the men and blue fox fur for the ladies.'

With a twinkle in his eye, Mortimer would cheerfully 'stretch the long bow' with his flamboyant yarns and exaggerated anecdotes. He gladly revealed being shipwrecked three times and once told a newspaper reporter how killer whales in the Antarctic had eaten one of Scott's ponies in a single mouthful. 'No one believes how big those whales were,' he announced with a broad grin. 'But I saw ponies, wearing snowshoes, swallowed whole!'[13]

At times he was joined at the bar by Bill Burton and Bill McDonald, two old shipmates from *Terra Nova* who also lived in Lyttelton and were always eager to share memories and spin their own yarns. Local historians, with an eye on posterity, once tried to record their florid stories on tape. But once the tape recorder was switched on the old sea dogs clammed up and no one could prise a word out of them.[14]

Mortimer regularly worked at sea up to the late 1950s, when he was well into his seventies. He served as an ordinary deckhand on such vessels as the *Port Waikato* and *Holmlea* and was reputedly New Zealand's oldest serving seaman. Even a fall, which resulted in a fractured skull, did not hurry McCarthy into retirement. In the early 1960s, with his sea-going days behind him, Mortimer took a job as night-watchman on vessels moored in Lyttelton Harbour, a short walk from home. He was around eighty years old and had been at sea for close to seventy years.

However, there was time for one last great adventure for the old salt. In 1962, Mortimer was invited to make a nostalgic return to the Antarctic. An injury had prevented him accepting an earlier invitation but he now leapt at the opportunity. The unexpected chance to go back to the ice came from the US Navy, who invited Mortimer, Bill Burton and Bill McDonald to sail on the freighter *Arneb*, which was taking supplies and equipment down to McMurdo Sound for Operation Deep Freeze, the large Antarctic scientific research programme. The three sprightly pensioners had a combined age of 223 years and Mortimer, at eighty, was the oldest man ever to set foot on the Antarctic continent.

The voyage was filled with many poignant moments and touching memories for the three veterans, who were among the handful of men still alive from the Heroic Age of Antarctic Exploration. Shortly before departure, McCarthy, Burton and McDonald gathered on the same quayside at Lyttelton from which *Terra Nova* had sailed fifty-two years earlier and chatted with well-wishers. Among those paying special attention was Peter Scott, the only son of Captain Scott, who was little more than a year old when *Terra Nova* left Lyttelton and who never knew his father.

Memories. (L–r): Mortimer McCarthy, Bill McDonald and Bill Burton reminiscing in Scott's expedition hut at Cape Evans on 19 February 1963. MCCARTHY FAMILY

(L–r): Mortimer McCarthy, Bill Burton and Bill McDonald examining a lamp at Cape Evans. Burton, a stoker on *Terra Nova*, was the longest-surviving member of the expedition. He died in 1988 at the age of ninety-nine. MCCARTHY FAMILY

Above: Descendants. The families of the Antarctic's most notable explorers came together at Kinsale in County Cork in 2000 to unveil a bust of Tim and Mortimer McCarthy. (L–r): Jonathan Shackleton, a cousin of Sir Ernest Shackleton; Gerard McCarthy, son of Mortimer McCarthy; Falcon Scott, grandson of Robert Scott; and Andrew McCarthy, grandson of Mortimer McCarthy.
McCARTHY FAMILY

Left: The memorial to Mortimer and Timothy McCarthy overlooking the sea in their native port of Kinsale, County Cork.
MICHAEL SMITH

Another link with the past emerged when Fred Parsons, another old hand from *Terra Nova*, wrote from England expressing his delight at Mortimer's planned trip on the *Arneb* to the 'old hunting ground' in McMurdo Sound. 'How often have I dreamed of such a ship and how I would like to meet some of the friends in Lyttelton that I knew then,' a wistful 84-year-old Parsons wrote. 'You lucky people.'[15]

Arneb, an armed 14,000-ton freighter, had much in common with her three well-seasoned guests. *Arneb* was among the longest-serving vessels in her class and had survived several potentially fatal encounters with the ice – a collision in 1957 resulted in a 12 ft (4 m) long gash in the hull – before being assigned to carry scientists and supplies to the Operation Deep Freeze station in McMurdo Sound.

The men from *Terra Nova* were eventually taken back to Cape Evans on 19 February 1963, where they sat in the atmospheric hut reminiscing about the old days, thumbing through yellowing newspapers and examining long-forgotten, touching relics of the expedition. It was a shade over fifty years to the day that *Terra Nova*, carrying the first news of the Scott disaster, sailed from McMurdo Sound for the last time.

McCarthy returned to New Zealand where other recognition soon followed. He was elected a life member of the New Zealand Antarctic Society and in 1964 Mount McCarthy, a 9,400 ft (2,865 m) peak in the Barker Range of Victoria Land, was named in his honour.

Mortimer 'Jack' McCarthy's long and eventful life ended tragically in August 1967. Feeling a chill in his old bones at night, Mortimer often switched on an electric heater to warm up his bedroom in Canterbury Street. During the night of 4 August, Mortimer tripped over the electric cord and was knocked unconscious. The upturned heater started a fire and the room was quickly filled with suffocating smoke. Mortimer never regained consciousness. He died of smoke inhalation and close inspection showed there was not a single burn or mark on his body. He was eighty-five years old and one of the last and most engaging survivors of the Heroic Age of Antarctic Exploration.

The McCarthy brothers were reunited in 2000 when memorial busts of the two men were unveiled in the port of Kinsale, County Cork. Among those present were descendants of the McCarthys and the men who served alongside the brothers in the Antarctic, plus representatives of Ireland's current generation of adventurers who came to pay tribute. In a fitting ceremony linking the past with the present, Mortimer McCarthy's son Gerard and grandson Andrew stood alongside Tom Crean's daughter, Scott's grandson and a cousin of Shackleton. Standing in the town's park, the statues are close to the shore and provide a clear view of the harbour and waterways the two men knew so well.

CARRYING THE TORCH

Ireland at the Pole. The all-Irish expedition celebrates reaching the South Pole on 8 January 2008. (L–r): Pat Falvey, Jonathon Bradshaw, Shaun Menzies and Clare O'Leary. PAT FALVEY

THREE GENERATIONS would pass before Ireland once more left distinctive footprints on the Antarctic ice. By the mid-1990s, seventy-five years after the Heroic Age of Exploration came to an end, there was a growing realisation that Irish explorers were significant figures in the great story of Antarctic discovery. Yet while the outstanding achievements of the early explorers were kept alive by a few enthusiasts and descendants of the men, there was little recognition among the general public, and most characters, with the exception of Shackleton, were peripheral figures in the grand sweep of Irish history.

Timing was against the older generation of explorers. The Heroic Age of Antarctic Exploration, in which Irishmen were influential characters, ended at the precise moment Irish independence was gained. Shackleton's death in January 1922, which signalled the end of the Heroic Age of Exploration, occurred two days before Dáil Éireann approved the Anglo-Irish Treaty and there were far more pressing matters than Antarctica for Ireland in the years immediately after independence.

Bransfield and Crozier, who had paved the way for the Heroic Age, were long forgotten, Shackleton was dead and the Irish survivors of the era were unable to speak openly about their exploits in the highly charged years after independence. Every voyage of exploration to the Antarctic, from Bransfield to Shackleton, was made under British rule and Ireland was in no mood to celebrate anything British.

Antarctica, in more ways than one, was very remote from Ireland in the 1920s and beyond. Almost all trace of Ireland's link with the Antarctic past began to fade in the following decades. Little was heard of Bransfield or Crozier, men like Crean and Forde lived and died in obscurity and even Shackleton, once the most acclaimed living explorer, drifted into the margins of awareness.

Appropriately, the first major reawakening of interest in Ireland's Antarctic legacy came from the ranks of the country's modern-day adventurers, the leading climbers and seafarers. These were the men and women whose appetite for adventure and pushing themselves to the limit in the most extreme conditions and terrain was a direct link with the feats of the early explorers. These are people who choose to confront their own limits and, more than anyone, know what special qualities it took to navigate the Southern Ocean or man-haul sledges across the Antarctic ice. To the modern generation of adventurers there was no more fitting way to commemorate the remarkable feats of the pioneers than to retrace the steps of the men who first went to the Antarctic.

The first notable attempt to link present-day adventurers with great Irish figures from Antarctic history came in 1996 when a group of experienced climbers and sailors from across Ireland put together the South Arís Expedition with the intention of replicating the momentous voyage of the *James Caird* and the overland crossing of South Georgia in 1916.

South Arís (South Again) was the first occasion that an all-Irish expedition had been assembled for the purpose of recreating an Antarctic voyage and the main purpose was to commemorate the role in the expedition played by the three Irishmen: Ernest Shackleton, Tom Crean and Tim McCarthy. But South Arís provided full confirmation that, while the equipment and support facilities are far superior in the modern day, the severity of Antarctic conditions and the immense physical challenges have not changed since men first went to the ice.

Sceptics argued that present-day extreme adventurers enjoyed considerable advantages over their predecessors and that comparing today's voyages with those of the early expeditions was scarcely credible. Advances in technology like Global Positioning Systems (GPS) satellite navigation and radio communications have changed the face of Polar travel, while the basic rations, specialised clothing and other up-to-date equipment are far superior to anything available to the men who first battled Southern Ocean storms in an open boat without waterproofs or who trekked across the ice in little more than fur boots, two pairs of trousers and an extra woolly jumper.

Another more welcome development is that modern-day travel to extreme climates is significantly safer than it was in the past, though sadly accidents still occur. Two men died on Scott's *Discovery* expedition, a further five perished on *Terra Nova* and three died on Shackleton's Imperial Trans-Antarctic Expedition. By contrast, no one has died on modern-day voyages to replicate the early expeditions, despite the risks.

A further benefit is that today's Antarctic journeys are invariably far shorter and travellers do not have to face the arduous return journey because a welcoming aircraft is revving up at the South Pole to carry them back to civilisation within hours of their arrival. An emergency airlift can also be summoned if necessary to evacuate an injured person off the ice. Today's travellers also possess the invaluable ability to study the terrain ahead in minute detail or download accurate and up-to-date weather forecasts before embarking on any journey – a luxury not available to those who first penetrated the Antarctic pack ice in sailing ships or crossed the Ross Ice Shelf in 100 °F of frost.

However, GPS or the latest windproof clothing count for nothing when pulling a 200 lb (90 kg) sledge in sub-zero temperatures and 30 mph winds or battling a hurricane in the Southern Ocean. To emphasise the point, each of today's crop of travellers to the Antarctic has returned home with an even deeper respect and admiration for the men who went before; discussing the technological advances seemed to miss the point. 'My estimation of these men went up one thousand per cent when I saw conditions first hand,' a recent traveller admitted.

The first step on the South Arís Expedition was to construct a replica of *James Caird*, the 22 ft (7 m) whaleboat which Shackleton, Crean and McCarthy – and three companions – sailed from Elephant Island to South Georgia. The boat was built by craftsmen at Tullaroan in Kilkenny and named *Tom Crean* after the quintessential unsung Irish hero.

Tom Crean during sea trials on Killary Lough in the west of Ireland in 1996 prior to the South Arís expedition.
JARLATH CUNNANE

The five-man crew of *Tom Crean* were: Paddy Barry, an experienced sailor from Cork; Jarlath Cunnane, a distinguished seaman from Mayo who built and fitted out the vessel; Jamie Young, a highly proficient canoeist and yachtsman from Cullyback, Antrim; Mike Barry, an accomplished Alpine and Himalayan climber from Kerry; and Frank Nugent, a leading climber from Dublin, who was deputy leader of the first successful Irish expedition to scale Mount Everest.

The 800-mile (1,200-km) journey of the *Tom Crean* began in mid-January 1997 at Cape Valentine on Elephant Island, the site where Shackleton's *Endurance* party had made their first landfall in April 1916 after more than a year drifting on an ice floe in the Weddell Sea. Thankfully the Southern Ocean was in relatively friendly mood at the start and the small craft coped well with 30 mph (48 kph) winds and lumpy seas, initially making about 75 miles (115 km) a day. Although wet and struggling to snatch proper rest, the five men were in good spirits and optimistic enough to make bets with one another on how long the voyage would take.

But the unpredictable Antarctic weather soon changed dramatically and after only a few days, a deep depression struck the area, with winds screeching to storm force 10.

The little boat reeled under the power of sustained wind speeds of 60 mph (100 kph) and gusts touching 70 mph (110 kph). Cunnane, a vastly experienced sailor, admitted: 'There is no doubt in my mind that the weather we encountered was the worst I or any of the crew ever encountered.'

There was no respite and in the space of a few hours, the *Tom Crean* capsized and rolled over three times. Water poured into the vessel and the men were thrown around in the raging seas. Only by a stroke of good fortune were they inside the tiny cabin when the boat capsized. The bulky frame of Cunnane was wedged into the entrance of the narrow living quarters and Mike Barry, who was asleep when the boat rolled over the first time, woke to find himself under water. He remembered: 'My first thought was "fuck this"! But then she popped up.' Paddy Barry, a master of understatement, estimated that the boat had capsized to 170° while his bemused companions wondered who had measured the other 10°.

Cunnane, a veteran of the sea, feared the worst. 'As *Tom Crean* lay upside down, I thought this was the end,' he recalled. 'We were lost without trace in the icy green sea, below us lay nearly 5,000 ft [1,500 m] of Antarctic sea and to my mind we were descending rapidly to the bottom.'[1] Fortunately, Cunnane had designed *Tom Crean* to be self-righting and the small craft suddenly flipped back upright. A volley of loud cheers could be heard above the roar of the seas as the shaken men disentangled themselves from the jumble of broken glass, wet bedding and assorted gear.

But there was no time to celebrate. Anxious colleagues on the support vessel, *Pelagic*, radioed even more disturbing news for *Tom Crean*. According to the latest forecasts, at least three further depressions were queuing up behind the storm and ready to hit the area in the coming days. 'It looks as though we will be hit by successive gales for the whole of next week,' the *Pelagic*'s log recorded. 'More strong winds and fierce seas are expected.'

In the darkness and heavy seas, *Pelagic* frequently lost sight of *Tom Crean* and the small vessel was even invisible on radar amidst the host of white dots that filled the screen from countless icebergs in the area. But, in a scene strongly reminiscent of Crean's cheerful reappearance in the *Stancomb Wills* in the same waters eighty years earlier, dawn broke with the reassuring sight of the boat emerging from the twilight and leaden seas.

Tom Crean's sea anchor had been ripped apart in the tumult and the vessel, lying broadside to the seas, was now at the mercy of the heavy breaking waves and the threat of new storms approaching the area. That night, *Tom Crean* capsized on two more occasions and the crew faced an agonising decision over whether to continue the voyage. The five men on board took the unanimous decision that continuing was futile. Nugent explained: 'We went down three times and I consider that a fair warning. I don't think the decision to abandon was made because of fear, but came out of a realistic evaluation of our chance of survival.'

Tom Crean disappears among the heavy seas of the Southern Ocean during the South Arís expedition. The boat, a 22 ft (7 m) replica of the *James Caird*, rolled over three times in violent storms and had to be abandoned.
JARLATH CUNNANE

At 5 a.m. on 26 January 1997 the voyage of *Tom Crean*, which had lasted nine days and covered about 450 miles (720 km) towards South Georgia, was reluctantly abandoned. While the disappointment was acute, the men were magnanimous in defeat. To them, the severe difficulties encountered in the Southern Ocean once again underlined the extraordinary achievement of Shackleton, Crean, McCarthy and three others on *James Caird* in 1916.

In winds touching 30 mph (48 kph) all gear was carefully transferred to *Pelagic*. Cunnane, who had spent a year nurturing *Tom Crean* from cradle to grave, was the last to leave. He respectfully drilled several holes in the bottom of the craft – to ensure the abandoned vessel was no hazard to shipping – and clambered aboard *Pelagic* to watch the final moments of his creation. All hands watched in silence as the little boat was slowly carried away by the mountainous seas and disappeared. 'The moment I left *Tom Crean* was for me very sad and emotional,' Cunnane admitted. 'The boat might have survived but we could have perished.'

Pelagic duly completed the voyage to South Georgia where a plaque was left at King Haakon Bay in honour of the six men from the *James Caird* – Shackleton, Crean, McCarthy, Worsley, Vincent and McNish – who landed there after sailing from Elephant Island.

The next task was to drop off the four men who planned to follow in the footsteps of Shackleton, Crean and Worsley and cross the island's mountains and glaciers to the abandoned whaling port of Stromness. The quartet – Frank Nugent, Mike Barry, Jamie Young and Paddy Barry – made the traverse in forty-eight hours, about twelve hours

Ireland's South Arís Expedition left a plaque at King Haakon Bay on South Georgia in February 1997 to commemorate the open boat journey of Shackleton, Crean, McCarthy and three others in the *James Caird*. Pictured at the spot where the *Caird* landed in 1916 are: (back row, l–r) Mike Barry, Paddy Barry and Jarlath Cunnane; (front row, l–r) Mick O'Rourke, Frank Nugent, Jamie Young and John Bourke. JARLATH CUNNANE

longer than it had taken the badly nourished, ill-equipped trio to make the crossing in 1916. However, the South Arís team camped twice during the traverse, unlike Shackleton, Crean and Worsley, who did not carry a tent and made the crossing without proper rest. Nugent radioed news of their arrival to the *Pelagic* and concluded with the suitable tribute: 'We still stand in awe of the great achievement of Shackleton, Crean and Worsley in crossing South Georgia.'

The journey, despite the modern equipment and technology, was an ordeal for the men and *Pelagic*'s log reported that all four had suffered during the trek. 'They were all extremely footsore from the plastic double mountaineering boots which were overspec for the terrain they had to cover. [They had] weather beaten faces, hair dishevelled and clothing filthy and somewhat in tatters,' the log noted.

Mike Barry, the Kerryman who had survived the traumatic sinking of *Tom Crean* and crossed South Georgia, was among those whose admiration for the achievement of the Irish pioneers had increased during the South Arís expedition. It was Barry who, quietly and without fanfare, put together the most ambitious of all projects linking the past with the present: to finish what Shackleton and Crean had never managed and become the first Irishman to walk to the South Pole. To Mike Barry, the Pole was unfinished business for Ireland.

Barry, a fifty-year-old businessman from Tralee, approached the challenge of the South Pole with an impressive pedigree. He had extensive experience of climbing in the Alps, Andes and Himalayas and in 1993 was an important member of the team which helped place Ulsterman Dawson Stelfox on the summit of Mount Everest, the first Irishman to achieve the feat.

His plan was a simple go-it-alone affair and markedly different to the many current-day expeditions which rely on heavy sponsorship and media publicity to generate interest. Barry's expedition did not have a major sponsor and instead he teamed up with an informal group of four other travellers whose only connection was a shared objective to stand at the South Pole. The informality is in keeping with Barry's own character. He is a modest, quietly spoken individual who rarely chases the limelight and someone who draws inevitable comparisons with fellow Kerry explorer Tom Crean. Barry, like Crean, is a man who lets his deeds do the talking.

Mike Barry, the climber from Tralee, carries the tradition of Irish Polar exploration into the twenty-first century as he embarks on his historic 731-mile (1,170-km) journey to the South Pole in December 2003. MIKE BARRY

The party's guide was Matty McNair, the much-travelled Canadian adventurer who led the first all-female team to the North Pole in 1997. The group was completed by three English trekkers, Alex Blyth, Ray Middleton and Ian Morpeth. Few of the group had met before and aside from some modest sponsorship deals, each paid for the expedition out of their own pocket. To emphasise the informality of the undertaking, the group did not bother with the traditional custom of naming the expedition and there were no television cameras to record the trek for posterity.

The stepping-off point for the trek, which began in early December 2003, was Hercules Inlet on the south side of the Ronne Ice Shelf and the Pole was a march of 731 miles (1,170 km) to the south. The group made good time at the start, often pulling their sledges for between seven and nine hours a day on the long slog over the ice leading to the snow-capped Thiel Mountains and up to the Polar Plateau. Christmas was celebrated halfway to the Pole and the weather was unusually kind. Some days the party managed to cover 16 miles (25 km) and it was so mild one evening that dinner was eaten outside the comfort of the tents.

Barry, undemonstrative and quietly confident, welcomed the new year of 2004 with the simple wish of tucking into homemade brown bread made by his children. His philosophy about surviving the long trek was equally simple. He cheerfully reminded his four companions of the old chestnut that walking 731 miles (1,170 km) to the Pole was like eating an elephant – 'best done a small bite at a time'.

The imposing Thiel Mountains which bar the way to the South Pole for modern-day adventurers who start their journeys at Hercules Inlet.

However, conditions turned against the group as they climbed up the Thiel Mountains and on to the Polar Plateau, which is nearly 9,000 ft (2,800 m) above sea level. Temperatures dropped sharply and strong winds cut into the party. Altitude sickness plagued McNair and after six weeks on the march, the combination of white-out, soft snow and the biting cold left all five increasingly drained. Staying warm became the major priority and one brief radio communiqué summed up the change in conditions on the plateau: 'It's cold here,' said the caller. Barry suffered badly from blisters and at one stage was forced to remove his skis, which made the going across soft snow even tougher. But, as Blyth observed in a radio message: 'He's a tough nut.'

The daily slog was a straightforward mixture of skiing, eating and sleeping. Nothing else invaded the routine. The party marched in single file for periods of one and a half hours before taking a break and the monotony of the endless and unchanging gleaming

Present-day adventurers, who enjoy the benefits of advances in technology and superior equipment, are far better equipped than the first men to explore the Antarctic. But as Mike Barry (above) showed on his South Pole journey, modern technology does not help to pull the heavily laden sledge over the ice. MIKE BARRY

white plain of ice was broken only by a regular change of procession leader. Even the modest comfort of relieving the tedium by chatting with a fellow hiker was prevented by the wailing winds.

By 14 January Barry had passed the milestone of 88° 23' S, overtaking Shackleton's 1909 record and bringing him closer to the Pole than any Irishman had managed overland. McNair, sensing the occasion, radioed a message containing Shackleton's famous apologetic remark to his wife in 1909 after turning back with the South Pole only 97 geographic miles (179 km) away: 'Better a live donkey than a dead lion . . .'

A week later, in the early hours of 21 January 2004, Mike Barry became the first Irishman to reach the South Pole by foot. It had taken fifty-one days to fulfil his ambition and Barry was greeted by temperatures down to a bone-chilling –39 °F (–38°C). He had little time to savour his triumph. The group lingered at the Pole for less than twenty-four hours before a Twin Otter ski plane picked up the tired but happy party and flew them back to the Patriot Hills base station, close to Hercules Inlet. On arrival, Barry discovered that he had shed 1½ stone (9.5 kg) on the seven–week march.

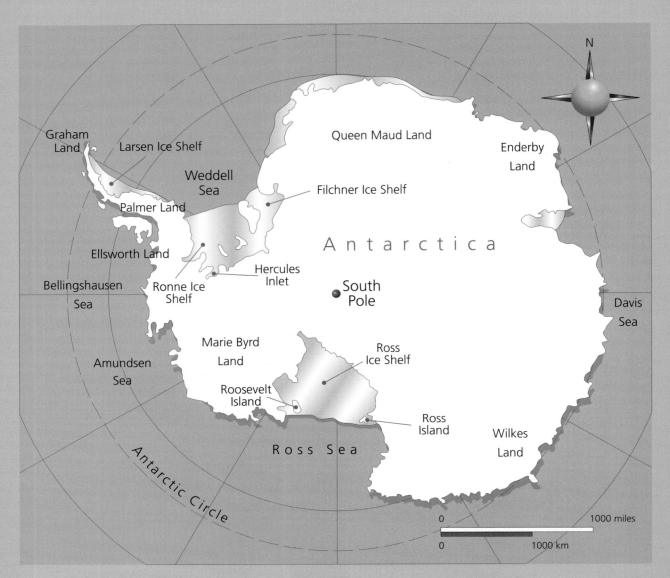

N

Graham
Land

Larsen Ice Shelf

Queen Maud Land

Enderby
Land

Weddell
Sea

Filchner Ice Shelf

Palmer Land

A n t a r c t i c a

Ellsworth Land

Hercules
Inlet

South
Pole

Bellingshausen
Sea

Ronne Ice
Shelf

Davis
Sea

Marie Byrd
Land

Ross
Ice Shelf

Amundsen
Sea

Roosevelt
Island

Ross
Island

Wilkes
Land

R o s s   S e a

Antarctic Circle

0   1000 miles

0   1000 km

Above: Hercules Inlet to the South Pole, the route taken by Mike
Barry when he became first Irishman to reach the Pole on foot.
This is now the standard overland route to the Pole for modern
adventurers, including the first all-Irish party to the Pole under
Pat Falvey.

Left: Mike Barry enjoys the questionable luxury of a quick wash
in sub-zero temperatures during a break on his way to the Pole.
MIKE BARRY

Pat Falvey, leader of the first all-Irish expedition to reach the South Pole. Falvey (left) is pictured with Broke Evans, the son of Lt Teddy Evans, whose life was saved by Tom Crean in 1912 in a remarkable feat of courage which inspired Falvey to launch his South Pole journey.
MICHAEL SMITH

Ireland did not have to wait very long before the first all-Irish expedition to the Pole was assembled. Within three years of Mike Barry's achievement, the Beyond Endurance expedition was under way. The driving force behind Beyond Endurance was fifty-year-old Pat Falvey, the hugely experienced and energetic mountaineer from the Gurranabraher suburb of Cork.

Falvey, a veteran of more than sixty expeditions, had a formidable track record and an unquenchable thirst for adventure after a tempestuous early life. A self-confessed workaholic, he left school at fifteen and had made and lost a fortune by the age of twenty-nine. Broke, depressed and hospitalised by panic attacks and chest pains, Falvey somehow turned his energies to climbing. He twice conquered Mount Everest, scaled the Seven Summits – the highest peaks in Africa, Antarctica, Asia, Australasia, Europe and North and South America – and emerged as one of the world's most experienced expedition leaders.

Falvey was ably supported by Clare O'Leary, a 35-year-old doctor from Bandon, Cork, with a passion for outdoor adventure, who is among the leading women climbers in the world. O'Leary ventured on to the ice for the first time only in 2001 and by 2004 had become the first Irishwoman to climb Everest. She achieved the remarkable feat of scaling the Seven Summits by the end of 2005 and only a few months before embarking on the South Pole journey, Falvey and O'Leary made the first crossing of Greenland's ice caps – a trek of 350 miles (560 km) – by an all-Irish party.

The South Pole team was completed by two Dubliners, Shaun Menzies, a 42-year-old IT consultant from Dublin, and Jonathon Bradshaw, a 35-year-old who, with a dash of old-fashioned romanticism, quit his job in the computer industry and turned to the Polar regions in search of a more adventurous life. One of Bradshaw's earliest ambitions was an audacious scheme to cycle across Greenland, which the authorities rejected as needlessly reckless. Instead he was urged to join an expedition skiing across the country, where he bumped into Falvey and O'Leary, who were training for the journey to the Pole. Working

Clare O'Leary, the doctor from Bandon, County Cork, who was the first Irishwoman to reach the South Pole on foot. O'Leary is one of the world's most accomplished female climbers who has also trekked to the North Pole and is among the small band of women to have scaled the Seven Summits.
PAT FALVEY

alongside them was Menzies, who had impressed Falvey on an earlier expedition to the mountains and glaciers of South Georgia and was selected for the Polar party.

Rigorous training was vital to Falvey's project, in stark contrast to the earlier generation of Antarctic explorers who did very little physical training before venturing forth on to the ice. Although men like Crean, Keohane and Shackleton were undoubtedly hardened to the conditions in Antarctica, the typical routine was to spend the long winter months before the main journeys confined in pokey base camp huts. They rarely ventured outside for very long and much of their time was spent on undemanding tasks like making sleeping bags, tending the animals or building sledges.

Falvey and O'Leary, by contrast, trained for almost three years before leaving for the Pole, including climbing mountains, spending weeks on cross-country skiing sorties in Norway and finally rounding off the preparations with a five-week traverse of Greenland. While the climate was warmer in Ireland, the training was no less rigorous and Falvey and O'Leary could be seen on practice runs through Killarney National Park dragging a tractor tyre behind them. Another major difference from the early expeditions was the reassuring presence of state-of-the-art back-up and communication facilities in Kerry under the watchful eye of expedition co-ordinator Niall Foley – the expedition's fifth member. Apart from organising much of the expedition's preparations, Foley was the vital link with the outside world during the trek and the conduit for the daily updates on the group's progress, which is an essential aspect of modern-day expeditions.

The Polar trek began from Hercules Inlet in mid-November 2007 and, in O'Leary's own words, they were 'hammered with bad weather' from the very start. Temperatures nudged -20 °F (-29 °C) in white-out conditions, but the severe wind chill made it feel significantly colder. Temperatures were soon down to -30 °F (-35 °C) and stiff winds sliced into them. The training regime could only partly prepare the marchers for the rigours of the daily slog. Each sledge weighed around 200 lb (90 kg). For O'Leary, who weighed a shade under 8 stone (50 kg), this was almost twice her body weight.

The target was to haul in single file for around seven hours a day, broken down into segments of seventy minutes' marching and a break of ten minutes, with the aim of covering about 15 miles (24 km) a day. Most of the team suffered blisters and other minor ailments from the start and Falvey soon discovered that his thumb was frostbitten, a serious setback so early in the trek. At worst, he feared he might lose at least the tip but, helped by the attention of Dr O'Leary, the injury stabilised and the thumb was saved. Menzies and Bradshaw added to the sick list by developing painful tendonitis in their Achilles tendons, which Bradshaw said was like having a drawing pin stuck under his heel.

Despite the setbacks, the party made reasonable progress and were ahead of schedule, frequently notching up 17 miles (28 km) a day. But the weather worsened as the group approached the Thiel Mountains and stretches of soft snow and troublesome white-out soon slowed progress. After a promising start, the group gradually fell behind schedule. Frustration began to nibble at morale as they dropped about 4 miles (6 km) a day behind schedule. In a radio message on 17 December, Falvey gloomily reported: 'We have really had a miserable ten days of white-out, no contrast, soft snow and pushing our resolve to the limits of our endurance. We know it just can't continue or it will burn us.'

Three days later, about thirty days into the trek, disaster struck when Falvey collapsed in pain. Lying prostrate in the snow 250 miles (400 km) short of the Pole, Falvey's ambitions were in tatters and the expedition in jeopardy. The drama began as Falvey stepped aside to take some video footage of his three companions. He felt a sudden shooting pain in his back and collapsed in agony, struck by a trapped or twisted nerve. To his alarm, he quickly realised that O'Leary, Menzies and Bradshaw were completely unaware of the crisis and purposefully trudging ahead in blissful ignorance. Falvey's frantic shouts for help were drowned out by the howling winds and in poor visibility it was only a matter of minutes before they would disappear from sight.

Falvey summoned all his strength to struggle to his feet and drag himself along. He repeatedly collapsed in pain. Fortunately, O'Leary stopped the march after a short distance to check their bearing and turned to see the plainly suffering Falvey staggering towards them in the hazy gloom. She quickly administered an anti-inflammatory shot and effectively took command. After a brief attempt to continue, she called a halt to the day's march after just 2 miles (3 km). 'I don't think hauling a 90 kg (200 lb) sled is part of the treatment for any kind of back pain,' O'Leary cheerfully reported back to base.

It was the pivotal moment of the expedition. Unless he recovered, Falvey would have to be evacuated off the ice, leaving O'Leary, Menzies and Bradshaw to continue without the expedition leader. Next morning his load was redistributed between O'Leary, Menzies and Bradshaw and he struggled along as best as he could manage, often wincing in agony. 'It would register 7 out of 10 on the pain scale,' he announced. The extra loads forced the party to reduce the daily schedule. The group, with Falvey hobbling alongside, would be fortunate to achieve 12 miles (20 km) a day. Plans for a well-earned rest and modest feast to celebrate Christmas Day were abandoned, while in Kerry, Foley sent a flurry of festive greetings in an attempt to bolster morale.

Pulling the extra weight was punishing and the expedition, growing increasingly fatigued, was at its lowest point. Menzies closed one day's hard labour by reporting: 'I'm shattered, absolutely shattered. The last eight days have been without doubt the toughest so far.' O'Leary, Menzies and Bradshaw would struggle to drag the extra weight all the way to the Pole and for the first time they discussed evacuating Falvey off the ice.

The crisis was made worse by the discovery that Bradshaw was feeling the effects of an old rib injury and Menzies had developed serious problems with one of his feet. The skin on the sole of his left foot was detached and the surplus flesh was bunched up around his heel. At the end of one painfully hard day, Menzies sat on his sledge and broke down in tears. Only O'Leary, the smallest of the quartet, remained reasonably fit, though the exhaustion of pulling more than twice her body weight was starting to tell. 'I don't know how she does it,' Bradshaw said. 'She is incredibly strong.'

Fortunately, Falvey's back pain began to ease a little and, drawing on his inner reserves, he managed to ease the burden on his companions by pulling a half-laden sledge. 'His recovery has been staggering,' Menzies reported. 'These are the toughest people I have ever met.' But as the group approached Shackleton's 'furthest south' temperatures plunged to almost -40 °F (-40 °C).

Although the pain was often excruciating, Falvey was determined to resume full-time duties and there was huge relief when he was finally able to drag his own load. His companions had been stretched near to the limit and Menzies welcomed Falvey's recovery by admitting: '. . . we were not sure how long we could keep going.' The new year of 2008 arrived with all four clearly drained by weeks on the march; altitude sickness, which caused nagging headaches and shortness of breath, added to the problems as the group advanced. With the Pole only around 60 miles (100 km) away, Falvey reported: 'Our energy is low, but our enthusiasm is high.'

The trek south had been hard won. Bradshaw noted that all four had lost considerable weight and now resembled 'zombies or skeletons' shuffling along on autopilot. It needed nine hours of hard slog to meet the restored daily target of 15 miles (23 km), which they had managed to make in seven or eight hours at the outset. Bradshaw's amusing assessment of his companions was: 'Pat [Falvey], previously a robust gentleman, looks like a malnourished

(L–r): Jonathon Bradshaw, Shaun Menzies and Clare O'Leary, members of the first all-Irish team on their way to the Pole in 2008. PAT FALVEY

teenager, Shaun [Menzies] a lanky beanpole with gaunt deep-set eyes. Clare [O'Leary], well, I can only see her when she is facing me – if she turns to the side she disappears.'

The gruelling 731-mile (1,170-km) journey of the first all-Irish party to the South Pole came to a welcome end on 8 January 2008. It had taken fifty-eight days, only a few days longer than scheduled.

Falvey, a burly 16 stone (100 kg) at the start, had lost 3½ stone (22 kg) – more than twice the weight loss anyone expected. O'Leary said the feeling of standing at the Pole was a mixture of relief and pride. 'It was an honour to be part of the first Irish team to achieve the Pole,' she said.

An outstanding feat of a slightly different kind was achieved in early 2009 when another Irishman, 32-year-old Mark Pollock, crossed the ice of Antarctica on foot and reached the South Pole. The distinction was that Pollock is blind. His story is the stuff of legend and would hardly be out of place in the tales of early Antarctic exploration. He hails from Hollywood, the small town on the shores of Belfast Lough, and was a natural athlete with a promising future in spite of being blind in his right eye since the age of five.

On the march. Mark Pollock, the blind adventurer, crossing Antarctica in sub-zero temperatures attached to rugby coach Simon O'Donnell by two carbon fibre poles. MARK POLLOCK

By twenty-two he was captain of the rowing club, picked to represent his country at the World Championships, and taking a business degree at Trinity College, Dublin. Suddenly, a detached retina in his left eye made him fully blind.

Pollock fought back and rebuilt his life, first by returning to the rowing boat and winning medals. More demanding and extreme endurance challenges followed, including six marathons in six days and the daunting North Pole and Everest marathons. In 2008, to mark the tenth anniversary of going blind, Pollock signed up to join a race to the South Pole. The Amundsen Omega 3 South Pole contest, which involved six teams, presented formidable problems to Pollock and his teammates, Simon O'Donnell and Inge Solheim. O'Donnell, a rugby coach from Dublin on his first voyage to a cold-weather environment, was attached to Pollock by two carbon fibre poles, and Solheim, a Norwegian survival specialist who had been to the North Pole seven times, provided the essential know-how on the ice.

After being dropped at around 83° S, some 500 miles (800 km) from the Pole, the teams started the race on 4 January 2009 and were greeted with ferociously cold weather.

Facing page: Mark Pollock, the first blind Irishman to walk to the South Pole. MARK POLLOCK

Triumph over adversity. Mark Pollock (right) stands at the South Pole with companions
Inge Solheim (left) and Simon O'Donnell (centre), on 26 January 2009.
SIMON O'DONNELL

Temperatures on the first day plunged to -25 °F (-32 °C) and within a few days the thermometer had sunk to a numbing -48 °F (-45 °C). The spirit of the race – and a very tight schedule to meet the aircraft pick-up from the Pole – called on the teams to travel at breakneck speed over the ice. Although helped by relatively light sledges of around 130 lb (60 kg), the tempo was remarkable and much faster than was possible for those on longer self-supporting marches with full loads of 90 kg (200 lb).

Pollock's team, which was called South Pole Flag, generally skied for at least thirteen hours and aimed to cover up to 21 miles (34 km) a day. At times, when the weather permitted, they skied for longer and the pace rocketed to nearly 30 miles (45 km) a day. The group quickly established a daily routine of ski, camp and snatches of sleep. The only prolonged break in the demanding routine was a compulsory 24-hour rest at the midway food supply depot. At night Pollock busied himself arranging matters inside the tent while the main burden of setting up the camp and unloading the sledges fell on the shoulders of O'Donnell and Solheim.

Both Pollock and O'Donnell adapted well to the potentially troublesome poles linking them together. Only as they neared the Pole did the attachment cause any difficulty. O'Donnell, in the lead, could see the outline of the American base at the Pole from many miles away and the adrenalin rush of reaching the end of the slog quickened his stride. Without seeing the goal in sight and not sharing the same adrenalin rush, a tired Pollock lagged a little and for the only time on the march slowed O'Donnell's pace.

The last leg of the journey was the most astonishing of all, despite the growing tiredness from the arduous daily grind and constant brushes with frostbite. The final 50 miles (80 km) to the Pole was covered in a hectic and exhausting non-stop trek of thirty-six hours without proper rest. Drained but elated, Pollock, O'Donnell and Solheim reached the South Pole on 26 January 2009 after a 500-mile (800-km) journey lasting twenty-two days. The winners had taken eighteen days, though the feat could never eclipse Pollock's unique achievement of being the first blind Irishman to reach the Pole.

There will be others. It is the very essence of explorers and travellers down through the ages that each new discovery or adventure merely feeds the appetite to find the next mountain, glacier or ocean and to stand where few humans have stood before. It is a process as old as discovery itself and no country has served the relentless quest with more courage and resolution than the admirable band of explorers from Ireland.

REFERENCES

1 EDWARD BRANSFIELD (1785–1852)

1. Sheila Bransfield's research is an important source of information on parts of Edward Bransfield's life: The Role of Edward Bransfield in the Discovery of Antarctica, Dissertation for University of Greenwich/Greenwich Maritime Institute.

2. R. J. Campbell, *The Discovery of the South Shetland Islands*, p. 198.

3. Sheila Bransfield.

4. Campbell, The *Discovery of the South Shetland Islands*, p. 131.

5. *Ibid.*, p. 132.

6. Midshipman Charles Poynter's original journal is kept at the Alexander Turnbull Library, National Library of New Zealand Te Puna Mátauranga o Aotearoa, Wellington, New Zealand.

7. Campbell, *The Discovery of the South Shetland Islands*, p. 202.

2 FRANCIS CROZIER (1795–C. 1848)

1. Roald Amundsen, *The South Pole*, p. 12.

2. M. J. Ross, *Ross in the Antarctic*, p. 206.

3. Michael Smith, *Francis Crozier – Last Man Standing*, p. 128.

4. Smith, p. 154.

5. Smith, p. 163.

3 ERNEST SHACKLETON (1874–1922)

1. Robert Scott, *The Voyage of the Discovery*, p. 501.

2. Ernest Shackleton, *The Heart of the Antarctic*, p. 205.

3. Shackleton, p. 209.

4. Shackleton, p. 210.

5. Hugh R. Mill, *The Life of Ernest Shackleton*, p. 145.

6. Shackleton, p. 215.

7. Beau Riffenburgh, *Nimrod*, p. 257.

8. Shackleton, p. 217.

9. Shackleton, p. 217.

10. Shackleton, p. 221.

11. Shackleton p. 222.

4 THOMAS CREAN (1877–1938)

1. British National Antarctic Expedition records, Royal Geographical Society.

2. BNAE records.

3. Robert Scott diary, October 1911.

4. Apsley Cherry-Garrard, *The Worst Journey in the World*, p. 196.

5. Tryggve Gran, *Kampen on Sydpolen*, p. 158; *The Norwegian With Scott*, p. 200.

6. Scott diary, 4 January 1912.

7. E. R. G. R. Evans, *South With Scott*, p. 240; *The Last Supporting Party*, (publication unknown).

8. Evans, p. 253.

9. Evans, p. 253.

10. Frank Hurley, *Argonauts of the South*, p. 264.

11. John Thomson, *Elephant Island and Beyond*, p. 196.

12. Frank Worsley, diary.

13. Tom P. Jones, *Patagonian Panorama*, p. 80.

14. Eileen and Mary Crean, interview with author.

5 PATRICK KEOHANE (1879–1950)

1. Robert Scott diary, 22 June 1911.

2. Herbert Ponting, *The Great White South*, p. 143.

3. Scott diary, 5 December 1911.

4. Scott diary, 14 December 1911.

5. Charles Wright, *Silas*, p. 221.

6. Patrick Keohane diary, 20 December 1911.

7. Scott diary, 22 December 1911.

8. Wright, p. 227.

9. Keohane diary, 13 January 1912.

10. Apsley Cherry-Garrard, *The Worst Journey in the World*, p. 483.

11. Patrick Keohane, field diary, 26 March 1912.

12. Scott diary, 29 March 1912.

13. Cherry-Garrard, pp. 483–84.

14. Keohane diary, 23 April 1912.

15. Edward Atkinson, *Scott's Last Expedition*, p. 316.

16. Atkinson, p. 396.

17. Cyril Hart, *Cornish Oasis*, p. 162.

18. Michael O'Brien, interview with author.

6 ROBERT FORDE (1875–1959)

1. Tryggve Gran, *The Norwegian With Scott*, p. 122.

2. *Ibid.*, p. 123.

3. E. R. G. R. Evans, *South With Scott*, pp. 154–5.

4. *Ibid.*, p. 157.

5. Gran, p. 126.

6. *Ibid.*, p. 126.

7. Robert Scott diary, 1 October 1911.

8. T. Griffith Taylor, *With Scott the Silver Lining*, p. 321.

9. Frank Debenham, *The Quiet Land*, p. 117.

10. *Ibid.*, p. 359.

7 MORTIMER McCARTHY (1882–1967) AND TIMOTHY McCARTHY (1888–1917)

1. Herbert Ponting, *Great White South*, p. 15.

2. Griffith Taylor, *With Scott the Silver Lining*, p. 431.

3. Taylor, p. 427.

4. Sir Ernest Shackleton, *South*, p. 197.

5. Frank Worsley, *Endurance*, p. 107.

6. Worsley, p. 145.

7. Shackleton, p.140.

8. Frank Worsley, *Shackleton's Boat Journey*, p. 138.

9. Worsley, p. 114.

10. Victor Campbell, *The Wicked Mate*, p. 13.

11. Mortimer McCarthy newspaper interview, 1960.

12. Baden Norris, personal recollection.

13. Mortimer McCarthy newspaper interview,1960.

14. Baden Norris, personal recollection.

15. Fred Parsons, letter to Mortimer McCarthy, 3 February 1963 (Canterbury Museum).

8 CARRYING THE TORCH

1. Jarlath Cunnane, interview with author.

BIBLIOGRAPHY

The following is a list of those books, magazines and other publications which have been helpful in compiling this book. It is not a comprehensive list and should be regarded as a personal selection.

BOOKS, MAGAZINES AND OTHER PUBLICATIONS

Aldridge, Don, *The Rescue of Captain Scott*, Tuckwell Press, 1999

Alexander, Caroline, *The Endurance*, Bloomsbury, 1998

Amundsen, Roald, *My Life As An Explorer*, Wm. Heinemann, 1927

Amundsen, Roald, *The South Pole*, Hurst & Co, 1976

Barrow, John, *Voyages of Discovery and Research Within the Arctic Regions*, John Murray, 1846

Barryroe Co-operative, *Patrick Keohane: Antarctic Explorer*, 2004

Barry, Dennis, *The Polar Crean*, Capuchin Journal, 1952

Bernacchi, Louis, *The Saga of The Discovery*, Blackie & Son, 1938

Burton, Robert & Stephen Venables, *Shackleton at South Georgia*, Robert Burton, 2001

Campbell, R. J. (ed), *The Discovery of the South Shetland Islands 1819–1820: The Journal of Midshipman C. W. Poynter*, Hakluyt Society, 2000

Campbell, Richard (ed), *The Voyage of HMS Erebus and HMS Terror to the Southern and Antarctic Regions. Captain James Clark Ross, R.N. 1839–1843. The Journal of Sergeant William K. Cunningham, R.M. of HMS Terror*, Hakluyt Society Journal, 2009

Cherry-Garrard, Apsley, *The Worst Journey in the World*, Penguin 1983

Connolly, Terry, *McCarthy Brothers – The Final Chapter*, Kinsale Record, Vol. 10, 2000

Connolly, Terry, *Mortimer McCarthy*, Kinsale Record, Vol. 10, 2000

Connolly, Terry, *Timothy McCarthy – A Kinsale Hero at the Antarctic*, Kinsale Record, Vol. 9, 1999

Cunnane, Jarlath, *Northabout*, The Collins Press, 2006

Debenham, Frank, *Erebus and Terror at Hobart*, Polar Record, No 3, 1942

— Debenham, Frank, *The Quiet Land*, Bluntisham Books, 1992
Tom Crean: An Appreciation, Polar Record, 1939

Dunnett, Harding, *Shackleton's Boat: The Story of the James Caird*, Neville & Harding, 1996

Dwyer, R. T., *Tans, Terrors and Troubles: Kerry's Real Fighting Story*, Mercier, 2001

Evans, E. R. G. R. (Lord Mountevans), *Adventurous Life*, Hutchinson, 1946
— *South With Scott*, Collins, 1924
— *The Last Supporting Party* (publication unknown), 1913

Falvey, Pat *A Journey to Adventure*, The Collins Press, 2007
— *Reach For The Sky*, The Collins Press, 1997

Fiennes, Sir Ranulph, *Captain Scott*, Hodder & Stoughton, 2003

Fisher, Margery and James, *Shackleton*, Barrie, 1957

Fleming, Fergus, *Barrow's Boys*, Granta Books, 1998

Fluhmann, May, *Second in Command: A Biography of Captain Francis Crozier*, Government of Northwest Territories, 1976

Fuchs, Sir Vivian, *Of Ice and Men*, Anthony Nelson, 1982

Gran, Tryggve, *The Norwegian with Scott: Tryggve Gran's Antarctic Diary 1910–13*, HM Stationery Office, 1984

Gurney, Alan, *Below the Convergence*, Pimlico, 1998

Hart, Cyril, *Cornish Oasis: A Biographical Chronical of the Fishing Village of Coverack*, Lizard Press, 1990

Huntford, Roland, Scott & Amundsen, Hodder & Stoughton, 1979

Huntford, Roland, *Shackleton*, Hodder & Stoughton, 1985

Hurley, Frank, *Argonauts of the South*, G. P. Putnam, 1925

Hurley, Micheál, *Home from the Sea: The Story of the Courtmacsherry Lifeboat 1825–1995*, Micheál Hurley, 1995

Hussey, Leonard, *South With Shackleton*, Sampson Low, 1949

Huxley, Elspeth, *Scott of the Antarctic*, Weidenfeld & Nicolson, 1977

Johnson, Anthony, *Scott of the Antarctic and Cardiff*, University College Cardiff, Press, 1984

Jones, A. G. E., *Polar Portraits*, Caedmon of Whitby, 1992

Lambert, Andrew, *Franklin: Tragic Hero of Polar Exploration*, Faber & Faber, 2009

Lansing, Alfred, *Endurance*, Granada Publishing, 1984

Lashly, William, *Under Scott's Command: Lashly's Antarctic Diaries*, Gollancz 1969

Markham, Sir Clements, *Antarctic Obsession: A Personal Narrative of the Origins of the British National Antarctic Expedition 1901–04*, Bluntisham 1986

McClintock, Sir Leopold, *The Voyage of the 'Fox' in Arctic Seas*, John Murray, 1859

Mill, Hugh R., *The Life of Sir Ernest Shackleton*, Heinemann, 1923

Mills, Leif, *Men of Ice*, Caedmon of Whitby, 2008
— *Frank Wild*, Caedmon of Whitby, 1999

Morrell, Margot & Stephanie Capparell, *Shackleton's Way*, Viking, 2001

Murphy, David, *The Arctic Fox*, The Collins Press, 2004

Nugent, Frank, *Seek the Frozen Lands*, The Collins Press, 2003

Parry, Ann, *Parry of the Arctic*, Chatto & Windus, 1963

Ponting, Herbert, *The Great White South*, Duckworth & Co, 1921

Poulsom, Neville Wright, *The White Ribbon: Medallic Record of British Polar Exploration*, Seaby 1969

Pound, Reginald, *Evans of the Broke*, Oxford University Press, 1963

Rosove, Michael (ed.), *Rejoice My Heart*, Adelie Books, 2007

Ross, Sir James Clark, *A Voyage of Discovery and Research in the Southern Antarctic Regions During the Years 1839–43*, John Murray, 1848

Ross, M. J., *Ross in the Antarctic*, Caedmon of Whitby, 1982

Savours, Ann, *The Voyages of The Discovery*, Virgin Books, 1992

Scott, Robert, *Scott's Last Expedition: The Journals*, Smith, Elder & Co, 1913
— *The Diaries of Captain Robert Scott* (facsimile edition), University Microfilms, 1968
— *The Voyage of the Discovery*, Smith, Elder & Co, 1905

Shackleton, Sir Ernest, *The Heart of the Antarctic*, Heinemann, 1909
— *South*, Century, 1983

Shackleton, Jonathan & John MacKenna, *Shackleton: An Irish in Antarctica*, Lilliput Press, 2002

Smith, Michael, *An Unsung Hero – Tom Crean, Antarctic Survivor*, The Collins Press, 2000
— *Captain Francis Crozier – Last Man Standing?* The Collins Press, 2006
— *I Am, Just Going Outside – Captain Oates*, The Collins Press, 2002
— *Polar Crusader – Sir James Wordie*, Birlinn 2004
— *Tom Crean – An Illustrated Life*, The Collins Press, 2006
— *Tom Crean – Iceman*, The Collins Press, 2002
Solomon, Susan, *The Coldest March: Scott's Fatal Antarctic Expedition*, Yale University Press, 2001
Taylor, T. Griffith, *With Scott: The Silver Lining*, Smith, Elder & Co, 1916
Thomson, John, *Elephant Island and Beyond: The Life and Diaries of Thomas Orde Lees*, Bluntisham, 2003
Thomson, John, *Shackleton's Captain: A Biography of Frank Worsley*, Hazard Press, 1998
Tyler-Lewis, Kelly, *The Lost Men*, Bloomsbury, 2006
Wild, Frank, *Shackleton's Last Voyage*, Cassell & Co, 1923
Wilson, Edward, *Diary of Discovery Expedition to the Antarctic 1901–04*, Blandford Press, 1966
Wilson, Edward, *Diary of the 'Terra Nova' Expedition to the Antarctic 1910–12*, Blandford Press, 1972
Woodward, Frances J., *Portrait of Jane: A Life of Lady Franklin*, Hodder & Stoughton, 1951
Worsley, Frank, *Endurance*, Philip Allan, 1931
— *Shackleton's Boat Journey*, The Collins Press, 2002
Wright, Charles, *Silas: The Antarctic Diaries and Memoir of Charles S. Wright*, Ohio State University Press, 1993
Yelverton, David, *Antarctic Unveiled*, University Press of Colorado, 2000

FILMS

Tom Crean – Kerryman on the Ice, Crossing the Line Films, Ireland
Escape from Antarctica (South Arís Expedition), Crossing the Line Films, Ireland
90° South, Herbert Ponting, National Film & Television Archive, UK
South, Frank Hurley, National Film & Television Archive, UK

ARCHIVE SOURCES

Many original diaries, letters, official records, ships' logs, and other published and unpublished papers were consulted during the research for this book, including collections found at the following sources:

Admiralty Library, Ministry of Defence, London, UK
Antarctic Treaty Secretariat
Banbridge Library, UK
Bank of England, UK
British Library, UK
British Library, Newspaper Library, UK
Canterbury Museum, Christchurch, New Zealand
Dundee Heritage Trust, Dundee, UK

Kerry County Library, Tralee, Ireland

Kerry County Museum, Tralee, Ireland

Lyttelton Museum, Lyttelton, New Zealand

McManus Galleries, Dundee, UK

Ministry of Defence, UK

National Archive, London, UK

National Maritime Museum, London, UK

Plymouth Central Library, UK

Royal Astronomical Society, London, UK

Royal Geographical Society, London, UK

Royal Naval Museum, Portsmouth, UK

Scott Polar Research Institute, Cambridge, UK

Archives Office of Tasmania, Australia

Alexander Turnbull Library, Wellington, New Zealand

The Gilbert White/Oates Museum, Selborne, Hampshire, UK

A large number of unpublished diaries and other documents were consulted in preparation of this book, including:

Barne, Michael: *Discovery* diaries and reports 1901–04, Scott Polar Research Institute

Bradshaw, Jonathon: Blog written on Beyond Endurance expedition November 2007–January 2008

Bransfield, Edward: Antarctic Voyage 1819–20 and the Discovery of the Antarctic Continent, *Polar Record*, 4(32), 1947

Bransfield, Sheila: *The Role of Edward Bransfield in the Discovery of Antarctica*, Dissertation for University of Greenwich/Greenwich Maritime Institute, 2002

Crean, Thomas: Royal Navy service record; letters; Kerry County Library/ Scott Polar Research Institute

Crozier family: Early Crozier Memorials (published privately, *c.* 1830–1870)

Crozier, Francis: Letters, papers, Royal Geographical Society; National Archives; Public Records Office Northern Ireland; Scott Polar Research Institute

Evans, E. R. G. R. (Lord Mountevans): Royal Navy service record, National Archives, UK

Falvey, Pat: Blog written on Beyond Endurance expedition, November 2007–January 2008

Forde, Robert: Royal Navy service record, National Archive, UK

Hennessy, John: Research into life of Robert Forde

Keohane, Patrick: Antarctic Journals, 1910–13: Log of the Cruise of the Terra Nova; Kerry County Museum; Scott Polar Research Institute; Royal Navy service record, National Archive, UK; Papers, letters and photographs, Keohane Family

McCarthy, Mortimer: Papers, letters, photographs, McCarthy Family; Letter from Frederick Parsons, 1963, Canterbury Museum, New Zealand

Menzies, Shaun: Blog written on Beyond Endurance expedition, November 2007–January 2008

Pelagic: Logbook of South Arís Expedition, 1996–97

Pollock, Mark: Blog written on South Pole Flag expedition, 2008–09

Ross, James Clark: Letters, Scott Polar Research Institute

Royal Society: Papers, re: Francis Crozier

Shackleton, Ernest: *Endurance* diaries, letters, papers 1914–16, Scott Polar Research Institute; Admiralty papers, National Archives

Terra Nova: Agreement and Account of Crew, Scott Polar Research Institute

Worsley, Frank: *Endurance* diaries, papers, 1914–16, Scott Polar Research Institute

INDEX

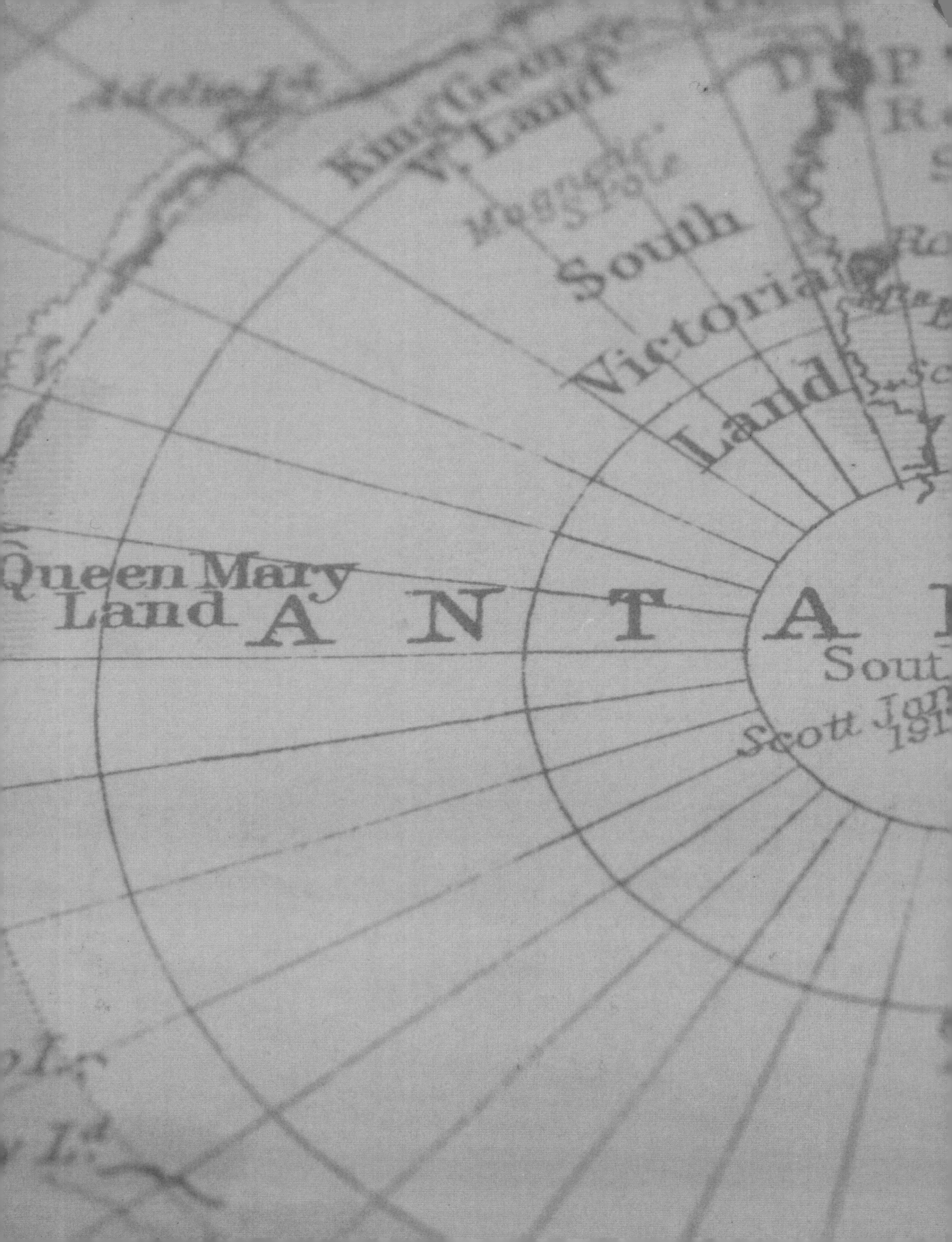

King George
V. Land

Maggate

South

Victoria

Land

Queen Mary
Land   A   N   T   A

Sout

Scott Jan.
191

Adelaide